Numismatic Auctions, Inc.

Dear Bidder,

Welcome to Heritage's second Platinum Night Signature catalog, with 435 lots being offered as Session Two of our official June 2004 Long Beach auction. Our inaugural Platinum Night auction took place at FUN, and was a resounding success, with tens of thousands of bids received. This special Platinum Night catalog features some of the very finest coins that we are auctioning at Long Beach, offered together in one sizzling session containing the rarest of the rare, on the night of June 3. More than sixty-five Long Beach consignors have their very special coins included in this catalog.

We invite your participation in our Long Beach auctions, and especially in this Platinum Night session. These are such wonderful coins that I am sure that you will want to witness this auction in person, while partaking of Southern California's hospitality. If you are participating through the Internet, make sure that you take full advantage of all of the features of our Interactive Internet™ bidding system at HeritageCoins.com. Either way, we welcome your patronage.

Sincerely,

Greg Rohan
President

TERMS and CONDITIONS of AUCTION

AUCTIONEER AND AUCTION:

1. This auction is presented by Heritage Numismatic Auctions. Inc. or its subsidiary Currency Auctions of America, Inc. or their affiliate, Heritage Auctions, Inc. through its divisions Heritage Comic Auctions, or Heritage Sports Collectibles Auctions, as identified with the applicable licensing information either on the title page of the catalog or on the Internet site (the "Auctioneer"). The auction is conducted under these Terms and Conditions of Auction and applicable state and local law.

BUYER'S PREMIUM:

2. On bids placed through Heritage, a Buyer's Premium of fifteen percent (15%) for Heritage Numismatic Auctions Inc, Heritage-CAA, and Heritage Comics Auctions or twenty percent (20%) for Heritage Sports Collectibles, Heritage-Odyssey and Heritage Galleries & Auctioneers of the hammer price will be added to the successful bid. If the bid is placed through eBay Live a Buyer's Premium equal to the normal Buyer's Premium plus an additional five percent (5%) of the hammer price will be added to the successful bid. There is a minimum Buyer's Premium of $6.00 per lot.

AUCTION VENUES:

3. Exclusively Internet, CurrencyAuction.com, Amazing Comics Auctions, and Bullet Auctions are auctions conducted on the Internet. Signature auctions accept bids on the Internet first, followed by a floor bidding session. Bids may be placed prior to the floor bidding session by Internet, telephone, fax, or mail.

BIDDERS:

4. Any person participating in or who registers for the auction agrees to be bound by and accepts these Terms and Conditions of Auction ("Bidder(s)").
5. All Bidders must meet Auctioneer's qualifications to bid. Any Bidder who is not a customer in good standing of the Auctioneer may be disqualified at Auctioneer's sole option and will not be awarded lots. Such a determination may be made by Auctioneer in its sole and unlimited discretion, at any time prior to, during, or even after the close of the auction.
6. If an entity places a bid, then the person executing the bid on behalf of the entity agrees to personally guarantee payment for any successful bid.
7. Auctioneer reserves the right to exclude any person it deems in its sole opinion is disruptive to the auction or is otherwise commercially unsuitable.

CREDIT REFERENCES:

8. Bidders who do not have established credit with the Auctioneer must either furnish satisfactory credit information including two collectibles-related references well in advance of the auction date or supply valid credit card information. All Bidders must meet Auctioneer's qualifications to bid. Any Bidder who is not a customer in good standing at Auctioneer may be disqualified and will not be awarded lots. Auctioneer reserves the right to disqualify any Bidder even after the close of the auction. Bids placed through our Interactive Internet program will only be accepted from pre-registered Bidders. Bidders who are not members of HeritageGalleries.com should pre-register at least two business days before the first session to allow adequate time to contact references.

BIDDING OPTIONS:

9. Bids may be placed for a Signature Sale as set forth in the printed catalog section entitled "Choose your bidding method." For Exclusively Internet, CurrencyAuction. Com, Amazing Comics Auctions, and Bullet auctions see the alternatives shown on each website. Review at www.HeritageCoin.com/Auctions/howtobid.asp.
10. The Auctioneer cannot be responsible for your errors in bidding, so carefully check that your bid is entered correctly. When identical mail or FAX bids are submitted, preference is given to the first received; Internet bids are evaluated as received first. The decision of the Auctioneer and declaration of the winning Bidder is final. The Auctioneer is not responsible for executing mail bids or FAX bids received on or after the day the first lot is sold, nor Internet bids submitted after the published closing time; nor is the Auctioneer responsible for proper execution of bids submitted by telephone, mail, FAX, e-mail, Internet, or in person once the auction begins. To ensure the greatest accuracy, your written bids should be entered on the standard bid sheet form and be received at the Auctioneer's place of business at least two business days in advance of the auction date. Internet bids may not be withdrawn until your written request is received and acknowledged by Auctioneer (FAX: 214-443-8425); such requests must state the reason, and may constitute grounds for withdrawal of bidding privileges. Lots won by mail Bidders will not be delivered at the auction unless prearranged in advance.

CONDUCTING THE AUCTION:

11. Notice of the consignor's liberty to place reserve bids on his lots in the auction is hereby made in accordance with Article 2 of the Texas Uniform Commercial Code. A reserve is an amount below which the lot will not sell. THE CONSIGNOR OF PROPERTY MAY PLACE WRITTEN RESERVE BIDS ON HIS LOTS IN ADVANCE OF THE AUCTION. ON LOTS SUBJECT TO A RESERVE, IF THE LOT DOES NOT MEET THE RESERVE THE CONSIGNOR MAY PAY A REDUCED COMMISSION ON THOSE LOTS. Reserves are generally posted online about 3 days prior to the auction closing on Internet-Only auctions, and 7 days prior to the auction on Signature auctions. IF THERE IS AN UNMET RESERVE BID POSTED ON A LOT, THE CURRENT BID DISPLAYED ONLINE WILL AUTOMATICALLY BE SET AT ONE INCREMENT BELOW THE RESERVE BID. The Auctioneer will not knowingly accept (and reserves the right to reject) live telephone or floor bids from consignors. Any successful bid placed by a consignor on his consigned lot on the auction floor or by telephone during the live session, or after the reserves for an auction have been posted, will be considered an unqualified bid, and in such instances the consignor agrees to pay full Buyer's Premium and Seller's Commissions on the lot(s) even if (s)he buys them back.
12. The highest qualified Bidder shall be the buyer. In the event of any dispute between floor Bidders at a Signature Sale, the Auctioneer may at his sole discretion put the lot up for auction again. The Auctioneer's decision shall be final and binding upon all Bidders.
13. The Auctioneer reserves the right to refuse to honor any bid or to limit the amount of any bid which, in his sole discretion, is not submitted in "Good Faith," or is not supported by satisfactory credit, numismatic references, or otherwise. A bid is considered not made in "Good Faith" when an insolvent or irresponsible person, or a person under the age of eighteen makes it. Regardless of the disclosure of his identity, any bid by a consignor or his agent on a lot consigned by him is deemed to be made in "Good Faith".
14. All items are to be purchased per lot as numerically indicated and no lots will be broken. The Auctioneer reserves the right to withdraw, prior to the close, any lot or lots from the auction. Bids will be accepted in whole dollar amounts only.
15. No "buy" or "unlimited" bids will be accepted. Bidders will be awarded lots at approximately the increment of the next highest bid. No additional commission is charged for executing bids other than the Buyer's Premium applied to all successful bids. Off-increment bids may be accepted by the Auctioneer at Signature auctions.
16. Estimates will be given upon written request. It is recommended that Bidders approach or exceed the estimates in order to increase the chances of bidding successfully.
17. Auctioneer reserves the right to rescind the sale in the event of nonpayment, breach of a warranty, disputed ownership, auctioneer's clerical error or omission in exercising bids and reserves, or otherwise.
18. Outage Policy: Auctioneer occasionally experiences Internet and/or Server outages during which Bidders cannot participate or place bids. If such outage occurs, we may at our discretion extend bidding for the auction up to 24 hours. At our discretion, Auctioneer may consider two outages that occur very closely to one another to be one outage when extending such auction. This policy applies only to widespread outages and not to isolated problems that occur in various parts of the country from time to time.
19. Scheduled Downtime: Auctioneer periodically schedules system downtime for maintenance and other purposes; this scheduled downtime is not covered by the Outage Policy.
20. The Auctioneer or affiliates may consign items to be sold in this auction, and may place reserve bids on those items or any other in the auction. The Auctioneer or affiliates expressly reserve the right to modify any such reserve bids on these items or any others at any time prior to the live auction or the online closing based upon data made known to the Auctioneer or its affiliate.
21. The Auctioneer may extend advances, guarantees, or loans to certain consignors, and may extend financing or other credits at varying rates to certain Bidders in the auction.

PAYMENT:

22. All sales are strictly for cash in United States dollars. Cash includes: U.S. currency, bank wire, cashier checks, travelers checks, and bank money orders, all subject to reporting requirements. Credit Card (Visa or Master Card only) payments may be accepted up to $10,000 from non-dealers at the sole discretion of the auctioneer, subject to the following limitations: a) sales are only to the cardholder, b) purchases are shipped to the cardholder's registered and verified address, c) Auctioneer may preapprove the cardholder's credit line, d) a credit card transaction may not be used in conjunction with any other financing or extended terms offered by the Auctioneer, and must transact immediately upon invoice presentation, e) rights of return are governed by these Terms and Conditions, which supersede those conditions promulgated by the card issuer, f) floor Bidders must present their card. Personal or corporate checks may be subject to clearing before delivery of the purchases.
23. Payment is due upon closing of the auction session, or upon presentment of an invoice. The Auctioneer reserves the right to void a sale if payment in full of the invoice is not received within 7 days after the close of the auction.
24. Lots delivered in the States of Texas, California, or other states where the auction may be held, are subject to all applicable state and local taxes, unless appropriate permits are on file with us. Lots from different auctions may not be aggregated for sales tax purposes.
25. In the event that a Bidder's payment is dishonored upon presentment(s), Bidder shall pay the maximum statutory processing fee set by applicable state law.
26. If the auction invoice(s) submitted by the Auctioneer is not paid in full when due, the unpaid balance will bear interest at the highest rate permitted by law from the date of invoice until paid. If the Auctioneer refers the invoice(s) to an attorney for collection, the buyer agrees to pay attorney's fees, court costs, and other collection costs incurred by the Auctioneer. If Auctioneer assigns collection to its in-house legal staff, such attorney's time expended on the matter shall be compensated at a rate comparable to the hourly rate of independent attorneys.
27. In the event a successful Bidder fails to pay all amounts due, the Auctioneer reserves the right to resell the merchandise, and such Bidder agrees to pay for the reasonable costs of resale, including a 10% seller's commission, and also to pay any difference between the resale price and the price of the previously successful bid.
28. The Auctioneer reserves the right to require payment in full in good funds before delivery of the merchandise to the buyer.
29. The Auctioneer shall have a lien against the merchandise purchased by the buyer to secure payment of the auction invoice. Auctioneer is further granted a lien and the right to retain possession of any other property of the buyer then held by the Auctioneer or its affiliates to secure payment of any auction invoice or any other amounts due the Auctioneer from the buyer. With respect to these lien rights, the Auctioneer shall have all the rights of a secured creditor under Article 9 of the Texas Uniform Commercial Code. In addition, with respect to payment of the auction invoice(s), the buyer waives any and all rights of offset he might otherwise have against the Auctioneer and the consignor of the merchandise included on the invoice.
30. If a Bidder owes Auctioneer or its affiliates on any account, the Auctioneer and its affiliates shall have the right to offset such unpaid account by any credit balance due Bidder, and it may secure by possessory lien any unpaid amount by any of the Bidder's property in their possession.
31. Title shall not pass to the successful Bidder until all invoices are paid in full. It is the responsibility of the buyer to provide adequate insurance coverage for the items once they have been delivered.

RETURN POLICY:

32. Signature Sales: The auction is not on approval. No certified material may be returned because of possible differences of opinion with respect to the grade offered by any third-party organization, dealer, or service. There are absolutely no exceptions to this policy. Under extremely limited circumstances, (e.g. gross cataloging error) a purchaser, who did not bid from the floor, may request Auctioneer to void a sale. Such request for evaluation must be made in writing detailing the alleged gross error, and submission of the lot to the Auctioneer must be preapproved by the Auctioneer. A Bidder must notify Ron Brackemyre, (ext. 312) in writing of the Bidder's request and such notice must be mailed within three (3) days of the mail Bidder's receipt of the lot. Any lot that is to be evaluated must be received in our offices within 30 days from the date of auction. Grading or method of manufacture do not qualify for this evaluation process nor do such complaints constitute a basis to challenge the authenticity of a lot. AFTER THAT 30-DAY PERIOD,

HERITAGE NUMISMATIC AUCTIONS, INC. PROUDLY PRESENTS THE

PLATINUM NIGHT SIGNATURE AUCTION

#349 • LONG BEACH, CALIFORNIA • JUNE 3, 2004

Featuring selections from:

The Harold W. Anderson Collection, Part One, The Jack R. Canniff #1 Registry Collection of Washington Quarters
The Barry Donnell Collection, The Virgil Farstad Collection, Part Two, The Garden State Collection,
The David J. Greene Collection of Buffalo Nickel Errors, The Greenwich Collection, Part One,
The Newark Mounds Collection, The Kyle Patrick Registry Collection of Lincoln Cents,
The Paulsboro Collection, Part One, The South Florida Collection

MAIN EXHIBITION OF LOTS

Long Beach Convention Center
100 S. Pine Avenue
Long Beach , CA 90802

Tuesday, June 1 • 12 pm-8 pm • Room 103-C
Wednesday, June 2 • 11 am-7 pm • Booth 400
Thursday, June 3 • 8 am-7 pm• Booth 400
Friday, June 4 • 8 am-7 pm• Booth 400
Saturday, June 5 • 8 am-noon• Booth 400

PUBLIC AUCTION, INTERNET AND MAIL BID AUCTION #349

Long Beach Convention Center
100 S. Pine Avenue
Long Beach , CA 90802
Room 103-B

Session 1 • Thursday, June 3, 1 pm • Lots 5001-5753

SESSION 2 • PLATINUM NIGHT
Thursday, June 3, 7 pm • Lots 6001-6435

Session 3 • The Harold W. Anderson Collection
Thursday, June 3, 9 pm (approx) • Lots 7001-7516
Session 4 • Friday, June 4, 1 pm • Lots 8001-8610
Session 5 • Friday, June 4, 7 pm • Lots 8611-9563
Session 6 • Saturday, June 5, 9 am • Lots 9564-10464

Lots are generally sold at the approximate rate of 200 per hour, but it is not uncommon to sell 150 lots or 300 lots in any given hour. Please plan accordingly so that you don't miss the items you are bidding on.

LOT SETTLEMENT AND PICK UP • Booth 400 • Friday-Saturday, 10am - 1pm

HERITAGE
Numismatic Auctions, Inc.

3500 Maple Avenue, 17th Floor, Dallas, Texas 75219-3941
214-528-3500 • 1-800-US COINS (872-6467)
e-mail: Bid@HeritageCoins.com

View full-color images at HeritageCoins.com

Heritage Numismatic Auctions, Inc 3S 3062 16 63
Auctioneer Sam Foose 3S 3062 16 65
Heritage Numismatic Auction Inc. Licensed by the State of California

Cataloged by:
Mark Van Winkle, Chief Cataloger • Brian Koller, Catalog Production Manager
Jon Amato, Jeff Ambio, Jason Bradford, Jim Jones, Greg Lauderdale, John Salyer, Warren Tucker

Photography by Jody Garver, Byron Carroll, Deign Rook, Tony Webb and Jason Young

Production and design by Keith Craker, Cathy Hadd, Mary Hermann, Kim Patterson, Mike Puttonen, Marsha Taylor, and Carl Watson

Price $50

FAX BIDS TO:
214-443-8425

FAX DEADLINE:
Wed., June 2, Noon CT

INTERNET BIDDING:
Closes at 10 pm CT
before the session on sale

Auction Results

Available Immediately
• Web site Results:
www.HeritageCoins.com

AUCTION #349

The owners of Heritage, left to right
Steve Ivy, Co-Chairman
Jim Halperin, Co-Chairman
Greg Rohan, President

HERITAGE
Numismatic Auctions, Inc.

3500 Maple Avenue, 17th Floor • Dallas, Texas 75219
Phone 214-528-3500 • 800-872-6467
www.HeritageCoins.com • e-mail: Bid@HeritageCoins.com
www.HeritageCurrency.com • e-mail: Bid@HeritageCurrency.com
www.HeritageGalleries.com • e-mail: Bid@HeritageGalleries.com

NO LOTS MAY BE RETURNED FOR REASONS OTHER THAN AUTHENTICITY. Lots returned must be housed intact in the original holder. No lots purchased by floor Bidders may be returned (including those Bidders acting as agents for others). Late remittance for purchases may be considered just cause to revoke all return privileges.

33.Exclusively Internet, CurrencyAuction.com, Amazing Comics Auctions™ and Bullet auctions: THREE (3) DAY RETURN POLICY. All lots (Exception: Third party graded notes are not returnable for any reason whatsoever) paid for within seven days of the auction closing are sold with a three (3) day return privilege. You may return lots under the following conditions: Within three days of receipt of the lot, you must first notify Auctioneer by contacting Customer Service by phone (1-800-872-6467) or e-mail (Bid@HeritageGalleries.com), and immediately mail the lot(s) fully insured to the attention of Returns, Heritage, 3500 Maple Avenue, 17th Floor, Dallas TX 75219-3941. Lots must be housed intact in their original holder and condition. You are responsible for the insured, safe delivery of any lots. A non-negotiable return fee of 5% of the purchase price ($10 per lot minimum) will be deducted from the refund for each returned lot or billed directly. Postage and handling fees are not refunded. After the three-day period (from receipt), no items may be returned for any reason. Late remittance for purchases revokes all Return-Restock privileges.

34.All Bidders who have inspected the lots prior to the auction will not be granted any return privileges, except for reasons of authenticity.

DELIVERY:

35.Postage, handling and insurance charges will be added to invoices. Please either refer to Auctioneer's web site www.HeritageGalleries.com for the latest charges or call Auctioneer.

COMPLETE SHIPPING AND HANDLING CHARGES

36.Auctioneer is unable to combine purchases from other auctions or Heritage Rare Coin Galleries into one package for shipping purposes. Successful overseas Bidders shall provide written shipping instructions, including specified customs declarations, to the Auctioneer for any lots to be delivered outside of the United States.

37.All shipping charges will be borne by the successful Bidder. Any risk of loss during shipment will be borne by the buyer following Auctioneer's delivery to the designated common carrier.

38.Regardless of domestic or foreign shipment, risk of loss shall be borne by the buyer following Auctioneer's delivery to a shipper.

39.Any claims for undelivered packages must be made within 30 days of shipment by the auctioneer.

40.In the event an item is damaged either through handling or in transit, the Auctioneer's maximum liability shall be the amount of the successful bid including the Buyer's Premium.

CATALOGING:

41.The descriptions provided in any catalog are intended solely for the use of those Bidders who do not have the opportunity to view the lots prior to bidding.

42.Any description of the lots contained in this auction is for the sole purpose of identifying the items.

43.In the event of an attribution error, the Auctioneer may, at the Auctioneer's sole discretion, correct the error on the Internet, or, if discovered at a later date, to refund the buyer's money without further obligation. Under no circumstances shall the obligation of the Auctioneer to any Bidder be in excess of the purchase price for any lot in dispute.

WARRANTIES AND DISCLAIMERS:

44.NO WARRANTY, WHETHER EXPRESSED OR IMPLIED, IS MADE WITH RESPECT TO ANY DESCRIPTION CONTAINED IN THIS AUCTION. Any description of the items contained in this auction is for the sole purpose of identifying the items, and no description of items has been made part of the basis of the bargain or has created any express warranty that the goods would conform to any description made by the Auctioneer.

45.Auctioneer is selling only such right or title to the items being sold as Auctioneer may have by virtue of consignment agreements on the date of auction and disclaims any warranty of title to the coins.

46.Auctioneer disclaims any warranty of merchantability or fitness for any particular purposes.

47.Auctioneer disclaims all liability for damages, consequential or otherwise, arising out of or in connection with the sale of any property by Auctioneer to Bidder. No third party may rely on any benefit of these Terms and Conditions and any rights, if any, established hereunder are personal to the Bidder and may not be assigned. Any statement made by the Auctioneer is a statement of opinion and does not constitute a warranty or representation. Any employee of Auctioneer may not alter these Terms and Conditions, and, unless signed by a principal of Auctioneer, any alteration is null and void.

48.Coins sold referencing a third-party grading service ("Certified Coins") are sold "as is" without any express or implied warranty, except for a guarantee by Auctioneer that the Certified Coins are genuine. Certain warranties may be available from the grading services and the Bidder is referred to the following services for details of any such warranties: ANACS, P.O. Box 182141, Columbus, Ohio 43218-2141; Numismatic Guaranty Corporation (NGC), P.O. Box 4776, Sarasota, FL 34230; Professional Coin Grading Service (PCGS), PO Box 9458, Newport Beach, CA 92658 and ICG, 7901 East Belleview Ave., Suite 50, Englewood, CO 80111. Comic books sold referencing a third-party grading service ("Certified Comics") are sold "as is" without any express or implied warranty, except for a guarantee by Auctioneer that the Certified Comics are genuine. Certain warranties may be available from the grading services and the Bidder is referred to the following services for details of any such warranties: Comics Guaranty Corporation (CGC), P.O. Box 4738, Sarasota, FL 34230. Currency sold referencing a third-party grading service ("Certified Currency") are sold "as is" without any express or implied warranty, except for a guarantee by Auctioneer that the Certified Currency are genuine. Certain warranties may be available from the grading services and the Bidder is referred to the following services for details of any such warranties: Currency Grading & Authentication (CGA), PO Box 418, Three Bridges, NJ 08887.

49.All non-certified coins and comics and currency are guaranteed genuine, but are not guaranteed as to grade, since grading is a matter of opinion. Grading is an art, not a science, and therefore the opinion rendered by the Auctioneer or any third party grading service may not agree with the opinion of others (including trained experts), and the same expert may not grade the same coin with the same grade at two different times. Auctioneer has graded the non-certified items, in the Auctioneer's opinion, to their current interpretation of the American Numismatic Association's standards as of the date the catalog was prepared. There is no guarantee or warranty implied or expressed that the grading standards utilized by the Auctioneer will meet the standards of ANACS, NGC, PCGS, ICG, CGC, CGA or any other grading service at any time in the future.

50.Auctioneer offers no opinion as to the validity of a grade assigned by any third-party grading service. Since we cannot examine C.G.A. encapsulated notes or Comics Guaranty Corporation (CGC) encapsulated comics, they are sold "as is" without our grading opinion, and may not be returned for any reason. Auctioneer shall not be liable for any patent or latent defect or controversy pertaining to or arising from any encapsulated collectible. In any such instance, purchaser's remedy, if any, shall be solely against the certification service certifying the collectible.

51.Due to changing grading standards over time and to possible mishandling of items by subsequent owners, the Auctioneer reserves the right to grade items differently than shown on certificates from any grading service that accompany the items. For the same reasons as stated above, the Auctioneer reserves the right to grade items differently than the grades shown in the catalog should such items be reconsigned to any future auction.

52.Although consensus grading is employed by most grading services, it should be noted as aforesaid that grading is not an exact science. In fact, it is entirely possible that if a lot was broken out of a plastic holder and was resubmitted to another grading service or even the same service, the lot could come back a different grade. Certification does not guarantee protection against the normal risks associated with potentially volatile markets.

53.The degree of liquidity for certified coins and collectibles will vary according to general market conditions and the particular lot involved. For some lots there may be no active market at all at certain points in time.

RELEASE:

54.In consideration of participation in the auction and the placing of a bid, a Bidder expressly releases Auctioneer, its affiliates, the Consignor, or Owner of the Lot from any and all claims, cause of action, chose of action, whether at law or equity or any arbitration or mediation rights existing under the rules of any professional society or affiliation based upon the assigned grade or a derivative theory, breach of warranty express or implied, representation or other matter set forth within these Terms and Conditions of Auction or otherwise, except as specifically declared herein; e.g., authenticity, typographical error, etc., and as to those matters, the rights and privileges conferred therein are strictly construed and is the exclusive remedy. Purchaser by non-compliance to its express terms of a granted remedy, shall waive any claim against Auctioneer.

DISPUTE RESOLUTION AND ARBITRATION PROVISION:

55.By placing a bid or otherwise participating in the auction, such person or entity accepts these Terms and Conditions of Auction, and specifically agrees to the alternative dispute resolution provided herein. Arbitration replaces the right to go to court, including the right to a jury trial.

56.If any disputes arise regarding payment, authenticity, grading or any other matter pertaining to the auction, the Bidder or a participant in the auction and/or the Auctioneer agree that the dispute shall be submitted, if otherwise mutually unresolved, to binding arbitration in accordance with the rules of the Professional Numismatists Guild (PNG) or American Arbitration Association (A.A.A.). The A.A.A. arbitration shall be conducted under the provisions of the Federal Arbitration Act with locale in Dallas, Texas. If an election is not made within ten (10) days of an unresolved dispute, Auctioneer may elect either PNG or A.A.A. Arbitration. An award granted in arbitration is enforceable in any court. No claims of any kind (except for reasons of authenticity) can be considered after the settlements have been made with the consignors. Any dispute after the settlement date is strictly between the Bidder and consignor without involvement or responsibility of the Auctioneer.

57.In consideration of his participation in or application for the auction, a person or entity (whether the successful Bidder, a Bidder, a purchaser and/or other Auction participant or registrant) agrees, that all disputes in any way relating to, arising under, connected with, or incidental to these Terms and Conditions and his purchases or default in payment thereof shall be arbitrated pursuant to the arbitration provision. In the event that any matter including actions to compel arbitration, construe the agreement, actions in aid or arbitration or otherwise needs to be litigated, such litigation shall be exclusively in the Courts of the State of Texas, in Dallas County, Texas, and if necessary the corresponding appellate courts. The successful Bidder, purchaser, or Auction participant also expressly submits himself to the personal jurisdiction of the State of Texas.

MISCELLANEOUS:

58.Agreements between Bidders and consignors to effectuate a non-sale of an item at auction, inhibit bidding on a consigned item to enter into a private sale agreement for an item, or to utilize the Auctioneer's auction to obtain sales for non-selling consigned items subsequent to the auction are strictly prohibited. If a subsequent sale of a previously consigned item occurs in violation of this provision, Auctioneer reserves the right to charge Bidder the applicable Buyer's Premium and consignor a Seller's Commission as determined for each auction venue and by the terms of the seller's agreement.

59. Acceptance of these terms and conditions qualifies Bidder as a Heritage customer who has consented to be contacted by Heritage in the future. In conformity with "do-not-call" regulations promulgated by the Federal or State regulatory agencies, participation by the Bidder is affirmative consent to being contacted at the phone number shown in his application and this consent shall remain in effect until it is revoked in writing. Heritage may from time to time contact Bidder concerning sale, purchase and auction opportunities available through Heritage and its affiliates and subsidiaries.

60.Storage of purchased coins: Purchasers are advised that certain types of plastic may react with the coin's metal and may cause damage to the coins. Caution should be used to avoid storage of coins in materials that are not inert.

STATE NOTICES:

61.Notice as to an Auction Sale in California. Auctioneer has in compliance with Title 2.95 of the California Civil Code as amended October 11, 1993 Sec. 1812.600, posted with the California Secretary of State its bonds for it and its employees and the auction is being conducted in compliance with Sec. 2338 of the Commercial Code and Sec. 535 of the Penal Code.9

Rev. 5/5/04

CHOOSE YOUR BIDDING METHOD

Mail Bidding At Auction

Mail bidding at auction is fun and easy and only requires a few simple steps. **1.** Look through the catalog, and determine the lots of interest; **2**. Research their market value by checking price lists and other price guidelines, or use our on-line archives; **3**. Fill out your bid sheet, entering your maximum bid on each lot using your price research and your desire to own the lot; **4**. Verify your bids!; **5**. Mail Early. Preference is given to the first bids received in case of a tie. **When bidding by mail, you frequently purchase coins at less than your maximum bid.**

On the floor of the auction, bidding is opened at 5% to 10% above the second highest mail bid; we act on your behalf as the highest mail bidder. If the auctioneer recognizes no other bids from the floor, you are awarded the lot at the opening bid. If bidding proceeds from the floor, we act as your agent, bidding in increments over the previous bid. This process is continued until you are awarded the lot or you are outbid.

An example of this procedure:

You submit a bid of $100, and the second highest mail bid is at $50. Bidding on the floor starts at $55 on your behalf. If no other bids are submitted by the floor, you purchase the lot for $55. If other bids come from the floor, we bid for you in increments set by the auctioneer, until we reach your maximum bid of $100. If bidding passes your maximum, we take no other action, and the bidding continues on the floor until the final bidder has been recognized by the auctioneer.

Interactive Internet™ Bidding

You can now bid with Heritage's exclusive *Interactive Internet*™ program, available only at our web site: www.HeritageCoins.com. It's fun, and it's easy!

1. Register on-line at http://Register.HeritageCoins.scom. We request that you pre-register at least one week before the sale! After we check your references, we will e-mail back your permanent User name & Password (you can later personalize your password).
2. View the full-color photography of every single-coin lot in the on-line catalog!

3 Construct your own personal catalog for preview.

4 View the current opening bids on lots you want; review prices realized archive.

5. Bid and receive immediate notification if you are the top bidder; later, if someone else bids higher, you will be notified automatically by e-mail.

6 *Interactive Internet*™ Bidding stops at midnight before the session starts. Then Heritage acts as your agent against the other bidding competition. Internet bids are recognized as the first bids received, so if there is a tie, you win!

7. After the sale, you will be notified of your success.

It's that easy!

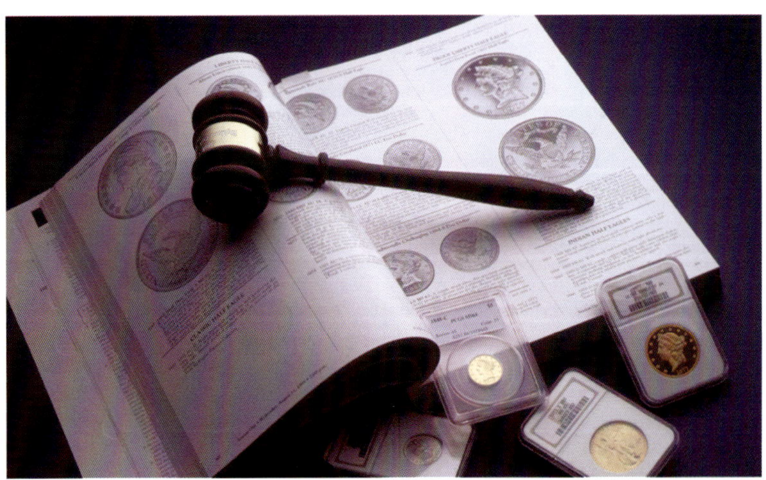

1. **Name, Address, City, State, Zip**

Your address is needed to mail your purchases. We need your telephone number to communicate any problems or changes that may affect your bids.

2. **References**

If you have not established credit with us from previous auctions, you must send a 25% deposit, supply valid credit card information, or list coin dealers with whom you have credit established.

3. **Lot Numbers and Bids**

List all lots you desire to purchase. On the reverse are additional columns, you may also use another sheet. Under "Amount" enter the maximum you would pay for that lot (whole dollar amounts only). We will purchase the coin(s) for you as much below your bids as possible.

4. **Total Bid Sheet**

Add up all bids and list that total in the appropriate box.

5. **Bid Higher to WIN**

Increase your bids automatically to increase your success.

6. **Sign Your Bid Sheet**

By signing the bid sheet, you have agreed to abide by the Terms of Sale listed in the auction catalog.

7. **Fax Your Bid Sheet**

When time is short submit a Mail Bid Sheet on our exclusive Fax Hotline. There's no faster method to get your bids to us *instantly*. Simply use the **Heritage Fax Hotline number: 214-443-8425**.

When you send us your original after faxing, mark it "Confirmation of Fax" (preferably in red!)

MAIL/FAX BID SHEET

FAX HOTLINE: 214-443-8425

Heritage Numismatic Auctions, Inc.
An affiliate of Heritage Rare Coin Galleries
1-800-US COINS (872-6467)
Heritage Plaza
100 Highland Park Village
Dallas, Texas 75205-2788
(All information must be completed.)

NAME WILLIAM STARK CUSTOMER NO.

ADDRESS 4739-B BRADFORD DRIVE

CITY/STATE/ZIP DALLAS, TX 75219

DAYTIME PHONE (A/C) (214) 555-8109 EVENING PHONE (A/C) (214) 528-3500

EMAIL ADDRESS

Dealer References (City, State)

Hamilton Coin Auctions - Tampa, FL

Carlson Coin & Stamp - San Francisco, CA

(Bid in whole dollar amounts only.)

You are authorized to release payment history information to other dealers and auctioneers so that I may establish proper credit in the industry. (Line out this statement if you do not authorize release).

LOT NO.	AMOUNT	LOT NO.	AMOUNT	LOT NO.	AMOUNT	LOT NO.	AMOUNT
143	200	3210	325				
221	75						
303	125						
1621	125						
2416	625						
							1475

PLEASE COMPLETE THIS INFORMATION:

1. IF NECESSARY, PLEASE INCREASE MY BIDS BY:
   ☑ 10% ❑ 20% ❑ 30%
   Lots will be purchased as much below bids as possible.
2. ☑ I HAVE BOUGHT COINS FROM YOU BEFORE (references are listed above)

I have read and agree to all of the Terms and Conditions of Sale: inclusive of paying interest at the lesser of 1.5% per month (18% per annum) or the maximum contract interest rate under applicable state law from the date of sale, (if the account is not timely paid), and the submission of disputes to arbitration.

William Stark

I have read and agree to the Terms of Sale in auction catalog.
(Signature required) Please make a copy of your bid sheet for your records.

SUBTOTAL

TOTAL from other side

TOTAL BID 1475

The official prices realized list that accompanies our auction catalogs is reserved for bidders, consignors, and HeritageCoins.com members. We are happy to mail others one upon receipt of $1.00. Written requests should be directed to Sonia Magdaleno.

NEW FEATURES

Registry Set Information

Because of the popularity of registry sets with coin collectors, Heritage has added relevant information after every US coin in our catalog listings. After each listing, you will see numbers such as the following: (#7100) (Registry values P4, N491). In order, these refer to the coin's Index number, the PCGS Set Registry weight, and the NGC Certified Coin Registry value.

PCGS Registry Numbers

The PCGS Set Registry(tm) allows collectors to list and virtually share their collections of coins certified by PCGS. Individual coins are identified by the unique numbers that appear on the PCGS insert. Collectors can interactively update their collections on the PCGS website at http://www.pcgs.com/new_set_registry/ as often as they wish. In addition, the collector can link images to his set to allow others to view his coins.

PCGS ranks sets by weighted average grade with rarer coins having a higher weight than common ones, by completeness, and by overall rating. This allows collectors to compete with others who share the same interests with the idea of creating the finest possible set. For purposes of comparison, the Registry also lists some of the finest collections ever assembled, such as Eliasberg, Norweb, and Garrett.

NGC Registry Numbers

NGC's Certified Coin Registry is a community for collectors where their sets can be displayed and ranked according to grade, rarity and other factors. The goal of NGC's Certified Coin Registry is to encourage coin collecting as a hobby, acknowledge the collectors who assemble truly remarkable sets, and inspire beginner hobbyists as they embark on the fun and rewarding hobby of building a coin collection.

NGC's Certified Coin Registry is the most inclusive system of its kind. It ranks coins from both major certification services, NGC and PCGS, so all of the coins in your set will be included.

Your set is ranked according to its true rarity, thanks to NGC's highly accurate weighted ranking system based on a number of factors including a coin's grade, rarity and census information. A value is placed on each coin that is based on the relative rarity of its type, date and grade. This value takes many factors into account such as grade, population, market value, eye appeal and expert opinion. In addition, a coin with the NGC Exclusive Star Designation is automatically assigned a Registry point premium in order to recognize its exceptional eye appeal for the grade. When a set is ranked in the registry, its rank is judged based on the total of the individual scores of all the coins.

NGC, the industry's leading coin certification company, has been the Official Grading Service of the ANA since 1995 and has been the only grading service ever to hold that distinction.

To find out more about NGC's Certified Coin Registry go to http://www.collectors-society.com/ or call 1-800-587-1897.

Index Number

Heritage has added coin index numbers at the end of each certified coin lot description in this catalog. These index numbers are used in some coin inventory software programs as well as in the bar code of most certified coins.

Rev. 2/25/04

TABLE OF CONTENTS

Early American Coins 6001-6008
Large Cents 6009
Small Cents 6010-6020
Three Cent Silver 6021-6023
Three Cent Nickels 6024
Nickels 6025-6032
Half Dimes 6033-6037
Dimes 6038-6056
Twenty Cent Pieces 6057-6060
Quarter Dollars 6061-6072
Half Dollars 6073-6103
Silver Dollars 6104-6126, 6133-6153
Trade Dollars 6127-6132
Gold Dollars 6159-6181
Quarter Eagles 6182-6218
Three Dollar Pieces 6219-6233
Stellas 6234-6235
Half Eagles 6236-6303
Eagles 6304-6349
Double Eagles 6350-6403
Territorial Gold 6407-6412
Gold Commemoratives 6154-6158
Silver Commemoratives 6404-6406
Patterns 6413-6428
Errors 6429
Proof and Mint Sets 6430-6435

BOLD AND RARELY ENCOUNTERED 1787 EXCELSIOR COPPER, VF35 PCGS

6001 1787 New York Excelsior Copper, Eagle Left VF35 PCGS. Eagle on globe facing left. Breen-980. Breen credits this design to John Bailey, who also helped engrave the similar eagle motif on the reverse of the legendary Brasher doubloons. According to Breen, only 15 to 20 survivors are known, "usually in low grades." This richly detailed piece has a well centered obverse, while the reverse is slightly off center toward 11 o'clock. The slightly granular dark walnut-brown fields complement the lighter mahogany devices. A generally unabraded example of this rare Early American piece. Listed on page 46 of the 2004 *Guide Book*.(#427)

PROBABLE FINEST KNOWN MARIS 14-J 1786 NEW JERSEY COPPER

6002 1786 New Jersey Copper, Narrow Shield MS64 Brown PCGS. Maris 14-J, R.1. Straight plow beam, sharp projection to the right. A spectacularly preserved example of this common variety. Perfect for a high grade type set, the surfaces are glossy medium brown with occasional flashes of original mint red still seen around the outer legends, especially NOVA CAESAREA. The striking details are also strongly defined with the only noticeable surface defect being a shallow planchet lamination over the UM in UNUM. Most likely the finest example known of the variety. Listed on page 50 of the 2004 *Guide Book*.(#496)

MS62 BROWN 1787 NEW JERSEY COPPER MARIS 46-E VARIETY

6003 1787 New Jersey Copper, Small Planchet, Plain Shield MS62 Brown NGC. Maris 46-e, R.1. This chocolate-brown representative is well struck aside from the lower right obverse border and the upper right reverse margin. A thin planchet streak through the upper right corner of the shield and a couple of reddish planchet flaws do not reduce the substantial eye appeal. Struck from a clashed obverse die. Listed on page 50 of the 2004 *Guide Book*.(#506)

BORDERLINE UNCIRCULATED 1786 VERMONTENSIUM COPPER

6004 1786 Vermont Copper, VERMONTENSIUM AU58 NGC. RR-6, Bressett 4-D, R.2. A virtually unabraded golden-brown representative that has bold definition on the major devices. A 2% curved rim clip (as made) is noted at 1 o'clock. The borders have a few moderate planchet flaws, as made, these mostly affect the BLI in PUBLICA and the CI in DECIMA. A mint-made die crack wanders below QUARTA. A decidedly lofty grade for a Landscape Vermont piece, and worthy of the finest specialized cabinet. Listed on page 51 of the 2004 *Guide Book*.(#545)

Ex: NORWEB 1786 VERMONTENSIUM COPPER RYDER-7 VARIETY

6005 1786 Vermont Copper, VERMONTENSIUM MS62 Brown NGC. RR-7, Bressett 5-E, R.3. A sharply struck and well centered representative that generally has medium brown patina, although portions of the reverse border possess more reddish maroon color. A couple of small mint-made planchet flaws above the P in PUBLICA and inside the M in DECIMA are noted as pedigree markers.

There are three VERMONTENSIUM Landscape varieties, Ryder-6 through 8. Among these, RR-6 is certainly the most available, and RR-8 is probably more obtainable than RR-7 since the former has many more appearances than the latter in recent Heritage sales. In the recent Stack's Ford sale, Michael Hodder mentions that he has seen 122, 74, and 83 examples respectively of the Ryder 6, 7, and 8 varieties. Thus, it is fair to state that Ryder-7 is the toughest of the VERMONTENSIUM marriages. Listed on page 51 of the 2003 *Guide Book.* *Ex: Norweb Collection (Bowers and Merena, 10/87), lot 1272; purchased earlier from Richard Picker on 3/22/55.*(#545)

FASCINATING DOUBLE STRUCK 1787 FUGIO CENT

6006 1787 Fugio Cent, STATES UNITED, Cinquefoils—Double Struck, 2nd 15% Off Center—MS64 Brown NGC. Newman 11-X, R.4. According to Breen (1988), many Mint State examples of this variety emerged from the Bank of New York hoard. Both sides are double struck, the second impression being 15% off center at 9 o'clock. There are two dates discernible on the obverse, although we note that the first date is somewhat off the flan. Mostly medium brown in color with the barest traces of faded mint red in a few of the more protected areas. Scattered planchet flaws (as struck) are noted, particularly on the reverse, although we stress that these features are anything but uncommon for the type. Listed on page 63 of the current *Guide Book.*(#883)

RED AND BROWN GEM
1787 UNITED STATES FUGIO CENT

6007 1787 Fugio Cent, UNITED STATES, Cinquefoils MS65 Red and Brown NGC. Newman 8-B, R.3. A gorgeously undisturbed Gem that is essentially free from the planchet flaws and impurities often encountered on this series. Orange color dominates the protected areas, while the highpoints of the devices and the exposed fields have medium lilac hues. Due to the die alignment, the upper obverse and the lower reverse are needle-sharp, while the upper right reverse and the right side of BUSINESS have softer definition, as made. Struck from a boldly clashed reverse die. Surely among the finest known survivors of this variety, which is seen less often than the various STATES UNITED reverses. Listed on page 63 of the 2004 *Guide Book*.(#890)

RED AND BROWN PREMIUM GEM
1787 FUGIO CENT, NEWMAN 8-B

6008 1787 Fugio Cent, UNITED STATES, Cinquefoils MS66 Red and Brown NGC. Newman 8-B, R.3. Crimson color fills the legends and sundial and outlines the rings. The devices offer original lavender patina. The lower obverse and upper reverse are not fully struck, which is the situation for most examples seen since the dies were slightly misaligned. A splendidly preserved representative of this interesting die marriage. A bold lintmark (as made) above AT in STATES will identify this piece in any future auction appearances. Struck from a heavily clashed reverse die, as is usual for the variety. Listed on page 63 of the 2004 *Guide Book*.(#890)

EXTRAORDINARY SPECIMEN MS65 BROWN S-6 1793 LARGE CENT

6009 1793 Wreath Cent—Vine and Bars—Specimen MS65 Brown NGC. S-6, R.3. The S-6 is one of the most frequently encountered and certainly most easily recognized of all 1793 varieties. Its "Sprung Die" in the left obverse field is immediately apparent and seen on all examples of the variety to one degree or another. On this example it is especially pronounced with a sharp ridge in the field. This, of course, is because the coin was struck from a later state of the dies. In fact, almost all the Die State VI characteristics are present on this piece, indicating it was one of the final coins struck in the run of 12,000 S-6 cents and most likely minted on April 9, 1793. The Breen reference states this piece is a Die State II coin, but we respectfully disagree.

Three exceptional S-6 cents are known as well as a couple of memorable S-5 coins. According to the EAC Condition Census, this piece is tied for second finest known with the ANS coin, which is permanently impounded. The coin that is considered the finest known is the Ex: Bement example and is known as "The King of the 1793 Cents."

The condition of this coin is truly extraordinary. It was Breen's contention in his 1977 reference on proofs that this particular coin was struck on a burnished blank for presentation purposes. The surfaces do indeed display a brightness and vibrancy that is not seen on other Wreath cents we have encountered. Again, according to Breen, the Harold Bareford coin (this piece) is the one S-6 that most clearly qualifies as a presentation piece. The fields are bright and glow with semi-reflectivity. The design motifs also show an unparalleled degree of definition in all areas. Although there is no direct evidence of heavy metal flow in the fields, indirect evidence can be seen from the strongly bifurcated lettering around the peripheries, leading one to suspect that this coin may have been double struck. As for surface flaws, there are really none that are immediately apparent. Examination with a glass does, however, reveal a speck of darker color to the left of the leftmost leaf above the date (a useful pedigree identifier), and a short angling mark on the cheek of Liberty. The color designation by NGC is Brown, and that is technically correct. However, in addition to the overall brown patina there is an overlay of olive with a strong presence of original red also.

This is the most perfectly preserved and singularly important early large cent we have ever had the privilege of offering at public auction. It will not be a bargain for its new owner, but then every time this coin has changed hands over the past 131 years it has cost its new owner dearly. A true "museum quality" coin.

Ex: George F. Seavy; William H. Strobridge (1873), lot 208; Lorin G. Parmelee (2/6/1892); Dr. Thomas Hall (9/7/1909); Virgil M. Brand; to Horace Brand in 1934; New Netherlands Coin Co., privately (7/30/51), to Harold Bareford; to Herman Halpern (9/13/85); Stack's (3/88), lot 6, for $46,750; Ed Milas (RARCOA); Martin Paul (The Rarities Group); Superior (8/92), lot 10, unsold; unknown intermediary; to the present consignor. The coin used by J.N.T. Levick who used it as a plate coin in an 1868 photo that was published in an 1869 issue of the American Journal of Numismatics for his plate of 1793 large cents. Also used as a plate coin in Sylvester S. Crosby's United States Coinage of 1793, published in 1897.(#1347) (Registry values: N10218)

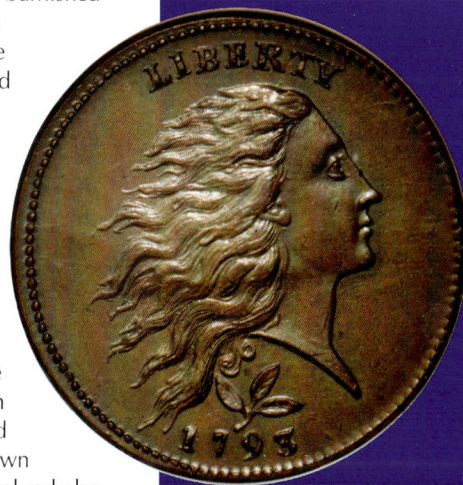

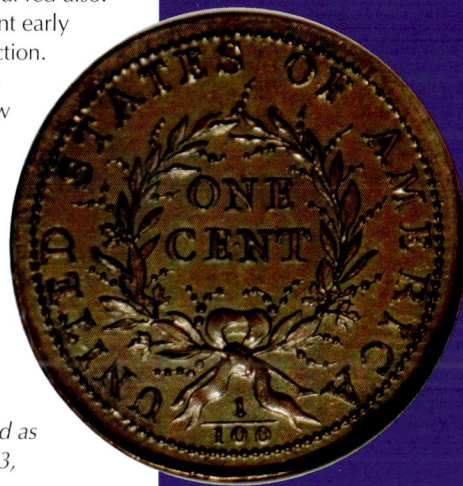

EVER-POPULAR 1856 FLYING EAGLE CENT

6010 1856 MS63 PCGS. Snow-9. On page 39 of Rick Snow's reference on the Flying Eagle series, he states: "Most of the examples from this die pair which exist in high grade show detail and edges which confirm their status as proofs. However, the overall quality of these pieces are not anywhere near that of the regular proof issues of the period. These usually have dull or nonexistent mirrors. Many show striking defects such as lint strike-throughs and planchet flaws. The probable reason for the poor quality is the relatively large production." The bold definition of this Select representative is consistent with a proof striking, but reflectivity on the streaky autumn-brown surfaces is almost non-existent and several planchet cracks are noted on each side.

From The Barry Donnell Collection.(#2013) (Registry values: N4719)

INTERESTING 1856 FLYING EAGLE CENT PROOF 61 NGC

6011 1856 PR61 ANACS. Snow-9 is technically a restrike that, according to Rick Snow (2001), was produced starting in 1858. The striking period for this die marriage probably went through 1860, if not later. These coins were prepared for solely for distribution to collectors at the time. Traces of modest, shimmering brightness are noted as the coin rotates under the light, but the outward appearance is one of even charcoal-gray coloration. Direct angles also reveal flickers of faint crimson and golden overtones. An expectantly sharp specimen striking with remarkably smooth surfaces for the assigned grade. A strike-through resembling a planchet flaw is seen at the center of the reverse. Close examination under a loupe reveals feather-like detail inside the cavity. We suspect a piece of an obverse flaked off, adhered to the reverse die, and was subsequently struck into this piece. An uncommon error, especially on an 1856 Flying Eagle Cent.(#2037) (Registry values: N4719)

RARE GEM PROOF 1856 FLYING EAGLE CENT

6012 1856 PR65 PCGS. Snow-9. The S-9 variety is the most frequently encountered die pairing for 1856 Flying Eagle Cents. These coins were produced from late 1857 until 1860. A considerable (but unknown) number were struck and apparently stockpiled in the mint for sale to collectors. Snow speculates that after the start of the Civil War, sales stagnated, and those pieces that remained were mistakenly released into circulation. This is a fully original example that has lustrous surfaces that display variegated golden, brown, and lilac coloration with the reverse being somewhat deeper in hue. A pleasing, high grade example of this fabled 19th century rarity. Population: 40 in 65, 5 finer (3/04).(#2037) (Registry values: N7079)

CLASSIC 1856 FLYING EAGLE CENT GEM PROOF

6013 1856 PR65 NGC. Snow-9. A richly colored golden-tan specimen that is subtly reflective and displays expectantly bold highpoint detail. The popularity of the 1856 Flying Eagle cannot be overstated. Its production marks the first deviation from the Mint's standards on copper coinage after it began losing money on Large Cent planchets earlier in the decade. Immediately successful, although still not officially authorized, restrikes became necessary to ensure that the many government officials and various "VIPs" received an example of the new smaller copper-nickel issue. Because of their distribution among the non-numismatic community, many survivors received either light circulation or have otherwise been impaired to some degree.(#2037) (Registry values: N7079)

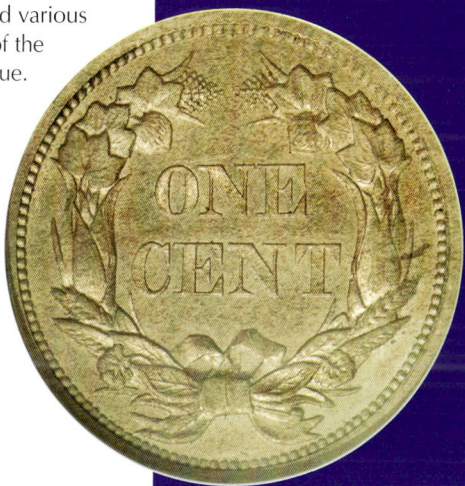

ELUSIVE 1857 FLYING EAGLE CENT PR64

6014 **1857 PR64 PCGS.** Snow-PR1. According to official Mint records, 485 proofs were struck of this issue. Most were apparently unsold and melted or released into circulation, however, as only a tiny fraction, perhaps fewer than 50 pieces, of the original number survives today as a recognizable proof. This specimen was produced from one of three proof dies known for the 1857 Flying Eagle, being characterized by a die file mark from the left serif of the top of the I in UNITED to the rim, and a die scratch that slants downward in the obverse field just below the eagle's beak. A thin veil of milky patina rests over both sides, leaving the viewer to angle the coin in order to appreciate the underlying reflective qualities. The obverse displays a few scattered carbon spots and tinges of forest-green color are seen about the wreath on the reverse. Population: 17 in 64, 11 finer (3/04).
From The Barry Donnell Collection.(#2040) (Registry values: N4719)

SPECTACULAR 1858 LARGE LETTERS FLYING EAGLE CENT PR67 DEEP CAMEO

6015 **1858 Large Letters PR67 Deep Cameo NGC.** Occasionally prooflike Flying Eagle cents are confused with the very rare proof strikings, but in this case there can be no confusion. The diagnostics for genuine proofs are listed in Snow's book that covers this series. They include: diagonal die file marks in the denticles below the first 8 and the 5 in the date. The date also slants up to the right. Minor doubling is also seen on UNI in UNITED. On the reverse, a minute die file mark is located in the denticles just left of 12 o'clock. These die markers are all very small and strong magnification is required to pick them out. However, they are present, and this die was not used on any business strikes.

As with all genuine proof Flying Eagle cents, the fields are deeply mirrored and the striking definition is razor sharp. This coin is truly a wonder to behold. The fields show unfathomable depth of reflectivity and the devices are nicely frosted, which yields an unmistakable two-toned cameo effect. The surfaces are hairline-free and we cannot locate any specks of carbon. There are a few tiny planchet voids on each side, probably lint marks from when the dies were wiped prior to striking. The only one that might be large enough to use as a pedigree identifier in the future is located just above the bottom of the E in ONE on the reverse.

Only 100 Large Letter proofs are estimated to have been struck. This number is based upon a known production of 80 silver proof sets plus a small number of pattern sets, probably no more than 20 pieces. Snow believes no more than 50 examples survive today in all grades, a number that would make an original mintage of 100 pieces seem like a reasonable estimate. This is the finest example certified by either of the two major services, and it is essentially an unimprovable coin. The pristine surfaces retain a generous amount of original whitish color from the copper-nickel alloy with the addition of a light overlay of pale reddish patina on each side. Population: 1 in 67 Deep Cameo (2 in 67 Cameo), 0 finer (4/04).(#92042)

UNSURPASSABLE 1858 SMALL LETTERS CENT PROOF 66 CAMEO NGC

6016 1858 Small Letters PR66 Cameo NGC. Low Leaves Reverse. Snow-PR-2. This is one of the finest known examples of this rare issue, and it is also one of the most aesthetically desirable. A stunning specimen, the devices are fully struck up with every feather and wreath element showing razor sharp detail. The fields are virtually flawless and show splendid mirrored reflectivity when held at direct angles. Characteristic striations are also evident when the coin rotates under the light, and they are suggestive of a very early die state. Aside from the outstanding condition of this piece, the eye appeal benefits from beautiful champagne, apricot, and pastel-lilac shadings. A small diagonal abrasion is noted above the 185 of the date, this being mentioned solely for future identification purposes.

The mintage of 200 pieces that many catalogers report for this proof issue seems to be somewhat higher than the actual number of coins produced. A more appropriate estimate would be somewhere in the range of 100 pieces. There is also some confusion surrounding the number of coins extant, particularly because auction records include prooflike business strikes that the mint issued in the 1858 12-piece pattern sets. These coins are still occasionally graded as proofs in error. Richard Snow believes that approximately 75 proof 1858 Small Letters Flying Eagle Cents are extant, a total that makes this issue similar in overall rarity to the proof 1857.

Collectors with enough curiosity to look at the reverses of their coins may discover the changes that the Mint implemented in 1858. At some time early in the year the design was changed in an effort to lower the relief. This would enable the coiner to lessen the striking pressure and extend working die life. The high relief design is called the "High Leaves Reverse" because the leaves inside the wreath at the C and T in CENT are fairly long. This design was in use in 1856, 1857, and early 1858 and may also be called the "Type of 1857." The lower relief design is called "Low Leaves Reverse" with the leaves by the C and T in CENT short and extending just above the base of each letter. This is also referred to as the "Type of 1858."

The proof 1858 Small Letters exists with both the High Leaves and Low Leaves reverses. The presently offered example is an example of the latter variety.(#2043) (Registry values: N10218)

CONDITIONAL RARITY: 1871 INDIAN CENT MS65 RED NGC

6017 1871 MS65 Red NGC. Razor sharp with satin-like fields and attractive amber-gold coloration evenly dispersed over the smooth surfaces. A couple of marks are visible on the principal obverse device. The 1871 is one of the most elusive Indian Cent issues in Red Uncirculated grades, of comparable rarity to dates such as the 1872 and 1877. Population: 4 in 65, none finer (4/04).(#2102) (Registry values: N7079)

NICELY MIRRORED GEM 1875 INDIAN CENT

6018 1875 PR65 Red PCGS. While the 1875 is normally found with only moderate reflectivity, this is a strongly mirrored example that shows rich red color except over the lower portion of the reverse where some deeper, iridescent mellowing is seen. An exceptionally pleasing example of this very scarce early proof issue. Population: 11 in 65, 2 finer (3/04).(#2314) (Registry values: N4719)

SELECT 1922 NO D WEAK REVERSE LINCOLN

6019 1922 No D Weak Reverse MS63 Red and Brown PCGS. Glossy with ample evidence of sunset-orange coloration in the protected areas. The wheat stalks display characteristic deficiency in strike and the D mintmark is only faintly visible, being positioned just to the left of the first 2 in the date. Population: 17 in 63, 7 finer (3/04).

From The Barry Donnell Collection.(#2541) (Registry values: N4719)

EXCEEDINGLY DIFFICULT 1970-S DOUBLED DIE CENT, MS64 RED PCGS

6020 1970-S Doubled Die MS64 Red PCGS. FS-029, DDO 1-O-I. A highly coveted variety that exhibits bold die doubling on LIBERTY and IN GOD WE TRUST. The 0 in the date is also clearly doubled. A nicely struck and lustrous near-Gem with magenta-red color and a few minor handling marks. This *Guide Book* variety is one of the major stoppers to a complete collection of Memorial Reverse Cents. Population: 14 in 64, 5 finer (3/04).(#92939)

BRILLIANT GEM CAMEO
1858 TYPE TWO THREE CENT SILVER PIECE

6021 1858 PR65 Cameo NGC. Breen estimates that 60-75 proof Trimes were produced this year, only about two or three dozen of which are extant. An early die state, this coin exhibits numerous striations (as produced) slanting down to the right in the obverse field. The finish is fully brilliant, and the surfaces shimmer with a very slight cameo effect noted on each side. A remarkable Gem proof Type Two Three Cent Silver piece.(#3705) (Registry values: N4719)

DESIRABLE 1858
THREE CENT SILVER PR66

6022 1858 PR66 PCGS. First year of commercially available proofs from the Mint, the 1858 is also generally the only year Type Two Three Cent Silver pieces are available in the proof format. This wonderfully preserved specimen is liberally striated on the obverse and both sides sparkle beneath a mixture of violet and aquamarine toning. Since Breen (1977) states that the diagnostic die striations of this issue fade with subsequent impressions, this Gem quality survivor is most likely one of the first few pieces produced. Population: 7 in 66, 0 finer (3/04).(#3705) (Registry values: N4719)

BEAUTIFUL 1858 THREE CENT SILVER PR66

6023 1858 PR66 NGC. A scarce Type Two proof issue, struck from a small but inexact mintage with estimates varying from 75 to 300 pieces. Both sides of this solid Gem specimen are toned in intermingles shades of steel-violet and aqua. The obverse is noticeably striated, a normal characteristic of proofs from this year.(#3705) (Registry values: N4719)

SUPERB CAMEO PROOF 1877 THREE CENT NICKEL

6024 1877 PR67 Cameo NGC. With an original mintage of only 510 pieces, all of which were proofs, the 1877 is one of the two stars in the three cent nickel series, only sharing the spotlight with the 1865 proof. This is an all-brilliant example that has moderately mirrored fields with a strong presence of mint frost on the devices. Exceptional technical preservation as well as eye appeal.(#83773) (Registry values: N4719)

GEM 1867 NO RAYS SHIELD NICKEL IN PROOF 66

6025 1867 No Rays PR66 Cameo PCGS. Reverse IIa. As a first year type candidate for the proof collector, we cannot overstate the importance of this gorgeous Gem. Watery, deeply reflective fields form a lovely backdrop to crisply delineated features. A few whispers of pale golden iridescence are evident at certain angles, but there is not a single mentionable blemish. One of only five so graded examples at PCGS, and unsurpassable at that service with a Cameo designation (3/04).(#83821) (Registry values: N2998)

CAMEO SUPERB GEM 1899 PROOF NICKEL, SINGLE FINEST CERTIFIED BY NGC

6026 1899 PR67 Cameo NGC. An occasional trace of tan color graces the meticulously struck surfaces of this undisturbed Premium Gem. Even the left ear of corn (located above the CE in CENTS) possesses sharp definition on the kernels. The white on black contrast is unmistakable, although Liberty's hair has greater frost than does the remainder of her portrait. The Cameo designation is elusive for 1899 proofs, since (as of 4/04) NGC has only certified six pieces as Cameo in all grades. The present specimen is the single finest certified by NGC, although the service has encapsulated 17 examples as PR67 without a Cameo designation.(#83897)

UNSURPASSABLE 1916-D NICKEL MS66 PCGS

6027 1916-D MS66 PCGS. Despite trivial incompleteness of detail on the Indian's hair and the bison's head, this is an attractive piece whose luster cartwheels gracefully beneath a blanket of warm champagne patination on the reverse. The accurately graded, pristine surfaces are indicative of the MS66 grade tier. Population: 8 in 66, none finer at either service (3/04).(#3932) (Registry values: N4719)

LOW POP 1920 BUFFALO NICKEL IN NGC MS67

6028 1920 MS67 NGC. While the 1920-P (63 million pieces produced) is a plentiful Buffalo Nickel in terms of total number of coins known, it is a rare issue at the Superb Gem level of preservation. Simply put, this is the most exquisite 1920 Nickel that this cataloger has handled. Untoned with a bright, lustrous sheen, the surfaces exhibit overall sharp striking definition that further enhances the already memorable eye appeal. Expertly preserved with nary a bothersome handling mark to report. NGC and PCGS combined report a mere six examples in MS67, and none are finer (3/04).(#3944) (Registry values: N4719)

EXTREMELY SCARCE 1925-S BUFFALO NICKEL MS65

6029 **1925-S MS65 PCGS.** One of the foremost strike rarities in the Buffalo Nickel series and a scarcity at any level of Mint State, the 1925-S emerges as one of the most challenging issues of this popular type at the Gem level of preservation. A soft, frosted sheen over both sides is complemented by delicate accents of golden and sky-blue patina. Just a trace of mushiness is noted on the highpoints of the obverse, although nothing like the deficiency that is normally encountered on Mint State representatives. The reverse, however, possesses an even stronger strike, sharp enough that the presence of the S mintmark almost defies belief. Any 1925-S Buffalo in Gem condition is of the utmost importance to the serious collector of this challenging series. Population: 12 in 65, 1 finer (3/04).(#3956) (Registry values: N7079)

LIGHTLY TONED GEM 1927-D BUFFALO

6030 **1927-D MS65 PCGS.** Rich green-gold patina is accented with multicolored iridescence, visible as the coin is turned under a light. Some typical softness shows on each side, but hardly detracts from this Gem's overall eye appeal. A small amount of wispy contact is evident near the center of each side, while the fields seem mark-free. An appealing, well preserved example. Population: 45 in 65, 1 finer (3/04).(#3961) (Registry values: N2998)

ELUSIVE GEM 1937-D THREE-LEGGED BUFFALO

6031 1937-D Three-Legged MS65 NGC. FS-020.2. One of most famous error issues in all of 20th century numismatics, the 1937-D Three-Legged gained almost instant notoriety when, in 1937-1938, C. L. "Cowboy" Franzen started offering examples for sale in The Numismatic Scrapbook. Franzen's coins probably came from Montana, the state in which most, if not all '37-D Three-Legged Nickels were distributed. The early discovery date would seem to indicate that most examples were removed from circulation after a relatively short period of time. Those that did escape circulation altogether nearly always display inferior luster and striking qualities. On this remarkable Gem representative, the soft, frosted luster is especially vibrant for the issue and only on the highest points of the design does the characteristic softness become evident. Population: 33 in 65, 13 finer (4/04).(#3982) (Registry values: N4719)

IMPECCABLE 1936 SATIN FINISH NICKEL PR68

6032 1936 Type One—Satin Finish PR68 NGC. Appealing pinkish-golden accents adorn shimmering, carbon-free surfaces with all the intricate detailing one expects of a proof. A virtually unimprovable example of Satin Finish type. Population: 14 in 68, 0 finer (4/04).(#3994) (Registry values: N2998)

AMAZING GEM 1794 HALF DIME MS66 NGC

6033 1794 MS66 NGC. V-3, R.5. A truly amazing first year Flowing Hair Half Dime, not only because of its lofty grade assignment, but also by virtue of its outstanding eye appeal. This beauty has it all: an abundance of natural luster, extraordinary sharpness of detail for the design type, and satiny surfaces that are free of all but the most trivial of mint-caused planchet voids. A pale golden wash of color heightens the appeal of this spectacular coin, highlighting the peripheral legends and devices in particular. This piece is from a late state of the reverse die, with prominent die cracks from the rim at 7 o'clock, across the eagle's tail, and then to the rim at 5 o'clock, with another crack dropping from the eagle's tailfeathers to the rim at 6 o'clock. This advanced state of the die affords a good look back into time at the early technology of the Mint, when die steel was at a premium and dies were frequently worked until they shattered. As might be expected, this is the second finest example of the date certified by NGC (one specimen is higher) and finer, for instance, than the Eliasberg coin, or any of the other examples of the date that have staked claims to Gem status.(#4250)

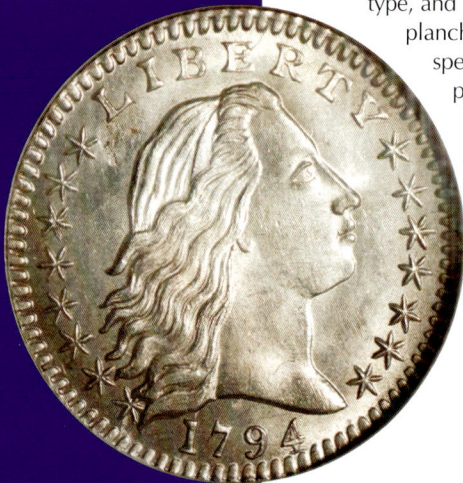

EXTREMELY SCARCE 1802 HALF DIME

6034 1802—Damaged, Bent—ANACS. Fair Details, Net Poor 1. V-1, LM-1, the only known dies, R.5. The 1802 Half Dime is unquestionably one of the first issues that comes to mind when making a list of the rarest silver issues in the 210-year span since their initial production. From an initial mintage of just 3,060 pieces, a figure that could easily have included pieces which were either back-dated or post-dated as was a common practice in the early years of the Mint, most specialists agree that no more than 40 to 50 pieces are extant. The rarity of the 1802 is further emphasized by the fact that deceptive electrotype counterfeits are known. While the irregularly worn example offered here ranks among the worst known survivors, this actually makes it accessible to a larger group of numismatists who would like to include an example of this great rarity in their collection. The planchet of this mostly bright silver-gray representative was severely bent at one time and later straightened. Fortunately, the reverse of the coin is the side that suffered the most, being worn smooth and displaying numerous small digs. Similar light pockmarks are noted on the obverse, but much of the detail was spared, including the final 3 digits of the date. The upper loop of the familiar nearly closed 2 that touches the portrait is unmistakable.(#4268)

PLATINUM NIGHT

SUPERB, ORIGINALLY TONED 1840 NO DRAPERY HALF DIME

6035 1840 No Drapery MS67 PCGS. This short-lived type had drapery added to Liberty's elbow late in 1840. While generally available in circulated grades and even the lower grades of Uncirculated, the 1840 is quite a challenge in MS67 condition. This is a pristine example. The surfaces are seemingly flawless with rose and sea-green patina scattered over each side. The devices are fully detailed in all areas. Outstanding quality. Population: 5 in 67, 1 finer (3/04).(#4321) (Registry values: N4719)

EXTREMELY RARE 1844 HALF DIME PR65

6036 1844 PR65 PCGS. Triple Date. V-3. Both the 1 and the 8 in the date are tripled punched while dramatic recutting is also seen on the first 4. A mere 4 specimens from this boldly repunched die are estimated by Breen to have been struck as proofs, and the number of proof strikings extant from all dies is thought to be in the neighborhood of 10 pieces. This noticeably striated specimen is intricately detailed and exhibits dappled violet toning that yields to flashes of sea-green at the margins. Population: 1 in 65, 3 at NGC, 1 finer, 1 finer at NGC (4/04).(#4420)

GEM CAMEO PROOF 1866 HALF DIME

6037 1866 PR66 Cameo PCGS. The 1867 Half Dime is a scarce issue whether it is in proof or business strike format. Only 10,000 business strikes were produced along with 725 proofs, making the proofs always in demand by collectors who need a high grade example and do not wish to spend the extra money for a more expensive business strike. This coin is clearly superior from a technical standpoint with deeply reflective fields that are partially covered with hazy-smoky color. The devices are lightly frosted yielding a noticeable cameo effect. A few small hairlines are noted on the obverse.(#84449)

SIGNIFICANT 1805 4 BERRIES DIME IN MINT STATE

6038 1805 4 Berries MS63 PCGS. JR-2, R.2. While JR-2 is the more plentiful of the two known die marriages of the 1805 Draped Bust Dime, examples that have survived the passage of time with fully Mint State surfaces must be considered rare. This is just such a coin, both sides displaying suitably bold striking detail that is perhaps most readily evident over the obverse portrait. The otherwise silver-gray features brighten a bit at more direct angles. Scattered adjustment marks (as produced) are seen through the centers, but neither side reveals any singularly mentionable abrasions. An important find for the Uncirculated type collector.(#4477)

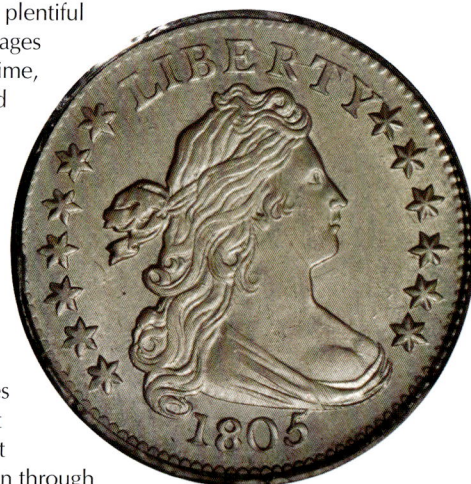

LUSTROUS 1807 HERALDIC EAGLE DIME MS63

6039 1807 MS63 PCGS. JR-1, R.2. This final year Heraldic Eagle issue is occasionally seen in Mint State, but most are rather drab examples that are invariably poorly struck on the left side. This brightly lustrous specimen is a welcome exception, being satiny and untoned with particularly sharp details over all but the left stars. The obverse displays numerous wavy clash marks in the field directly in front of Liberty's face. Population: 47 in 63, 31 finer (3/04).(#4480)

DEEPLY TONED MS66 1807 DRAPED BUST, HERALDIC DIME, ONE OF THE FINEST KNOWN

6040 1807 MS66 PCGS. JR-1, the only known dies, R.2. The reverse die for the 1807 dime had previously been used to strike four quarter eagle issues: the 1805, 1806/4, 1806/5, and 1807. Once it was converted to use for dimes dated 1807, well over 100,000 pieces were produced. As a result, most of the examples known today display multiple die problems, including weak definition on the left side of the obverse, die clashing in the right obverse field, repolishing, and missing peripheral details on late strikings. This particular coin shows softness on the left obverse stars, and close examination with a magnifier reveals die clashing on the right side of the obverse—minimal Mint-made problems for this issue. Post-striking impairments are virtually non-existent. The mint luster is thick and frosted, being strongly in evidence beneath the deep violet and blue toning that covers each side. An exquisite type coin and virtually unexcelled in technical grade (NGC has certified one piece finer). Population: 2 in 66, with none finer (3/04).(#4480)

EXCEPTIONAL GEM PROOFLIKE 1827 DIME, EX: PITTMAN

6041 1827 MS65 Prooflike NGC. JR-12, R.1. A bright specimen with little or no color. The fields are quite reflective as might be expected on a proof of the time and most probably a result of some unusual die preparation and polishing at the mint. Interestingly enough, proof 1827 dimes are known with this same die paring. Close examination reveals lack of highpoint definition on the eagle's leg and claw, also Liberty's hair on the obverse. In our opinion, this coin was not struck with multiple blows of the coining press (as a proof might have been) to further define the smaller details. Still, an exceptionally clean, noteworthy example that should be closely examined by prospective buyers.

Ex: John J. Pittman Collection (David Akers, 10/1997), lot 558 where it realized $16,500. Purchased in 1952 from Mike Kolman for $21.50.(#4504) (Registry values: N4719)

ORIGINALLY TONED, SUPERB GEM 1857 SEATED DIME

6042 1857 MS67 NGC. This richly toned example displays competing swirls of deep cobalt-blue and crimson-magenta colors throughout. Some of the highpoint detail at the top of the obverse is softly impressed, the balance of the features are sharp and distraction-free. Currently (4/04) this is the single finest example graded by NGC and is tied with one other MS67 at PCGS. A perfect candidate for inclusion in an originally toned, Superb Gem quality type set.(#4614) (Registry values: N1)

FINEST KNOWN 1858-O SEATED DIME MS66 NGC

6043 1858-O MS66 NGC. The '58-O is one of more underrated dates in the Seated Dime series, and possibly the most underrated O-mint issue. Often confused with the much more common dates such as 1857-O and 1859-O, 290,000 pieces were struck of this issue. However, few of those managed to survive over the years, and now it is quite elusive above VF condition with Gems being considered extremely rare.

Originally purchased by the consignor at the 1982 Stack's Robison Sale, where it was described as a "pristine Gem," this example is one grade finer than the Norweb specimen that had several small ticks on the obverse. Unusually strong definition for the issue shows overall, with both the head of Liberty and the bow knot sharply detailed. Exceptionally lustrous for a New Orleans product, the surfaces are colorfully tinted in original shades of moss-green, turquoise-blue, crimson, gray, and rose. This represents the single finest example thus far certified by either service (4/04). Accompanied by an NGC *Photo Proof* certificate.(#4617) (Registry values: N1)

FINEST CERTIFIED 1863 DIME MS67

6044 1863 MS67 NGC. Only 14,000 business strikes were produced of this Civil War era issue, and even similarly dated proofs, of which just 460 pieces were produced, greatly outnumber the few surviving Uncirculated pieces. This Superb representative exhibits pinpoint striking details and radiant, untoned surfaces that lack the prooflike qualities often found on high grade pieces. It is always a bit risky to come forward with the "finest known" superlative, but one cannot dispute the finest certified status of this outstanding 1863 Dime. Population: 1 in 67 (none at PCGS), 0 finer (4/04).(#4637) (Registry values: N1)

NEARLY UNSURPASSABLE 1874 ARROWS DIME, MS67 NGC

6045 1874 Arrows MS67 NGC. The increase in weight from 2.49 grams to 2.50 grams resulted in arrows being placed at the date of the 1873-1874 Seated Dime issues. While the branch mint coins are scarce to rare in all grades, P-mint representatives are encountered with enough frequency to serve as type coins for most collectors. This status does not, however, apply to the present Superb Gem. One of only seven MS67 examples known to both NGC and PCGS (4/04), this coin exudes both originality and perfection. Both sides are richly frosted and free of even the most trivial abrasion. In addition to its technical superiority, this coin's original toning scheme also places it head and shoulders above all 1874 Arrows Dimes that we have handled in recent memory. Areas of antique-gold, blue-green, and dusky-gold color are noted over the otherwise silver-gray surfaces. A conditionally rare coin of singular beauty. Population: 2 in 67, 2 finer (4/04).(#4668) (Registry values: N1)

VERY SCARCE 1896-O DIME MS66 QUALITY

6046 1896-O MS66 PCGS. The 1896-O is similar to the 1896-S in that both are low mintage issues, the O-mint having a production run of only 610,000 pieces. It was also not saved in any significant numbers with this piece tied with several others as second finest known. The surfaces display exceptionally bright, satin-like mint luster and both sides are covered with gray, rose, and sea-green toning. Sharply, but not fully defined in all areas. Population: 4 in 66, 0 finer (3/04).(#4810) (Registry values: N4719)

PLATINUM NIGHT

PRISTINE 1893 BARBER DIME PR68

6047 1893 PR68 NGC. Both sides of this impeccable second-year proof are layered in a rich blend of cobalt-blue and violet toning, along with an occasional flash of bright rose. Even careful inspection with a glass fails to root out the most inconsequential blemish. Population: 6 in 68, 1 finer (4/04).(#4877) (Registry values: N4719)

DAZZLING PR68 CAMEO 1895 DIME

6048 1895 PR68 Cameo NGC. Sometimes overlooked by collectors, the 1895 proof dime is a key issue in the series. This is not because of the low mintage of proofs (880 pieces), but because of the scarcity and low mintage of business strikes with only 690,000 pieces produced. As a result, there is additional date pressure on high grade 1895 proofs. This is a spectacular cameoed example that is brilliant throughout with surfaces that approach technical perfection. Close examination shows that the dies were heavily polished with subsequent thinning of the ribbon below Liberty's hair on the obverse. The heavy die polish also resulted in deeply reflective fields which set up a "black" background against the dazzling white mint frost on the devices.(#84879) (Registry values: N4719)

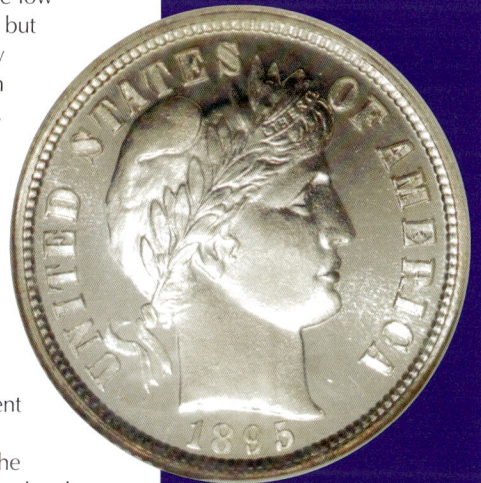

VERY RARE FULL BANDS GEM 1918-D DIME

6049 1918-D MS65 Full Bands NGC. Even though more than 22 million pieces were struck, the 1918-D is generally acknowledged today as the most challenging strike rarity in the Mercury dime series. No doubt this was a result of hurried wartime conditions. Gems are very elusive and Full Bands pieces are virtually non-existent at any grade level. This is an untoned example that has pronounced granularity to the surfaces. Sharply defined throughout, not just on the bands, there are no obvious or distracting blemishes on either side of this satiny coin. Population: 7 in 65, 1 finer (4/04).(#4919) (Registry values: N7079)

CHOICE BRILLIANT UNCIRCULATED 1919-D MERCURY DIME WITH FULL BANDS

6050 1919-D MS64 Full Bands PCGS. This conditionally scarce D-mint dime is rather difficult to locate with Full Bands definition. This is a noteworthy specimen whose untoned, bright surfaces show pinpoint striking definition throughout. The central bands are fully separated and the surfaces show only a few minor marks on the obverse. A definite find for the Mercury Dime specialist.(#4925) (Registry values: N2998)

CONDITIONALLY RARE 1919-D DIME, MS65 FULL BANDS

6051 1919-D MS65 Full Bands NGC. A conditionally rare early Mercury that is extremely elusive with fully split bands. This is a strongly detailed coin that also has well defined peripheries. The thick, satiny luster is covered with colorful hues of green, crimson, russet, and gold that deepens at the borders over both sides. There are no distracting blemishes, just a few microscopic ticks in the center of the obverse. Population: 3 in 65, 0 finer (4/04).(#4925) (Registry values: N4719)

THE SINGLE FINEST PCGS-CERTIFIED 1919-S DIME, MS66 FULL BANDS

6052 1919-S MS66 Full Bands PCGS. This issue's original mintage of 8.8 million pieces is on the scarce side for the Mercury Dime series. Add to this the fact that most extant '19-S Dimes are worn to one degree or another and one can easily appreciate the scarcity of this date in Mint State. As specialists in this widely collected 20th century series know, the 1919-S is also a major strike rarity. In fact, David Lange (1993) ranks this issue the second rarest S-mint Mercury with Full Bands definition.

This is one of the most important Mercury Dimes of **any** issue that we have handled in recent memory. First, the strike. The all-important central reverse crossbands are fully split from end-to-end. What's more, the definition remains crisp throughout virtually all other features. Now for the surface preservation. It is equally as impressive as the strike with smooth, lustrous surfaces that are devoid of grade-limiting abrasions. Untoned save for a few flickers of pale tinting at the borders, and a no-questions Gem that is sure to find its way into an important Registry Set. Population: 1 in 66, 0 finer (3/04).(#4927) (Registry values: N7079)

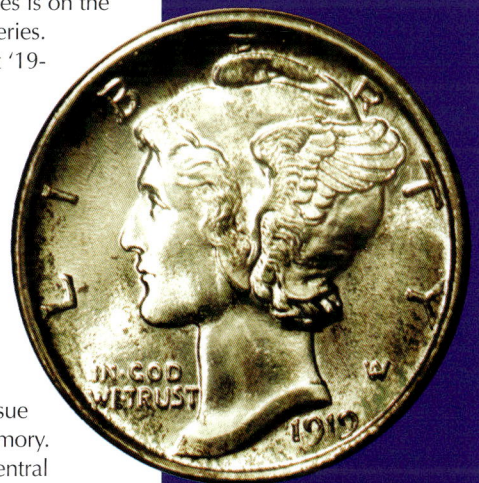

GEM HIGH GRADE 1921 MERCURY DIME MS66 FULL BANDS PCGS

6053 1921 MS66 Full Bands PCGS. The 1921 usually shares the spotlight in the popular series of Mercury Dimes, along with the '16-D, '21-D, and the overdates. Mint State pieces are generally well struck through the centers, as is the Gem example offered here. Only a hint of the normal border weakness on the obverse is visible. Delicate silver-gray patina is light enough that most would view this outstanding '21-P as brilliant.(#4935) (Registry values: N4719)

OUTSTANDING 1921 MERCURY DIME EX: STARR

6054 1921 MS66 Full Bands PCGS. Ex: Starr. An exquisite, sharply detailed example of this desirable key, with delicate, dappled violet toning in the peripheral areas. The only blemishes of note are a few tiny contact marks on the fasces.
Ex: Floyd Starr Collection (Stack's, 10/92), lot 387.(#4935) (Registry values: N4719)

SPARKLING 1925-S DIME MS66 FULL BANDS

6055 1925-S MS66 Full Bands PCGS. The 1925-S has a relatively low mintage within the context of the series, one of 5.8 million pieces produced, and is easily among the most poorly struck issues in the entire run of Mercury Dimes. Even those coins that display Full Bands definition are apt to possess indistinct peripheral detail and/or numerous die polishing lines. The extraordinary representative offered here leaves most of the high quality survivors we have seen in the dust. Both sides of this shimmering-white Premium Gem are strongly detailed in all areas and boast radiant luster that is perhaps its most outstanding attribute. Population: 19 in 66, 3 finer (3/04).(#4953) (Registry values: N4719)

1926-S MERCURY DIME MS67 NGC

6056 1926-S MS67 NGC. Sharply struck save for a little bit of bluntness in the center of the reverse, this lustrous Superb Gem displays some mottled olive-green and crimson-red iridescence overall. The underlying fields are frosty and exceptionally smooth. We are unable to find more than a single tiny abrasion, that being on Liberty's neck. Population: 2 in 67, 0 finer (4/04).(#4958) (Registry values: N4719)

COLORFULLY TONED GEM 1875-S TWENTY CENT PIECE

6057 1875-S MS66 NGC. A highly lustrous example that is beautifully toned in shades of sea-green, reddish-russet, and gold with only one mentionable abrasion visible on Liberty's thigh. Well defined over most of each side with occasional softness on the stars and the top of the eagle's left (facing) wing. A splendid, Gem high-grade type coin. Population: 30 in 66, 6 finer (4/04).(#5298) (Registry values: N4719)

LUSTROUS MS66 1875-S TWENTY CENT PIECE

6058 1875-S MS66 PCGS. The twenty cent piece is not rare in the strict sense of the word. However, it is a very popular coin for type collectors and the 1875-S has the largest mintage and is the most available issue in this short series. This is a highly lustrous example that displays streaky gray-brown patina over each side. A bit weakly detailed over the highpoints of the devices, the only marks of note are a cluster of tiny abrasions on the upper reverse below OF. Outstanding quality.(#5298) (Registry values: N4719)

FLASHY CAMEO GEM PROOF 1876 TWENTY CENT PIECE

6059 1876 PR65 Cameo NGC. The snow-white surfaces offer breathtakingly beautiful contrast between the glittering fields and chalky devices, being fully detailed and free from all but the most discreet hairlines. Fantastic quality and eye appeal for this briefly minted, odd denomination type coin. Population: 8 in 65, 5 finer (4/04).(#85304) (Registry values: N4719)

FINAL YEAR 1878 TWENTY CENT PIECE

6060 1878 PR65 PCGS. The 1878 is a well known, conditionally scarce, proof-only issue. Only 600 pieces were sold by the mint out of the 760 proofs that were produced. Most of each side is toned in mottled shades of charcoal-gray, russet, and blue-green. The underlying fields shimmer with mirror-like reflectivity. A worthwhile and obviously original example of this Twenty Cent rarity.(#5306) (Registry values: N4719)

POPULAR FIRST-YEAR 1796 BUST QUARTER

6061 1796 AU Details, Repaired, NCS. B-2, R.3. A perfectly centered example of the country's first Quarter Dollar, and the only year of issue for this particular design type. Evidence of a repair is seen at the top of the obverse and at the base of the reverse. Flat, gunmetal-gray patina covers most of each side with deeper charcoal-gray color in the protected areas. Weakly struck on the breast of the eagle and on the head, as always.(#5310)

CONDITIONALLY RARE 1838 NO DRAPERY SEATED QUARTER MS65 NGC

6062 1838 No Drapery MS65 NGC. The device punches for what would become the Seated Liberty Quarter were completed by Christian Gobrecht during the summer of 1838. After 20 "specimens" were sent to Treasury Secretary Levi Woodbury, regular production commenced on September 29. The Philadelphia Mint produced at least 466,000 examples this year, all of which, like their 1839 and 1840-O No Drapery counterparts, lacked obverse drapery folds at Liberty's right (facing) elbow. All three of these issues are scarce in problem-free Uncirculated preservation, and what few coins have been certified at the upper reaches of the Mint State grading scale are usually snatched up quickly by type collectors when they appear on the market.

Writing in 1991, Larry Briggs says of this issue: "Head, stars, and obverse dentils are poorly struck." Obviously, the author did not have the opportunity to examine the present example, as most detail on both sides is fully brought up, save for some of the denticulation. There are also remarkably few abrasions for the type. Fully frosted, completely untoned, and undeniably attractive. NGC and PCGS combined report only six coins in MS65 and seven finer (4/04).(#5391)

THE ULTIMATE 1867-S QUARTER, MS67 THE FIRST OFFERING OF THIS COIN AT PUBLIC AUCTION IN 18 YEARS

6063 1867-S MS67 NGC. The demand for silver coins in California had begun with the influx of '49ers eighteen years before and continued unabated out west throughout the Civil War. However, only 48,000 quarters were struck in the San Francisco mint in 1867—nowhere near the quantity needed to meet the demands of commerce in the booming post-war western economy. Only 150-200 pieces are believed known today in all grades, and the 1867-S is the sixth rarest quarter in overall rarity from 1855 to the present date. In XF and better grades it is considered R.6, and R.7 in mint condition. Most were heavily circulated, and this issue can be considered underrated above VF. Only three other pieces have been certified by NGC and PCGS combined in Mint State, with this piece the finest known by three points. In fact, this coin is one of only ten rarest Seated quarters in Superb condition. This distinguished roster includes the 1841-O, 1842-O, 1855-O, 1864-S, 1865-S, 1866-S, 1873-CC No Arrows, and 1891-O. It is interesting to note that the Eliasberg and James A. Stack collections account for six of these pieces. To further extend the high grade analysis of this issue, the combined populations for this issue from both PCGS and NGC (3/04) make it rarer than any other Seated quarter except for the "non-collectible" 1873-CC No Arrows. The only issue that is close to it is the 1860-S. All the other rare Carson City dates have far more coins certified. In Gem condition, the 1867-S is on par with the 1870-CC, 1871-CC, 1872-CC, and the aforementioned 1873-CC No Arrows. Just one piece is known for each of these issues in Gem condition.

This is a fabulous coin. The original, untoned, satiny "skin" is intact and both sides are essentially untoned. The central devices are fully struck, but the peripheral stars are not completely brought up—a trait seen on all known 1867-S quarters. The surfaces are essentially perfect with the only mentionable flaw being a small planchet flake to the right of the 7 in the date. Also, a fine die crack is seen up and to the left of the 1 in the date.
Ex: James A. Stack Sale (Stack's, 3/75); I. Kleinman (1975-?); Corky Vena (?-1977); New England Rare Coin Fund I (1977-1980), where it brought $30,000; Marty Haber (1980-1986); Auction '86, purchased by Jay Miller for the present consignor. Accompanied by an NGC Photo Proof.
From the Collection of Brian Keefe.(#5471)

SUPERBLY TONED GEM PROOF 1874 ARROWS QUARTER

6064 1874 Arrows PR67 NGC. Exceptional toning with hues of violet, cobalt-blue, reddish-gold, rose, and turquoise-blue. The strike is bold and this outstanding piece is almost devoid of imperfections. The short-lived Arrows series was used to signify a slight weight increase when the mint changed to the metric system. Lower graded proofs of this popular issue are not rare, but this Superb example is extremely scarce with only eight pieces thus far certified PR67 by NGC and PCGS combined, with none finer (4/04).(#5575)

WHITE ON BLACK 1896 QUARTER, PR68 ULTRA CAMEO NGC

6065 1896 PR68 Ultra Cameo NGC. The spectacular contrast between the icy-white devices and the deeply mirrored fields on this untoned specimen generates immense eye appeal. Meticulously struck and seemingly immaculate. A minute mint-made planchet flaw in the field below the S in PLURIBUS will identify this gorgeous piece in future auction appearances. Population: 11 in 68 Ultra Cameo, 2 finer (4/04).(#95682) (Registry values: N4719)

KEY DATE 1916 STANDING LIBERTY QUARTER IN BU

6066 1916 MS62 NGC. Among 20th Century silver rarities, the 1916 Standing Liberty Quarter is at the top of the list for popularity. With an original mintage of only 52,000 pieces, survivors are eagerly sought at all levels of preservation. It is our pleasure to offer a Mint State representative in the present lot. The otherwise medium gray features reveal a bit of pale apricot tinting toward the borders when the coin dips into the light. The luster is perhaps a bit subdued, but the surfaces are uncommonly free of distracting abrasions for a BU quality silver coin of this size. The reverse eagle is particularly well struck with bold delineation over most feathers.(#5704) (Registry values: N2998)

1916 STANDING LIBERTY QUARTER MS64 FULL HEAD

6067 1916 MS64 Full Head PCGS. A splendid near-Gem example of this widely recognized 20th century rarity. Only 52,000 pieces were struck of the 1916 and few were preserved in any grade with high grade examples being especially rare and desirable. The surfaces on this piece are bright and satiny with a tinge of peripheral color present and pronounced matte-like finish on the reverse. *From The Barry Donnell Collection.*(#5705) (Registry values: N4719)

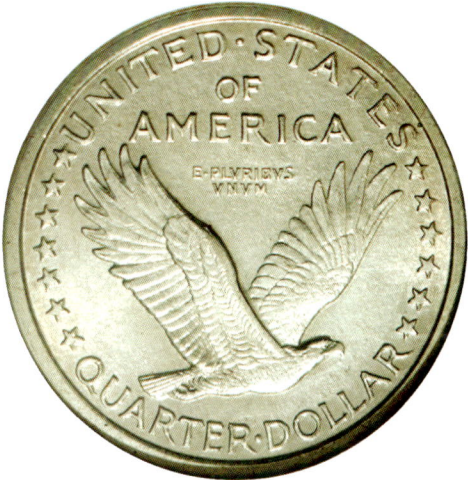

LUSTROUS, ORIGINALLY TONED MS66 FULL HEAD 1916 QUARTER

6068 1916 MS66 Full Head NGC. Seemingly everything conspired to make the 1916 quarter one of the premier rarities in 20th century American numismatics. It was the first year of issue for a new design by an accomplished sculptor, it had a very low mintage, and was not saved in significant numbers as the public's attention was focused on possible American involvement the European conflict. This is one of the finest examples known of this rarity, and it is almost perfectly preserved. Thick mint luster covers each side and the surfaces display deep, speckled, multicolored toning of unquestionable originality with significant underlying mint brilliance on the obverse. An exceptional, high grade 1916 quarter. Population: 15 in 66, 2 finer (4/04). (#5705) (Registry values: N7079)

SUPERB FULL HEAD 1929 STANDING LIBERTY QUARTER

6069 1929 MS67 Full Head NGC. The Standing Liberty quarter is known for strong eye appeal when found in high grades. This piece takes that concept to another level. Mostly brilliant, the surfaces exude a shimmering, satin-like mint luster and are virtually unaffected by post-striking impairments. Exceptional quality and well worth the premium this coin will surely bring. Population: 4 in 67, 0 finer (4/04).(#5773) (Registry values: N2998)

NICELY TONED, NEAR-GEM 1932-D WASHINGTON QUARTER

6070 1932-D MS64 PCGS. Each side exhibits a partially toned appearance with golden-charcoal shades being accented with multicolored iridescence as the coin is turned under a light. The surfaces are very lustrous and only a couple of tiny abrasions are noted on the obverse device.(#5791) (Registry values: N491)

NO-QUESTIONS GEM 1932-S QUARTER, MS65 PCGS

6071 1932-S MS65 PCGS. The mint luster shines brightly over each side and is unaffected by the light, opaque-white toning that partially covers each side. Surely there must be abrasions on this coin, but we cannot locate them with the unaided eye. Population: 60 in 65, 4 finer (3/04).
From The Jack Canniff Collection.(#5792) (Registry values: N991)

ONE OF THE FINEST PCGS-CERTIFIED 1935-S WASHINGTON QUARTERS

6072 1935-S MS67 PCGS. Billowy mint luster shines forth from both sides in the virtual absence of abrasions. The otherwise silver tinged iridescence yields to golden-tan patina in a few areas toward the central reverse. Well struck with exceptional eye appeal. With only 13 examples graded MS67 at PCGS and none finer (3/04), this '35-S Quarter is sure to elicit strong bids from Registry Set collectors.(#5799) (Registry values: N991)

FIRST YEAR 1794 HALF DOLLAR AU DETAILS

6073 1794 AU Details, Mount Removed, Damaged, NCS. O-101a, R.4. A later die state of this more obtainable die pairing, now thought to be among the last 1794 Half Dollars struck, The O-101a is most easily distinguished by the 10-11 berry arrangement on the reverse, and the die crack through the F in OF that takes a sharp turn toward the final S in STATES. This scarcely worn example has pearl-gray centers that yield to deeper gunmetal coloration at the margins. The coin has been so skillfully repaired that much of the damage can only be detected by the unnatural grainy texture of the surfaces.(#6051) (Registry values: N7079)

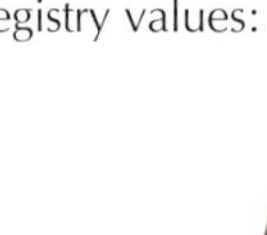

RARE 1797 DRAPED BUST, SMALL EAGLE HALF

6074 1797—Scratched, Damaged—ANACS. Good Details, Net AG3. O-101, R.5. Long known to be the most difficult type coin of the denomination, these Draped Bust, Small Eagle Half Dollars have enjoyed nearly legendary status and are perhaps the most avidly sought type in all of U.S. numismatics. This design was coined for only two years, 1796 to 1797, with a total mintage of 3,918 pieces. Most survivors are well circulated. Just four die marriages are known for the type, two for each of the dates of production. A lilac-gray piece with pinscratches in the right obverse field and a few tiny digs on the small eagle. AMERICA and the denominator are heavily worn, all other peripheral elements are clear. An early die state without the breaks that eventually shatter both dies. A certificate of authenticity with photo from the ANA Authentication Bureau, Number AB 5931, dated 12-10-97, accompanies the lot.
Ex: Bowers and Merena, 5/97, lot 1146.
From The Paulsboro Collection.(#6060) (Registry values: N4719)

SPLENDID GEM 1807 50 OVER 20 HALF DOLLAR

6075 1807 Large Stars, 50 Over 20 MS65 PCGS. O-112, R.1. The more obtainable of the 50/20 die pairings, particularly in higher grades, being distinguished by a well defined left foot on the 1 in the date and a partially detached upper serif of the E in E PLURIBUS. The die cutting blunder for which this popular *Guide Book* variety is named is clearly visible. While AU and better examples of the O-112 appear with some regularity, Gems such as this are of the greatest rarity and importance. The Condition Census example offered here is well struck and highlighted in coppery-orange toning.(#6086) (Registry values: N1)

WILDLY TONED CHOICE 1809 HALF DOLLAR

6076 **1809 MS64 NGC.** O-115a, R.3. Die cracks through the sixth star and the 0 in the date affirm the late die state. Cartwheel luster readily penetrates the exuberant ruby-red, aquamarine, lilac, and sky-blue patina. Well struck aside from the eagle's left (facing) shoulder. A beautifully preserved near-Gem, and surely within the Condition Census for the variety. Struck from a multiply clashed reverse die.(#6092) (Registry values: N2998)

CONDITIONALLY RARE 1812/1 BUST HALF, MS65 NGC

6077 **1812/1 Small 8 MS65 NGC.** O-102a, R.2. Easily identified as the later die state by the die crack that runs through the base of the second 1 to the stand of the overpunched 1. Surprisingly frosty surfaces, the central striking details are well brought up with some localized peripheral softness, most notably on the stars on the lower part of the reverse. Each side is moderately toned with reddish-gray hues that deepen to russet and deep sea-green at the borders. Noticeably die clashed on the obverse, the opposite side is virtually free of mentionable clashing. This conditionally rare example is finer than both the Eliasberg (MS 60) and Overton examples (MS 63), and is bettered by only one other at NGC (4/04).(#6101) (Registry values: N4719)

CHOICE 1813 50C OVER UNI HALF DOLLAR

6078 1813 50C Over UNI MS64 NGC. O-101, High R.3. A popular *Guide Book* variety with a blundered reverse, the UNI in UNITED was engraved in place of the denomination before the error was discovered and partially effaced. The obverse is lightly toned in silver-gray colors, while the reverse features vivid orange, powder-blue, and olive patina. Beautifully preserved, and well struck aside from the left side stars. Struck from heavily clashed dies. Combined O-101 and O-101a NGC Population: 6 in 64, 1 finer (4/04).(#6104) (Registry values: N4719)

EXQUISITE 1824 HALF DOLLAR, MS66 NGC

6079 1824 MS66 NGC. O-117, R.1. Two mint-made spikes from the left (facing) wing identify this die pairing. Golden-brown and dove-gray patina graces the obverse, while the reverse has aqua-tinged borders and orange-gray color throughout the centers. A well struck and lustrous premium Gem with clean surfaces and outstanding eye appeal. Combined NGC Population for all 1824 Overton varieties: 12 in 66, 2 finer (4/04).(#6137) (Registry values: N4719)

NEAR GEM 1827 SQUARE BASE 2 HALF DOLLAR BETTER O-108 VARIETY

6080 **1827 Square Base 2 MS64 NGC.** O-108, R.4. A tiny dot above the inner point of star 1 and numerous vertical stripes below the shield affirm this scarce Overton marriage. A well struck and shimmering near-Gem with rich lavender, apricot, and apple-green patina. 1827 provides the most challenging date for those who collect Capped Bust Halves by die pairing, since there are 49 varieties and two of those are extremely rare.(#6144) (Registry values: N2998)

SHIMMERING 1828 SQUARE 2, SMALL 8 HALF, MS66 NGC

6081 **1828 Square Base 2, Small 8, Large Letters MS66 NGC.** O-115, R.2. A wandering slender die crack through UNITED STATES attributes this Overton marriage. The horizontal shield lines extend into the left (facing) wing, as made. Waves of honey-gold and steel-blue patina endow this lustrous and virtually unabraded premium Gem. Combined NGC Population for all 1828 varieties: 14 in 66, none finer (4/04).(#6151)

IMPORTANT 1836 REEDED EDGE HALF DOLLAR, MS62 NGC

6082 1836 Reeded Edge MS62 NGC. The 1836 Reeded Edge Half Dollar is an important transitional year issue, not only because it meant a design change for the largest production silver coin at the time, but also because it marked an updated change in the Mint's technology to the new steam press. Just 1,200 pieces were reportedly struck and it appears that, not only did most enter circulation, they stayed in commercial channels for decades before their rarity and significance was documented. The example offered here is one of just 20 to 30 pieces known to survive at the Mint State level. Each side is boldly detailed, including the peripheral areas, and displays a mildly reflective sheen under medium gray-lilac toning. Population: 5 in 62, 8 finer (4/04).(#6175) (Registry values: N4719)

HIGHLY COLLECTIBLE GEM 1837 REEDED EDGE HALF DOLLAR

6083 1837 MS65 NGC. The 1837 is one of only two issues of Christian Gobrecht's Reeded Edge, 50 CENTS Reverse Half Dollar. The scarcity of the low mintage (1,200 pieces) 1836 explains the desirability of the 1837 among high quality type collectors. In 1836 the use of the "new" steam coining press necessitated a design change from John Reich's Capped Bust design to a somewhat similar design by Christian Gobrecht. The obsolete lettered edge was replaced by a reeded edge in 1836, however, as previously stated, only a limited number were struck. General production began the next year with over 3.6 million 1837 examples being coined (50 CENTS on the reverse), and these have become the most available date for this two year type. The latter issue is also a condition rarity in its own right, and few survivors possess the relatively abrasion-free surfaces of this richly toned representative. Warm copper-gray toning overlays the centers with gunmetal-blue patination interspersed. Fully struck in all areas, an exceptionally smooth example. Population: 32 in 65, 16 finer (4/04).(#6176) (Registry values: N4719)

IMPORTANT HIGH GRADE 1853 ARROWS AND RAYS HALF DOLLAR

6084 1853 Arrows and Rays MS66 NGC. While Arrows and Rays Halves are relatively available in the better grades of AU and lower-end Uncirculated, there are very few truly Gem, upper-end Mint State examples known. All too often the pieces seen are darkly toned or show indifferent luster. This piece, however, has thick, satin-like surfaces that are nearly flawless. In fact, the only surface anomalies we can see are some pronounced clash marks on each side that occurred at the time of striking. The coin is fully brilliant and untoned with a soft white appearance. A truly remarkable Arrows and Rays Half and the finest we have offered for sale in the last four years. Population: 13 in 66, 1 finer (4/04).(#6275) (Registry values: N1)

VERY SCARCE GEM 1854-O ARROWS HALF

6085 1854-O Arrows MS65 PCGS. The Arrows type was only struck in two years. It is easily obtainable in lower grades, but Gems such this piece are rarely seen and always in demand by advanced and knowledgeable collectors. Sharply defined throughout, the surfaces of this piece have thick, satiny mint luster and are attractively toned with golden-gray coloration over most of each side and aqua tints around the margins. Population: 11 in 65, 13 finer (3/04).(#6280) (Registry values: N4719)

HISTORIC 1861 CONFEDERATE STATES OF AMERICA RESTRIKE HALF DOLLAR

6086 1861 Scott Restrike MS61 PCGS. Acquiring the somewhat rusted reverse die for the Confederate Half Dollar from coin dealer Ebenezer Locke Mason, Jr. in the late 1870s, J. W. Scott hit upon the idea of restriking this rare Southern issue. He obtained 500 examples of 1861-dated Seated Half Dollars (supposedly all from the New Orleans Mint), planed off their reverses, and restruck them with the Confederate reverse. The pressure required to bring up the generally bold reverse definition resulted in flat and distended features on the obverse—a feature that the present example displays. Nonetheless, the date is clearly evident, and Liberty's portrait exhibits adequate definition on all but the highest points. Both sides are toned in natural slate-gray and pale orange shades.(#340402)

SUPERB 1879 SEATED HALF DOLLAR

6087 1879 MS67 NGC. The initial year of drastically reduced Half Dollar production and a popular issue as such. This is an outstanding representative that shows intermingled swirls of copper-green, pink, and electric-blue toning throughout. The surfaces are smooth and subtly prooflike beneath the toning. Population: 6 in 67, 1 finer (4/04).(#6361) (Registry values: N1)

COLORFUL 1882 HALF DOLLAR MS67

6088 **1882 MS67 NGC.** The 1882 is one of the more challenging of the popular 1879-1890 Half Dollar issues, being one of a mere 4,400 business strikes produced. This remarkably preserved example is typically sharp with prooflike tendencies beneath a coating of aquamarine and steel-violet toning. Population: 9 in 67, 1 finer (4/04).(#6364) (Registry values: N1)

CONDITIONALLY RARE 1895-S BARBER HALF, MS66 NGC

6089 **1895-S MS66 NGC.** Although the diligent numismatist can turn up several lower Mint State 1895-S Half Dollars after a year or so of searching, a lifetime of collecting could probably not produce another Gem whose eye appeal matches that of this specimen. Both sides present a bright, snow-white appearance without even a hint of patina. The strike is bold with none of the details getting too comfortable with their backdrop. A couple of tiny milling marks are reported on the primary obverse device. With otherwise placid surfaces and vibrant luster, this conditionally challenging Half Dollar is an important offering for the Barber coinage specialist. Population: 5 in 66, 1 finer (4/04).(#6473) (Registry values: N4719)

UNRIVALED 1899-S BARBER HALF, AN ORIGINALLY TONED AND ATTRACTIVE MS68 EXAMPLE

6090 1899-S MS68 PCGS. This exceptional Barber Half effortlessly puts forth the strong luster quality and crisp striking detail for which the 1899-S is known. In fact, these features are readily evident at all angles despite an overlay of warm, original, silver-gray patina. A few blushes of golden color are evident at more direct angles, but not even a loupe calls forth an abrasion that is worthy of undue concern. The high grade rarity of this issue is perhaps due to the fact that many examples were exported for use in the Philippines (this per Lawrence, 1991). This is the only MS68 example known to NGC and PCGS, and, perhaps not surprisingly, it has yet to be bettered at either service (3/04).(#6485) (Registry values: N7079)

VERY SCARCE MS65 1903-O HALF A SATINY GEM

6091 1903-O MS65 NGC. Even though 2.1 million pieces were struck of this issue, very few pieces were set aside high grade. This is the first MS65 or MS66 example we have offered in a Signature Sale since the 1999 ANA Sale. This is a bright and satiny Gem that shows uncommonly smooth surfaces with an especially clean cheek on Liberty. Most of each side is still brilliant with deep russet and cobalt-blue toning framing the rims. Sharply defined throughout. Population: 8 in 65, 4 finer (4/04).(#6496) (Registry values: N4719)

EYE-CATCHING 1909-S HALF DOLLAR MS66 ★

6092 1909-S MS66 ★ NGC. The 1909-S Half Dollar is a somewhat overlooked issue within the Barber series at the Gem level of preservation, being even more scarce in better Mint State grades than its mintage of more than 1.7 million pieces would suggest. The outstanding technical merits of this vibrant representative are perhaps exceeded by the coin's aesthetic appeal. Untoned centers give way to vivid shades of russet and turquoise iridescence at the margins. Population: 5 in 66, 1 finer (4/04).#6518) (Registry values: N2998)

RICHLY TONED, SUPERB GEM PROOF 1892 BARBER HALF

6093 1892 PR67 NGC. The 1892 has an enduring popularity with collectors as the first year of issue for the Barber series, and it is also one of the most available dates. This is an obviously original and untampered coin that has deeply reflective fields beneath multiple layers of toning. The obverse has golden-champagne central coloration with a sea-green periphery, while the reverse is toned a deeper shade of crimson with a thalo blue margin. Population: 14 in 67, 3 finer (3/04).(#6539) (Registry values: N4719)

SUPERB PROOF CAMEO 1893 HALF

6094 1893 PR67 Cameo NGC. Deeply mirrored fields and frosty textured devices shine forth in the virtual absence of toning. With sharp-to-full striking detail and carefully preserved features, this Superb Gem would make a lovely addition to a type set of specimen coinage. Population: 8 in 67 Cameo, there is only one finer with this finish (4/04).(#86540) (Registry values: N4719)

DAZZLING SUPERB PROOF 1895 BARBER HALF

6095 1895 PR67 NGC. As a date, the 1895 Barber half dollar is not a rare coin in either business strike or proof formats. Since specimen strikings were generally well preserved by collectors at the time, one might expect that survivors of the 800 piece proof delivery are relatively obtainable in today's market. They are, at least in grades up to and including the PR64 level of preservation. Gems, however, are scarce, and Superb Gems are of the utmost rarity and desirability. This silver-white example is untoned and both sides are fully brought up with frosted devices and reflective fields that are worthy of a Cameo designation, at least on the reverse. The nicest proof 1895 half that this cataloger has seen in quite some time. Population: 20 in 67, 10 finer (4/04).(#6542) (Registry values: N4719)

SUPERB, PERIPHERALLY TONED PROOF 1914 BARBER HALF

6096 **1914 PR67 NGC.** The 1914 has the lowest mintage in the Barber Half series, both as a business strike (124,610 pieces) and as a proof (just 380 pieces). This meticulously struck Superb Gem offers gorgeous honey-gold and electric-blue peripheral patina that frames the steel-blue centers. Population: 11 in 67, 2 finer (4/04).(#6561) (Registry values: N4719)

INTERESTINGLY TONED PR66 1915 BARBER HALF

6097 **1915 PR66 PCGS.** Final year of issue for the series and a coin with an impressively low mintage of only 450 proofs. The obverse is brightly reflective with an off center oval of shimmering golden color that is surrounded by deep blue elsewhere. The reverse, on the other hand, has a uniform dark blue patina. Essentially perfect surfaces. Population: 8 in 66, 6 finer (2/04).(#6562) (Registry values: N2998)

PLATINUM NIGHT

GEM 1917-S WALKING LIBERTY HALF WITH REVERSE MINTMARK

6098 **1917-S Reverse MS65 PCGS.** Produced in sizeable numbers, the 1917-S Reverse is plentiful in grades up to and including AU. Mint State survivors, however, are scarce, and Gems are rare. This fully lustrous representative is bathed in delicate silver and gold iridescence that allows full appreciation of a softly frosted finish. The otherwise sharp strike wanes a bit in the centers, and one or two out-of-the-way abrasions are noted toward the rims, but the eye appeal and technical quality are both equally deserving of the Gem designation.(#6573) (Registry values: N4719)

SHARPLY STRUCK 1919-D HALF DOLLAR MS64 PCGS

6099 **1919-D MS64 PCGS.** The 1919-D and '21-S are the two foremost keys in the widely collected Walking Liberty half series. A problem that seems common to virtually all 1919-D halves is that of weakness of strike, especially on the hand and head area of the obverse. Surprisingly, the hand is fully brought up on this coin and the head detail is nearly complete. From the standpoint of strike, this coin is unexcelled in our experience. Both sides are moderately toned with argent-gray and mottled russet patina, satiny underlying luster, and no singularly mentionable abrasions. A conditionally rare, key date coin with extraordinary striking definition. Population: 56 in 64, 11 finer (3/04).(#6578) (Registry values: N4719)

WELL STRUCK, NEAR-GEM 1920-D HALF DOLLAR

6100 1920-D MS64 PCGS. The 1920-D is a very scarce early Walker with a low mintage of only 1.5 million pieces to prove it. In addition to being an absolute rarity it is also a condition rarity and a strike rarity. This piece is remarkably well defined. Liberty's head, hand, and skirt lines as well as the eagle's feathers along the left leg are remarkably well struck. The mint luster is bright and softly frosted, each side presents a thin coating of silver-gray patina. An important 1920-D that is sure to be the object of much bidding attention by Walking Liberty specialists.(#6581) (Registry values: N2998)

GEM UNCIRCULATED 1928-S HALF DOLLAR

6101 1928-S MS65 PCGS. Superb mint luster overall, some mottled russet color has gathered over each side to add to the coin's fully original appearance. A few scattered abrasions are confined to the obverse, but these are nearly obscured by the patina. Slightly above average and a nice looking example of this scarcer issue.(#6588) (Registry values: N4719)

CONDITION CENSUS 1928-S HALF DOLLAR, MS66 NGC

6102 1928-S MS66 NGC. When offered in Mint State at all, the 1928-S (1.9 million pieces produced) is apt to grade no finer than MS63. An obviously important Gem, this coin is faintly toned on the obverse in dappled russet shades, the reverse is fully brilliant. Both sides are softly frosted in finish with solid luster quality and surface preservation for the assigned grade. The strike is not full over the highpoints, but, then again, there are virtually no '28-S Walkers that display this feature. Population: 4 in 66, 0 finer (4/04).(#6588) (Registry values: N4719)

SCARCE 1953-S FRANKLIN HALF DOLLAR GEM FULL BELL LINES

6103 1953-S MS65 Full Bell Lines PCGS. Most serious collectors of Franklin Half Dollars agree that, while available without any difficulty as a Gem, the 1953-S is the single greatest strike rarity in the series. This radiant, virtually untoned example does have some unavoidable softness on the details of the Liberty Bell, but near the base it is possible to follow each line all the way across without interruption. Extremely scarce as such. Population: 19 in 65, 1 finer (3/04).(#86666) (Registry values: N4719)

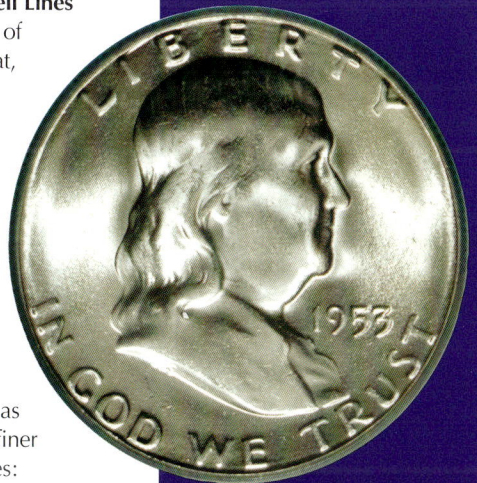

VERY FINE 1794 FLOWING HAIR DOLLAR RARITY

6104 1794 VF Details, Repaired NCS. B-1, BB-1, the only known dies. It is difficult to locate a 1794 Flowing Hair Dollar in today's market that is completely problem-free. The coin in this lot is not perfect, but it does possess some noteworthy and desirable features besides the 1794 date. Of obvious importance is the striking definition along the lower left obverse periphery. Stars 1, 3, and 4 are discernible, if not complete, and only star 2 can be described as being totally absent. All four digits in the date are readily evident, this despite a little softness of detail over the 1. The reverse die was also misaligned at the time of striking with the result that the TED in UNITED and STATE in STATES are more or less absent. All other design features are at least present, and there is some bolder definition in the more protected areas of the obverse portrait and reverse eagle. Now for the surface preservation. Both sides reveal some scattered circulation marks, but none are particularly noteworthy given the amount of wear that this coin saw. Much of the surfaces display not unattractive dove-gray coloration, although we do note a few areas of variegated color around the peripheries. This last feature brings us to this coin's most significant detraction: a plug through the upper obverse. This repair was rather well executed on the reverse, yet markedly less so on the obverse as far as the E in LIBERTY is concerned. Nevertheless, as a mid-grade survivor of this fabled numismatic rarity that offers relatively good overall definition, this coin represents a bidding opportunity that one should consider most carefully.(#6851)
(Registry values: N10218)

PLEASING VF 1794 DOLLAR

6105 1794 VF30 Repaired, Cleaned Uncertified. Well defined for a 1794 dollar, with the exception of the stars on the left side of the obverse and lower portions of the date. This is a striking defect that was caused by the dies slipping out of alignment, apparently after the first coin was struck. Even though the coin has been slightly repaired and cleaned, as noted above, this is still a desirable 1794 dollar that has light gray surfaces that deepen to a grayish-brown around the margins. Each side is covered with numerous small abrasions, but the only ones of any note are a small planchet void below the eagle's head and a short, angling scratch on the upper portion of the eagle's breast. A few of the denticles on each side show very fine scratches and tooling marks which enhance this design element, but actually do very little to detract from the overall appeal of the coin. Fine hairlines give the coin a somewhat dull, gray appearance. However, we have to emphasize that this coin represents an opportunity for the advanced collector to acquire a well detailed, nice appearing 1794 dollar with minor problems.
Ex: Phillip Flannagan Collection (Bowers and Merena, 11/01), lot 4203. From The Paulsboro Collection.(#6851) (Registry values: N10218)

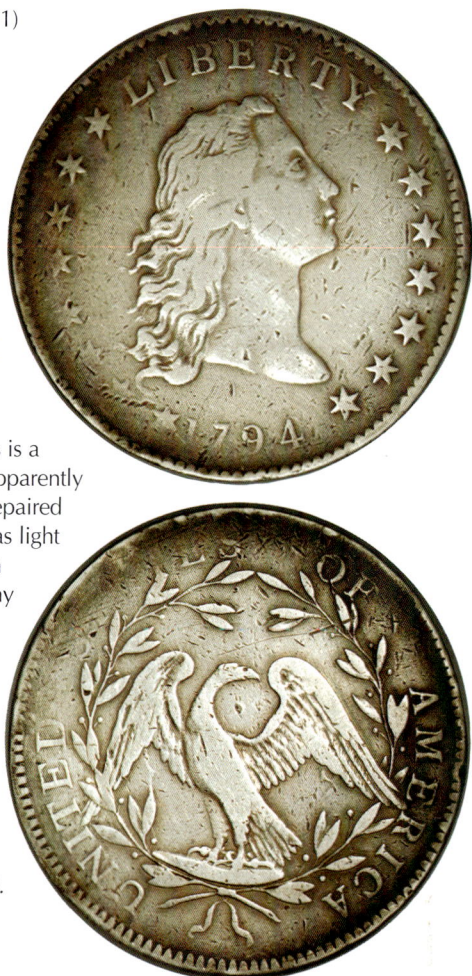

HISTORIC AND WELL DETAILED 1794 DOLLAR

6106 1794—XF Details, Obverse Repaired—NCS. We are not aware of another opportunity collectors have ever had to choose between so many 1794 dollars. As a rule, silver dollars from this year are rarely offered at public auction, and the demand for these coins far outdistances the supply. This particular coin shows evidence of minor repair in the upper obverse field, and yet numismatists for many generations have been willing to accept or overlook this defect as this piece has been in major collections since the 1870s. The surfaces are medium gray with much lighter accents over the highpoints on the reverse. Weakly struck on the stars on the obverse stars, as always, with the left side of the reverse also weak from having been struck from misaligned dies. The only mentionable surface defect is a diagonal scratch across the eagle's neck that continues into the field below. The repair was done on the obverse in the field at 1 o'clock and it affects a couple of stars. Apparently this area was smoothed in order to lessen the effect of a deep planchet flaw; however, the flaw is still obvious. A well detailed and historic 1794 dollar. *Ex: Michael Moore Collection (Edward Cogan, May 1-2, 1879), lot 611; John C. Lighthouse Collection (J. C. Morgenthau & Co., February 18-19, 1936), lot 208; F. S. Guggenheimer Collection (Stack's, January 22-24, 1953), lot 945.*(#6851) (Registry values: N10218)

6107 No lot.

SHARPLY DEFINED, NEAR-MINT 1794 DOLLAR

6108 1794—Light Scratches, Old Cleaning—AU58 SEGS. Mint records indicate that only 1,758 silver dollars were minted in the initial year of production, 1794. Of that number probably no more than 130-140 pieces are believed extant today in all grades. Needless to say, most are nowhere near as well defined as this piece. The central portions are boldly brought up and the coin was struck on a rough planchet. As always, the lower left portion of the obverse (specifically the first few stars and the lower digits in the date) are weakly defined, as is the left side of the reverse. This, of course, is from the coin being struck from misaligned dies, as was almost all the mintage. But we must point out that strike-wise this piece is far superior to almost all other 1794 dollars in existence. Close examination reveals numerous shallow scratches in the fields, most notably the left obverse field, which is also faintly tooled. A few minor adjustment marks are also located over the figure of Liberty. The fields and more recessed areas of the design have taken on a light gold coloration while the higher portions of the coin show steel-gray patina. A very well defined example of this numismatic classic and the first year of issue for the basic monetary unit of the newly-formed United States.(#6851) (Registry values: N14284)

CLASSIC HIGH GRADE 1795 DOLLAR 3 LEAVES, AU53 NGC

6109 1795 Flowing Hair, Three Leaves AU53 NGC. B-5, BB-27, R.1. Easily attributable as a noticeable die line (bar) shows behind the highest curl in the obverse field. The Flowing Hair type was produced for only two years and this is considered an important type coin, as the 1794 is now a classic rarity. The eagle's wing feathers are sharp and both sides are well centered with nearly full peripheral detail. Minimal abrasions and light steel-gray toning round out the picture. Uncommonly attractive for both the grade and the issue.(#6852) (Registry values: N4719)

LOVELY ALMOST UNCIRCULATED 1795 FLOWING HAIR DOLLAR, B-5

6110 1795 Flowing Hair, Three Leaves AU53 NGC. B-5, BB-27. Die State III. The most commonly encountered 1795 die variety, most easily attributed by the angling die scratch behind Liberty's head. Curiously sharp around the peripheries on each side, the centers are noticeably weak in definition. Lightly abraded and also equally light in color, one is almost tempted to say "brilliant." The reverse shows slight streakiness from tiny specks of grease that were struck into the planchet at the time of manufacture. An outstanding Flowing Hair dollar and an excellent type coin.(#6852) (Registry values: N4719)

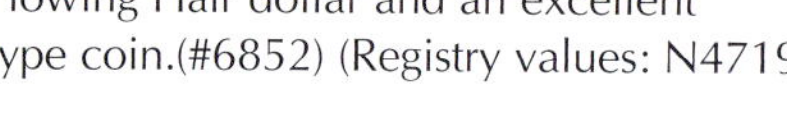

POPULAR HIGH GRADE 1802/1 BUST DOLLAR

6111 1802/1 Wide Date AU50 NGC. B-3, BB-234, R.3. Easily identified by the small die lump in the field between Liberty's forehead and stars 8 and 9. This is a scarcer die state per Bowers, with some of the arrowheads disconnected. Each side is toned a medium gray color with darker charcoal accents in some of the protected areas. The reverse exhibits a couple of small grease marks (as struck). Remaining luster is visible on both sides, but is especially pronounced on the reverse.(#6899)

EXTREMELY RARE AND VALUABLE NAME BELOW BASE 1836 GOBRECHT DOLLAR

6112 1836 Name Below Base, Judd-58 Restrike, Pollock-61, R.5, PR66 NGC. Die Alignment III. Plain Edge. Silver. On the obverse, Liberty is seated on a rock with a shield and a Liberty Cap on pole held in her left hand. The word LIBERTY is embossed on a ribbon that drapes over the shield, and C. GOBRECHT. F. (i.e., C. Gobrecht fecit, where fecit is Latin for "made this") appears in the field between the base of Liberty and the date. This variety, with Gobrecht's name appearing below the base of Liberty is an American numismatic classic. Nevertheless, criticism concerning the prominent placing of Gobrecht's name on a U.S. coin forced director Robert M. Patterson to have this signature moved to a less conspicuous place. In particular, Gobrecht's signature was impressed in small letters at the base of Liberty, creating the Judd-60 issue, or standard 1836 dollar which was then released to the public in December 1836.

All Gobrecht dollars, including the patterns, were struck with a proof finish (i.e., were struck at least twice to bring up the details of the low relief design). This particular coin exhibits excellent mirrored surfaces and is uniformly toned in colors of gray and blue with an undertone of reddish patina. Some doubling of the letters within the reverse legend is noted, and the coin may be unique as such. Since this coin was clearly struck at least twice, it is possible that the observed doubling occurred as a result of planchet rotation between strikes. This is the only Judd-58 specimen that we are aware of that shows this type of doubling.

The original dies for this pattern dollar were produced in 1836 by Christian Gobrecht (as an engraver at the U.S. Mint) from sketches made by Titian Peale and Thomas Sully. On the reverse, an American eagle flies to the left in a field of twenty-six stars. Thirteen large stars represent the thirteen original colonies, and thirteen smaller stars depict the subsequent states admitted to the Union (with Michigan expected to be admitted in 1837). The legend UNITED STATES OF AMERICA and ONE DOLLAR appears around the circumference. On the present coin, the head of Liberty is nearly opposite the O in ONE, with the eagle flying level to slightly downward after a normal coin turn (i.e., rotation around the coin's horizontal axis). A die crack unites the tops of NITED STATES O, and a second smaller crack is located at the bottom of DOLLA in DOLLAR. The Die Alignment III configuration, and the presence of reverse die cracks, indicate, according to the most recent and ongoing research by Mike Carboneau and James Gray, that this coin is a restrike, probably made between 1857 and 1869. However, since no "original" Judd-58 coin has been authenticated; it appears that all, or nearly all, of the Judd-58s are restrikes. Had the U.S. Mint not made these coins for collectors in the late 1850s and 1860s, then for all practical purposes, this pattern would be a non-collectible item. Therefore, the only collectible Gobrecht dollar patterns are the restrikes, and even these are very difficult to locate. In fact, no Judd-58 specimen exists in the Smithsonian Collection. Although the exact mintage of Judd-58 coins is unknown, recent estimates based on the observed population of Judd-60 coins (and their known mintage) suggest that if any Judd-58s were made in 1836, then fewer than six originals were struck (however, all of these examples seem to have vanished from the numismatic community). In addition, approximately 80 restrikes are estimated to have been made sometime after 1857. Although PCGS has recently begun to classify some Judd-58 coins as "originals," it is not clear that these newly identified coins are in Die Alignment I orientation and were made on 416 grain planchets; or if they represent other die alignment configurations made from an uncracked reverse die. In any case, after 18 years of grading and encapsulating coins, only 22 Judd-58s have been certified: sixteen by PCGS and six by NGC. Two coins have been graded Proof-66 by NGC and none by PCGS. No coins have been graded higher.

Finally, the current coin is a spectacular specimen representing one of the best preserved examples of one of the greatest rarities in numismatics. Simply an incredible coin and an incredible opportunity.(#11217)

MID-GRADE 1836 GOBRECHT DOLLAR, XF DETAILS

6113 1836 Name on Base, Judd-60 Original, Pollock-65, R.1—Cleaned—ANACS. XF Details, Net PR30. Silver. Plain Edge. Die Alignment I, issue of 1836. The present variety has C. GOBRECHT F. inscribed on the base of the rock. Based on the coin's die alignment, this piece represents one of the 1,000 Gobrecht dollars that were struck in December of 1836, and are routinely called "first originals." The Gobrecht dollars made in 1836 were struck on heavy weight (416.5 grain) planchets, the standard in effect since 1794. The present coin shows the cumulative effects of wear typical of circulation, illustrating that many Gobrecht dollars actually circulated within the channels of commerce; and therefore, represent "business strikes" even though they were originally struck as proofs. The Gobrecht dollars of 1836 and 1837 were also made with a plain edge (a somewhat unique situation for U.S. coins), indicating that a reeded collar for these coins was not ready in 1836. In fact, the Mint was changing from lettered edges to reeded edges at about this time. Unlike the reeded edge half dollars made in November 1836, all Gobrecht dollars made between 1836 and 1839 were produced on a screw press. The surfaces of the present coin are untoned and are non-reflective due to cleanings that must have occurred over the last 167 years. It was a normal practice for many decades for people to occasionally clean or polish their coins. In fact, the Gobrecht dollars that reside in the Smithsonian Collection, which were acquired from the U.S. Mint Collection, have also been cleaned several times by Mint personnel. Even though all Gobrecht dollars were produced with a proof finish and are listed in the Judd and/or Pollock pattern books, it is now generally accepted that the 1,000 coins minted in 1836, the 600 made in 1837, and the 300 struck in 1839 are standard issue coins made for circulation; and therefore, are not patterns. Nevertheless, the Judd and Pollock catalog numbers for these coins are routinely supplied for technical and historical reference.

The present coin represents a well circulated Gobrecht dollar that should be compatible with a introductory level or general type collection.

From The Paulsboro Collection.(#11225)

ELUSIVE 1838 GOBRECHT DOLLAR RESTRIKE IN SILVER JUDD-84

6114 1838 Name Omitted, Judd-84 Restrike, Pollock-93, R.5, Impaired Proof, Polished, Artificially Toned, NCS. Silver. Reeded Edge. Die Alignment III (head of Liberty opposite the NE of ONE; or equivalently, coin-turn with the eagle flying level). Both sides are unnaturally bright, even for a proof striking, with tinges of orange-gold and violet toning in the recesses. Classified as a "restrike," this term seems superfluous as it appears that all 1838 Dollars that exist today are restrikes. No "original" 1838 Dollar has been authenticated to our knowledge, and it is believed by some numismatists that no 1838 Dollars were actually struck in 1838. If this is correct, then all 1838 Dollars are restrikes.

Of the three die cracks normally found on the reverse, only the short crack connecting the bases of the letters LAR (of DOLLAR) can be detected here with any certainty. The presence and size of these die cracks, when compared with other Gobrecht Dollars struck with the same reverse die, indicate that this piece was probably made during one of Linderman's two terms of office. Most Gobrecht Dollar restrikes are known to have been made between 1857 and 1860 (during Snowden's term of office), or from 1867 to 1869 (during Linderman's first term), or from 1873 to 1878 (during Linderman's second term as U.S. Mint Director). Even though their origin is a bit hazy, the scarcity of these 1838 Restrikes when combined with the popularity of the Gobrecht design make them sought-after numismatic commodities.(#11352)

VERY RARE, TONED GEM PROOF 1838 GOBRECHT DOLLAR

6115 1838 Name Omitted, Judd-84 Restrike, Pollock-93, R.5, PR65 NGC. Die Alignment III. Reeded Edge. Silver. Like the Judd-58 above, all 1838 dollars are considered patterns. Unlike the circulation issues of 1836 (Judd-60) and 1839 (Judd-104), no 1838 dollars were intentionally made for public distribution. The 1838 dollars were made to test two new design features: (1) a reeded edge, and (2) the removal of the 26 stars from the reverse of the 1836 dollar and the placing of 13 new stars around the obverse. It is clear that the *dies* for the 1838 dollar were made in 1838; however, it is not certain how many (if any) 1838 dollars were actually struck in 1838. Only one original specimen is known, and that coin is a part of the U.S. Mint Collection now retained by the Smithsonian. However, the Smithsonian specimen exists in Die Alignment IV orientation (not Alignment I, as asserted by Breen), and was struck from an uncracked reverse die. All 1838 dollars that have been observed in private collections or museum holdings appear to be restrikes made in the late 1850s under the authority of Director James Ross Snowden, or in the late 1860s by Director Henry R. Linderman. Like the present specimen, the restrikes were made to satisfy collector demand for these beautiful coins. The restrikes are generally found in Die Alignment III orientation (i.e., head of Liberty opposite the NE of ONE) as on this coin; however, a few restrikes were also made in Die Alignment IV. Although the exact mintage of 1838 dollars is unknown, recent estimates suggest that fewer than 250 coins were ultimately made, and that only a small fraction of these coins survive today. The restrikes can be distinguished from the originals by the presence of a faint die crack through portions of MERI, which is faintly seen on this coin.

The present coin also exhibits deeply mirrored surfaces and is pleasingly toned with deep cobalt and gray-purple toning—evenly balanced from one side to the other. Only a small number of hairlines are evident on either side, and are consistent with the Proof 65 grade. A small area of planchet roughness is noted next to the denticles between 7 and 8 o'clock on the obverse, which easily serves as a pedigree identifier for future researchers.

A total of fifty-two 1838 dollars have been certified by PCGS (30) and NGC (22), with only seven coins at the Proof 65 level, and none higher. The present specimen is certainly among the finest known 1838 dollars.(#11352)

IMPAIRED 1839 GOBRECHT DOLLAR IN DIE ALIGNMENT IV

6116 1839 Name Omitted, Judd-104 Original, Pollock-116, R.3—Tooled, Polished—ANACS. AU Details, Net PR20. Silver. Reeded Edge. Die Alignment IV, original issue of 1839. The head of Liberty is directly opposite the letters OF in the reverse legend. According to Walter Breen's definition of die alignments for Gobrecht dollars, this coin is a Die Alignment IV specimen (i.e., eagle level after a rotation around the coin's vertical axis, or "medal turn"). Toned in deep shades of gray and navy blue with underlying brightness from polishing. The letters LIBERTY in the shield are unusually sharp, as are some other central features. While the overall detail of the coin is more consistent with a higher grade coin, some portions appear to have been tooled (e.g., the obverse stars have been worked) and the surfaces burnished (or polished). Nevertheless, no reverse die crack is visible in AMERI. Although impaired, the coin shows the typical die state characteristics of an "original" 1839 dollar; and as such, is believed to be one of the 300 dollars that were originally issued for general circulation in December 1839. Due to the small mintage for that year, "original" 1839 dollars are usually difficult to locate. Many 1839 dollars seen today (and most of those that have been certified) are actually restrikes made in the late 1850s and 1860s. Although not a particularly attractive coin, the present 1839 Gobrecht dollar does represent one of the rarest regular issued U.S. silver dollars ever made, and in its current state of preservation, should be an affordable specimen for a circulated type set.

Ex: Rarities Sale (Bowers and Merena, 8/01), lot 266.

From The Paulsboro Collection.(#11444)

SELECT PROOF 1839 GOBRECHT DOLLAR

6117 1839 Name Omitted, Judd-104 Original, Pollock-116, R.3, PR63 PCGS. Silver. Reeded Edge. Die Alignment IV, "original" issue of 1839. The head of Liberty is nearly opposite the F in OF, and therefore is in Die Alignment IV orientation. A full figure of Liberty, with pole and shield, is the main design element on the obverse. The 26 stars that had been placed on the reverse of the 1836 dollars have now been removed, and 13 stars are now seen around the figure of Liberty on the obverse. A majestic flying eagle (symbolizing the United States) adorns the reverse surrounded by the legend UNITED STATES OF AMERICA and the denomination: ONE DOLLAR.

This coin has been identified by PCGS as an "original;" that is, a coin that was made in 1839. This new classification methodology adopted by PCGS is consistent with the latest information published in the "Red Book." However, not all Die Alignment IV coins are originals, but all originals are in Die Alignment IV. Those coins that exhibit a microscopic die break through the top of MERI are normally associated with restrikes (including both Die Alignment III and IV coins). Likewise, those coins in Die Alignment IV with a perfect (uncracked) reverse die are believed to be the originals from 1839 (and are usually found in low grades). The present coin is attractively toned on both sides with subtle gray, golden, and lilac iridescence and strong reflectivity in the fields. The devices also exhibit an excellent strike on each side. Only 300 1839 dollars were reported to have been made in 1839, and an unknown number of restrikes were struck after 1857 to meet collector demand at that time. All of the 1839 dollars made in 1839 are thought to have been deposited into the US banking system. Therefore, by default, the Gobrecht dollars issued 1839 dollars are regular issued coins (even though they were struck in proof format). Although considered a rare coin today (in fact rarer than 1794 dollars), we are very fortunate to have three 1839 dollars to choose from in this sale. The present coin is an attractive specimen that should fit nicely into any high grade collection that includes regular issued US dollars. As previously noted, all Gobrecht dollars are assigned Judd numbers, suggesting that these coins are patterns. However, this conclusion is not correct. In fact, the Gobrecht dollars made in 1836, 1837, and 1839 are regular issued coins, and therefore are not patterns. Nevertheless, for historical reasons, it appears that these coins will continue to be incorrectly identified as patterns. The only real Gobrecht dollar pattern coins are the Judd-58 (name below base) and the J-84 (1838 dollar). Gobrecht dollars represent a short, 3-year series, with two different "types" of coins. The first type consists of the issue of 1836 with the no-star obverse design, and the second type includes the 1838 and 1839 dollars with obverse stars but no reverse stars. Another interesting observation is that Gobrecht dollars are the only Proof coins intentionally made for general distribution. Gobrecht dollars are one of the most fascinating and yet confusing series of silver dollars ever made by the US Mint. Due to the small number of 1839 dollars that exist today, very few coin collectors will ever own an 1839 Gobrecht dollar. The current coin certainty represents a high grade example that should please most collectors.(#11444)

ANOTHER EXCEPTIONAL, HIGH GRADE 1839 GOBRECHT DOLLAR

6118 1839 Name Omitted, Judd-104 Restrike, Pollock-116, R.3, PR64 NGC. Silver. Reeded Edge. Die Alignment IVa. Head of Liberty opposite the right side of the F in OF, with the eagle flying level following a medallic turn. Fully struck in all areas with complete definition on Liberty's foot and sandal. Richly toned with gray-golden toning over both sides and a wide swath of cobalt-blue at the top of the obverse. The proof surfaces are deeply mirrored and only interrupted by a few crisscrossing hairlines in the right obverse field. Double punched on stars 5 and 8, as evident on all 1839 dollars.

Recent research by M. L. Carboneau and James C. Gray indicates that the original 1839 dollars were made entirely in Die Alignment IV (not Die Alignment I) from perfect reverse dies. The original 1839 dollars can therefore be distinguished from the restrikes by the presence of microscopic die cracks at the top of MERI in AMERICA, at the base of LAR in DOLLAR, and through the top of TE in UNITED. Not all die crack combinations are present on all restrikes. This is due to either weakness of strike or the emission sequence of the specific coin relative to when the die cracks developed. Except for a few presentation pieces, most "original" 1839 dollars were intentionally placed into circulation at face value and therefore are regular issue coins and not patterns, although they are listed in the Judd and Pollock pattern books. Today, many 1839 dollars are found in circulated, impaired, or damaged condition. The present 1839 dollar has a faint die crack through the top of MERI in AMERICA. At least 20x magnification and proper lighting are necessary to see this crack. The existence of this die crack indicates that the coin is a "restrike" probably made between 1857 and 1859. From this die crack we can imply that this particular coin is from a small number of restrikes made under the authority of James Ross Snowden. During the late 1850s, there was a large demand for U.S. coins, which was spurred on in part by the elimination of the large cent in 1857. However, collectors quickly discovered that many coins made just a few years earlier (e.g., the Liberty Seated dollars of 1851, 1852, the Gobrecht dollars of 1836-1839, and several other issues) were impossible to find in circulation. Inquiries to the U.S. Mint for these coins led Snowden to realize that he could satisfy this demand by producing restrikes, and that the proceeds from these "private" sales could finance the purchase of coins and medals for the U.S. Mint Collection. Of course, Snowden was discreet about this operation, and at first there were no problems. Eventually, however, a scandal ensued which brought an end to Snowden's restriking activities. It was not until Linderman's tenure in office in 1867-1869 (and then again in 1873-1878) that the Gobrecht dollar dies were taken out and a small number of additional restrikes were made. In any event, many of the restrikes that Linderman made went into his own personal collection. In fact, several Gobrecht dollar rarities were still in Linderman's estate as late as 1887 (he died in 1879 while under investigation by a congressional subcommittee concerning charges of misconduct which were never resolved). In spite of all of the restriking that occurred during the 1850s and then later in the 1860s, relatively few Gobrecht dollars were made and only a small fraction of these coins still survive. Almost all the high grade 1839 dollars found today are "restrikes." The present specimen is an excellent coin that should fit in any high grade early dollar collection.(#11446)

LOW MINTAGE 1859-S SEATED DOLLAR SIGNIFICANT BU PRESERVATION

6119 1859-S MS62 NGC. Breen-5462. This is the first Silver Dollar issue produced in the San Francisco Mint, and it is a scarce-to-rare date in all grades. Since most '59-S Dollars were exported, Mint State survivors such as the present example undoubtedly fall into the latter category. While some examples of this issue display bothersome striking incompleteness over Liberty's head on the obverse and the eagle's left (facing) leg on the reverse, this coin is boldly, if not sharply defined in all areas. A mottled overlay of silver-gray and apricot toning overlays golden-blue highlights, these colors allowing appreciation of a semi-prooflike finish at direct angles. A few scattered abrasions are noted, but we stress that none are sizeable or individually distracting. NGC has seen a total of only seven examples in MS62, and a mere two are finer (3/04). This coin is an early die state of the Breen-5462 marriage with repunching evident on the 18 in the date.(#6948) (Registry values: N7079)

ELUSIVE HIGH GRADE 1861 SEATED DOLLAR

6120 1861 MS64 NGC. The mintage for the 1861 Seated Dollar was a generous 77,500 pieces. However, a significant number were exported overseas, and a large percentage of the mintage was also melted by private citizens during the years of the Civil War. We know that 40,000 Silver Dollars with this date were also melted in 1861 to provide bullion for subsidiary silver coinage. As a result, the 1861 is very scarce in all circulated grades. In fact, proofs appear at auction more often than XF or AU coins. Mint State pieces are also seldom seen. This piece is well defined throughout with even, satin-like luster that has taken on an overlay of rich, medium density gray toning with an undertone of rose that is apparent when held beneath a light. Population: 14 in 64, 3 finer (4/04).(#6951) (Registry values: N4719)

HIGHLY COLLECTIBLE 1871-CC SEATED DOLLAR

6121 1871-CC VF35 PCGS. One of only four CC-mint Seated Dollars, the 1871-CC boasts the lowest mintage (1,376 pieces) of all branch mint issues in this challenging series. Although it loses the top rarity title to the 1873-CC, the '71-CC is a genuinely rare coin in all grades with an extant population of perhaps 85-125 pieces. A bisecting swath of dark brown patina on the reverse interrupts the otherwise slate-gray coloration. There are scattered circulation marks, none of which stand out for the grade. The wear is even and the devices retain ample striking definition. Both the Carson City specialist and the Seated dollar collector would be wise to pay special attention when this coin crosses the auction block.(#6967) (Registry values: N2998)

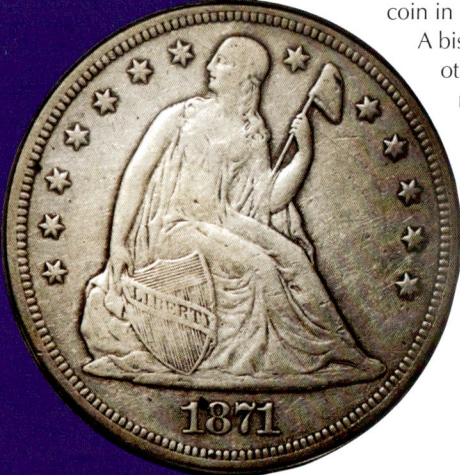

VERY RARE 1855 SEATED DOLLAR, PR64

6122 1855 PR64 NGC. Rarely seen in either business strike or proof format, the proofs of this date are very rare with estimates of survivors ranging from 30-40 pieces (equivalent of the number of proof sets sold that year) to as many as 75 examples (speculation based upon the number of proof sets sold plus an unknown number of coins sold individually by the Mint). If indeed pieces were sold individually outside sets attrition has taken a fearsome toll on the original mintage as only 33 pieces have been certified by both of the major services minus, of course, an unknown number of resubmissions. This is a flashy, deeply reflective example that shows no obvious or distracting contact marks, just a few discreet hairlines beneath the finely speckled gray-olive and golden toning.(#6998) (Registry values: N7079)

ORIGINAL GEM PROOF 1862 SEATED DOLLAR

6123 1862 PR65 NGC. A grand total of 12,090 Dollars were struck in 1862, only 550 of which were proofs. This is one of the very few Gems that remain today. The fields are deeply mirrored and they add significantly to the brightness of the gray, cobalt-blue, and rose-red toning that graces both obverse and reverse of this spectacular coin. The surfaces are essentially smooth with no obvious contact marks or other post-striking impairments on either side. A unquestioned Gem proof and thoroughly original. Population: 18 in 65, 8 finer (4/04).(#7005) (Registry values: N4719)

IMPORTANT PROOF 1869 SEATED DOLLAR IN GEM

6124 1869 PR65 PCGS. Proof Motto Seated Dollars are popular among type collectors with examples more-or-less available in grades up to and including PR64. Gems, however, are conditionally scarce. Housed in an older PCGS slab, this originally preserved specimen is awash in rich copper-gray toning. Direct angles reveal more vivid cobalt-blue and lavender undertones, as well as the glistening fields that one would expect for proof production methods. Sharply, if not fully struck in all areas, and devoid of even a single mentionable blemish. A high quality survivor of a Philadelphia Mint Silver Dollar delivery that is challenging to locate as a high grade business strike.(#7017) (Registry values: N4719)

INTERESTING GEM PROOF 1870 SEATED DOLLAR

6125 1870 PR65 NGC. Scarcer than the four preceding dates in the With Motto series, the 1870 presents the collector and researcher with the question of why this so. The mintage of proofs was notably high for the era with 1,000 pieces struck. The most obvious answer to the question posed above is that this date was not as popular as Mint officials estimated it would be (as happened in 1860) and many were melted as unsold at year's end. This is a flashy, deeply mirrored example that is light in color overall with powder-blue accents around the peripheries. There are very few technical flaws on either side. One interesting aspect of this coin is the irregular striking definition. The obverse displays the pinpoint striking details one would expect from a proof, but on the reverse the center is notably weak on the eagle's left (facing) leg, left wing, upper shield, and neck feathers. Population: 26 in 65, 9 finer (4/04).(#7018) (Registry values: N4719)

NICELY TONED GEM PROOF 1871 SEATED DOLLAR

6126 1871 PR65 NGC. This technically high grade and aesthetically pleasing proof is earmarked for inclusion in a collection of originally toned Gems. The smooth, virtually blemish-free obverse is layered in soft mint-green with antique-copper and red toning at the border. A more even layer of medium blue overlays the reverse. Fully struck, both sides reveal noteworthy reflective qualities as the coin turns into the light. A conditionally scarce offering from the later proof Seated Dollar series. Population: 16 in 65, 10 finer (4/04).(#7019) (Registry values: N4719)

LUSTROUS 1875-S/CC TRADE DOLLAR, MS64 CHOP MARK PCGS

6127 1875-S/CC MS64 Chop Mark PCGS. FS-012.5. Type One Obverse and Reverse. A deep chopmark at 8 o'clock on the reverse affects the obverse border near 10 o'clock. This otherwise carefully preserved near-Gem has booming luster and light tan patina. Well struck aside from Liberty's hair and the D in DOLLAR. Although two 1875-S/CC varieties are known, FS-012.5 is the most obvious since most of the second C in the original mintmark is intact. PCGS has a Registry Set devoted to chopmarked Trade Dollars, and the 1875-S/CC is a key to this specialized series.(#7040) (Registry values: N7079)

OUTSTANDING 1877-S TRADE DOLLAR MS66 ★

6128 1877-S MS66 ★ NGC. The 1877-S has the highest mintage in the Trade dollar series with 9.5 million pieces produced, and it is a popular type coin. Uncirculated pieces are not that difficult to locate but high grade examples such as this one are very rare. Fully struck throughout, the surfaces have dazzling mint luster and are brilliant throughout. It would be misleading to call this a perfect coin; however, there are no obvious or distracting abrasions on either side and this piece is as close to perfection as we can remember in a Trade dollar.(#7046) (Registry values: N7079)

BRILLIANT GEM 1878-S TRADE DOLLAR

6129 1878-S MS65 PCGS. The '78-S Trade Dollar is considered a common issue in Uncirculated grades. However, in this superior Gem state of preservation it is anything but common. This is an absolutely wondrous coin. Brilliant throughout, save for areas of subtle, mottled brown color on the reverse, the striking details are complete on most all of the devices. The mint frost is thick and races around each side unbroken by only the tiniest of abrasions. One of the more attractive Trade Dollars we have had the privilege of handling. Population: 15 in 65, 25 finer (3/04).(#7048) (Registry values: N4719)

GLITTERING 1879 TRADE DOLLAR PR66 CAMEO

6130 1879 PR66 Cameo PCGS. First of the proof-only years at the end of the Trade Dollar series. Only 1,541 proofs were produced of this date, and today only a small handful exist in such pristine condition as this one. The dazzling white surfaces show just the slightest hint of golden toning around the denticles and rims. The fields are intensely mirrored and light frost is noted on the devices, just enough to give the coin a mild cameo contrast. Population: 5 in 66 Cameo, 1 finer (3/04).(#87059) (Registry values: N4719)

GEM CAMEO PROOF 1880 TRADE DOLLAR

6131 1880 PR66 Cameo PCGS. The 1880 Trade Dollar is an issue with which we are very familiar. We typically offer at least one example in each of our Signature Sales, and, among others, our April 2002 sale of the Morris Silverman Collection included multiple Gem quality representatives. This example, however, is quite superior to the Gems we often see. Not only are the surfaces smooth and virtually pristine, but the stark cameo contrast enhances the eye appeal even further. The devices are not only richly frosted, but they are fully struck up over all features. A little dappled, golden-orange iridescence clings to the denticles and peripheral areas of the otherwise untoned surfaces. This issue is always in demand among specialists, and advanced collectors are sure to line up for the opportunity to bid on this lovely and seemingly immaculate specimen. Population: 10 in 66, 3 finer (3/04).(#87060) (Registry values: N4719)

SPLENDID 1881 TRADE DOLLAR PR66 CAMEO

6132 1881 PR66 Cameo PCGS. After a series high 1,987 proof Trade Dollars were struck in 1880, only 960 coins were minted of the proof-only 1881. Peerless, glassy surfaces present an essentially untoned appearance although a diagonal swath of milky patina is seen on the obverse when viewed at the proper angle. The contrast on this premium Gem representative is unmistakable. Population: 4 in 66 Cameo, 1 finer (3/04).(#87061) (Registry values: N4719)

SCARCE CHOICE BU 1879-CC MORGAN DOLLAR

6133 1879-CC MS64 PCGS. Perfect Dies. A lustrous and highly attractive example of this scarce and important Carson City key. The surfaces are bright with a glimmer of semi-reflectivity in the fields. The striking details are, however, a bit deficient, just missing complete definition over the central obverse. The coin presents as brilliant because of the lack of any mentionable color on either side. Several minor luster grazes in the obverse field prevent a full Gem grade.(#7086) (Registry values: P7, N2998)

SPLENDID 1879-CC DOLLAR MS63 PROOFLIKE

6134 1879-CC MS63 Prooflike NGC. The frosty-white devices contrast nicely with reflective, subtly striated fields, being further accented by colorful russet and blue peripheral hues. Every feature is quite crisp for this difficult Carson City issue and the surfaces are free of all but a few wispy abrasions.(#7087) (Registry values: P7, N2998)

ATTRACTIVE SELECT 1879-CC DOLLAR, MS63 DPL NGC

6135 1879-CC MS63 Deep Mirror Prooflike NGC. The frosty devices and watery fields combine to produce a stunning cameo image on this moderately abraded CC-mint Dollar. The borders are decorated with mottled shades of reddish-russet and sprinklings of cobalt-blue. The '79-CC is always in demand, and is quite scarce in any grade.(#97087) (Registry values: P7, N2998)

HIGHLY ELUSIVE GEM 1879-O MORGAN DOLLAR

6136 1879-O MS66 ICG. The '79-O is a favorite among collectors of Morgan Dollars and O-mint coinage alike, being the first of its kind from the New Orleans Mint. While seemingly abundant in AU and only modestly scarce in lesser Uncirculated grades, the availability of Gem or better examples is extremely limited. The nicely toned example offered here is as clean as we have recently seen for the issue and its vibrant luster is greatly enhanced by an area of blue, gold, red, and green toning at the top of the obverse.(#7090) (Registry values: P5, N4719)

1888 MORGAN DOLLAR MS67, EX: BINION

6137 **1888 MS67 NGC.** Ex: Binion Collection. Attractive amber and cobalt-blue toning adorns the reverse. Precious few examples of this otherwise available issue have received this lofty grade. Population: 21 in 67, 0 finer (4/04).(#7182) (Registry values: P2, N4719)

1889-CC PROOFLIKE DOLLAR, MS62 NGC

6138 **1889-CC MS62 Prooflike NGC.** The glassy, reflective fields are not uncommon for this issue, but the level of surface preservation is of the utmost importance for high quality specialists. A crisply impressed Morgan, the central highpoints are equally as sharp as the more recessed areas of the design. There are scattered bagmarks on both sides, and the surfaces present as mostly brilliant with the exception of milky haziness in the obverse field.(#7191) (Registry values: P9, N4719)

KEY 1889-CC MORGAN DOLLAR MS64 PROOFLIKE

6139 1889-CC MS64 Prooflike PCGS. While the occasional Mint State 1889-CC Morgan is not particularly uncommon with prooflike fields, such coins are in constant demand by collectors as they represent the ultimate in aesthetic appeal for this key date Carson City issue. The glassy surfaces on the important near-Gem example offered here possess enough reflectivity that a DMPL rating had to be a consideration, and are untoned save for a few irregular splashes of peripheral color on the obverse. Just a touch of light chatter is seen here and there in the fragile fields, while a few shallow facial disturbances rule out a higher classification. One of the finer examples of this well known Morgan Dollar rarity that we have offered in quite some time. Population: 4 in 64, 0 finer (3/04).(#7191) (Registry values: P9, N7079)

ELUSIVE BRILLIANT GEM 1890-CC DOLLAR

6140 1890-CC MS65 PCGS. The 1890-CC had a substantial mintage of 2.3 million pieces. Many were distributed at the time of minting and many thousands more were paid out on both coasts in bag quantities between the early 1930s and 1964. This is a partially reflective Gem that is brilliant throughout. The mint luster is thick and frosted, as always seen on Carson City Dollars. Fully struck, the only marks of note are a few tiny abrasions over the obverse.(#7198) (Registry values: P5, N2998)

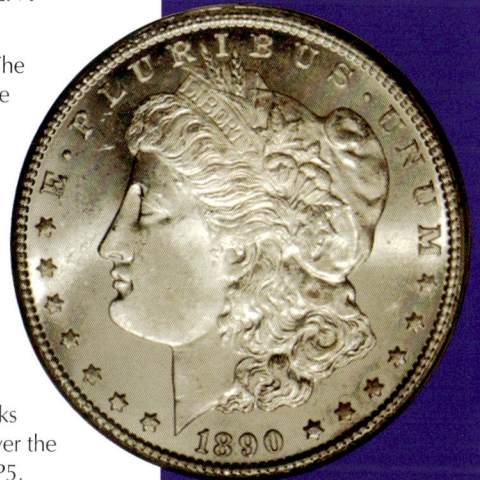

SCARCE GEM QUALITY 1893-CC MORGAN DOLLAR

6141 1893-CC $1 Morgan Dollar MS66 SEGS (MS65). The '93-CC Morgan is immensely popular in all grades, being the final year of issue from the Carson City Mint and sporting a reduced production figure of only 677,000 pieces. Rolls of mostly substandard Uncirculated pieces were available on an occasional basis until the 1970s, but very few quantity offerings have been available in recent years. Bowers relates that a bag of 1,000 coins was released into circulation in Great Falls, Montana. Additionally, the Redfield hoard contained a modest quantity of '93-CC's. Over the years, we have noticed a curious tendency for '93-CC Dollars to either have a flat-as-a-pancake strike or to be very sharply struck. There seems to be little middle ground on this issue. This particular Gem example is powerfully struck and brilliant, with flashy, semi-reflective fields. Only a few wispy blemishes are found in the left obverse field and in the vicinity of Liberty's chin. The serious collector of Morgan Dollars would have to search long and hard to locate an 1893-CC of equal eye appeal and technical merit.(#7222) (Registry values: P8, N10218)

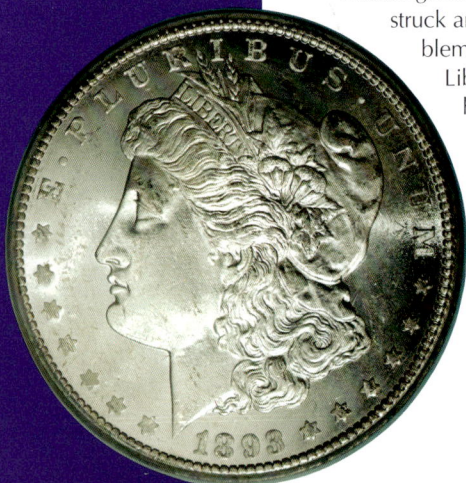

ATTRACTIVE 1893-S MORGAN DOLLAR XF40

6142 1893-S XF40 ANACS. Light to medium gray surfaces with bits of gunmetal color immediately surrounding the devices along with traces of hidden luster. Unlike some key issues in other series, the '93-S is an extremely saleable coin in any grade, whether it be a problem-laden Good or a nice looking XF piece such as this one. *From the Virgil Farstad Collection, Part Two.*(#7226) (Registry values: P10, N2998)

LUSTROUS 1893-S MORGAN DOLLAR XF45

6143 1893-S XF45 PCGS. Both sides of this bright silver-gray example have respectable amounts of surviving luster in the areas surrounding the devices. Surface marks are minimal for a lightly circulated Morgan and the only reportable distraction we can find is a trivial rim bruise on the reverse at 12 o'clock. Terrific collector grade quality for this well known scarcity.

From The Barry Donnell Collection.(#7226) (Registry values: P10, N2998)

ELUSIVE NEAR-GEM 1895-S DOLLAR, MS64 PCGS

6144 1895-S MS64 PCGS. Generally considered a semi-key date in the Morgan dollar series, the 1895-S is scarce in all conditions. This near-Gem complies fully with all of our expectations for the assigned grade. The surfaces are fully brilliant, showing a light silvery-white haze, and the fields are semi-prooflike, with myriad die polishing marks that impart a pleasing sheen to the coin. Sharply struck, but lacking some detail over the ear for a full strike, there are a couple of neck abrasions that seemingly define the coin's grade. Still a very pleasing example overall.(#7238) (Registry values: P8, N2998)

VERY SCARCE MS64 1897-O DOLLAR

6145 1897-O MS64 NGC. Even though 4 million pieces were struck of the 1897-O, it is an important condition rarity in the Morgan dollar series. This is because examples, even technically Uncirculated ones, are usually seen with a weak strike, indifferent or outright dull luster, and numerous abrasions. This particular coin has uncommonly strong definition in the centers, just shy of "full strike" designation on the obverse, and the reverse is unquestionably complete. The mint luster is subdued and satiny, as almost always seen, with pearl-gray surfaces and no obvious or distracting abrasions.(#7248) (Registry values: P7, N4719)

ATTRACTIVE GEM UNCIRCULATED 1903-S MORGAN DOLLAR

6146 1903-S MS65 PCGS. One of the more conditionally rare issues in the series, the 1903-S is most often seen well worn and, at best, XF in grade. Mint State survivors are very scarce, but tend to grade MS63 or higher when available. Gems are very elusive and highly sought after by advanced collectors. This piece has soft, satin-like mint luster and is modestly toned with attractive reddish-golden peripheral color. Well struck overall with just a bit of central softness noted over the ear of Liberty and on the eagle's breast. Both sides are nearly free of mentionable abrasions.(#7288) (Registry values: P7, N4719)

SUPERB GEM PROOF 1880 MORGAN DOLLAR

6147 1880 PR67 NGC. The 1880 had an original mintage of 1,355 proofs, and survivors tend to be either mishandled and low grade or attractive and very well preserved. Few of the high grade 1880s can compare to this coin, though. From a technical standpoint there are no obvious flaws on either side. Also, the surfaces are richly and originally toned with deep orange-rose color in the center of the obverse and cobalt-blue around the margin, while the reverse is nearly brilliant in the center with golden-russet and blue rings of toning around the periphery.(#7315) (Registry values: N4719)

BEAUTIFUL 1881 MORGAN DOLLAR PR67

6148 1881 PR67 PCGS. Luminous apricot, electric-blue, sea-green and orange-red colors alternate across the obverse, while the reverse has deeper peach, olive, and navy-blue hues. A razor-sharp specimen that reveals every breast feather and talon knuckle. A virtually pristine Superb Gem. Just 984 pieces were struck, and most survivors are found in PR62 to PR64 grades. Population: 7 in 67, 2 finer (3/04).(#7316) (Registry values: N4719)

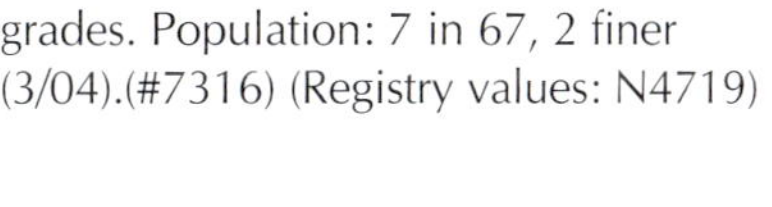

PEERLESS 1881 MORGAN DOLLAR PR68

6149 1881 PR68 NGC. A meticulously preserved proof Morgan Dollar that comes temptingly close to "as struck" status for a specimen striking of this popular issue. Both sides display full, glassy brilliance over peerless surfaces and, while not quite deserving of a Cameo designation, are endowed with an appreciable degree of contrast from fields to devices. Population: 5 in 68, 2 finer (4/04).(#7316) (Registry values: N7079)

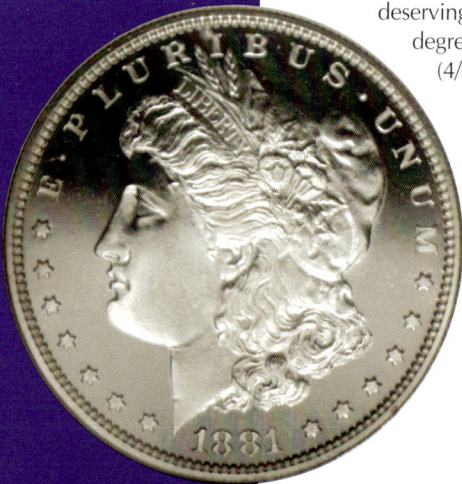

1883 SUPERB PROOF MORGAN DOLLAR TIED FOR FINEST KNOWN

6150 1883 PR68 NGC. The 1883 is a widely collected proof type coin and is a Morgan date that can often be located in near-Gem and Gem grades. However, it appears this is the second Superb proof we have ever offered and the single finest example thus far certified by NGC (4/04). The surfaces are seemingly perfect, even under the scrutiny of a 10x magnifier. This coin was obviously well cared for since the year of issue and is mostly brilliant with only the lightest shading of champagne-gold color at the border areas. While not noted on the insert, the devices are also nicely frosted, this being most apparent on the reverse. An important opportunity for the Morgan specialist.(#7318) (Registry values: N7079)

LEGENDARY KEY 1895 MORGAN DOLLAR PR63

6151 1895 PR63 NGC. Although Mint records indicate that 12,000 business strike Morgan Dollars were delivered in 1895, not a single example *dated* 1895 has surfaced. Either all 12,000 coins were stored at the Mint and melted in later years, or the coins delivered were dated 1894. Regardless of which, if either, of these theories is correct, the lack of business strike 1895 Morgan Dollars has propelled proofs of this date to the pinnacle of rarity and desirability in today's hobby. Without a doubt, this issue is now the key to the long-lived and widely collected Morgan Dollar series. The Select specimen offered here displays full, glassy reflectivity beneath a thin veil of milky patina. Wispy hairlines on each side stand in the path of a higher grade.(#7330) (Registry values: N7079)

REMARKABLY TONED 1898 DOLLAR, SUPERB PROOF 68 NGC

6152 1898 PR68 NGC. A mesmerizing proof Morgan that glitters with near-perfect, mirror surfaces and is literally awash in color, the kind of multihued, iridescent toning that never fails to impress even those with a preference for brilliant coins. Vibrant shades of turquoise-blue circle most of the coin, with areas of deep rose visible at the central regions. The underlying fields show the non-mistakable flash they are well known for. Simply spectacular eye appeal and quality. Population: 9 in 68, 1 finer (4/04).(#7333) (Registry values: N7079)

MEMORABLE SUPERB GEM PROOF 1903 MORGAN DOLLAR

6153 1903 PR67 NGC. The 1903 is one of the more frequently encountered dates in the proof series. Of course, the usual proviso with PR67 coins applies here also: it certainly is not common in this grade. Struck in the no-contrast method of proofing popular in the early years of the 20th century, the fields on this piece are exceptionally deep in their mirrored reflectivity and the devices are equally bright and shimmer with die polish, except on the reverse where the devices present a bit of light frost. Apparently this may have been one of the first hundred or so coins struck and the frost that is inherent in a new set of dies had not had time to fully erode from the reverse. Pinpoint striking details, the surfaces are mostly brilliant throughout and there are no obvious hairlines or contact marks present on either side. Population: 24 in 67, 3 finer (4/04).(#7338) (Registry values: N4719)

UNSURPASSABLE 1903 JEFFERSON GOLD DOLLAR, MS67 NGC

6154 1903 Louisiana Purchase/Jefferson MS67 NGC. Unknown any finer at either service, this coin represents ultimate technical superiority for the issue. The strike is exceedingly sharp, and the clean, satiny surfaces display a hint of green-golden patina near the borders. A coin whose positive attributes include originality and tantalizing eye appeal. Population: 43 in 67, 0 finer (4/04).(#7443) (Registry values: N4719)

RARE GEM 1905 LEWIS & CLARK GOLD DOLLAR, MS66 PCGS

6155 1905 Lewis and Clark MS66 PCGS. This is a coin that should make any commemorative gold collector sit up and take notice. Not only is this the key 1905 issue of the Lewis and Clark, but it is offered here in nearly unsurpassable condition. The surfaces are almost perfect (as one would expect from the grade), but what grabs the attention of the viewer first is the thick mint frost and pale-amber coloration that covers each side. One tiny mark is seen at certain light angles on the obverse near Lewis' nose, this being the only pedigree identifier that is visible. Population: 53 in 66, 3 finer (3/04).(#7448) (Registry values: N7079)

SUPERB 1915-S PANAMA-PACIFIC GOLD DOLLAR

6156 1915-S Panama-Pacific Gold Dollar MS67 PCGS. One of the nicer Pan-Pac Gold Dollars one is ever likely to encounter, with satin-like, peerless surfaces that have a few light splashes of coppery-orange patina on the obverse. Unlike entry level Gems of this issue, the miner's cap is essentially without friction. Population: 40 in 67, 0 finer (3/04).(#7449) (Registry values: N4719)

IMPRESSIVE 1915-S PANAMA-PACIFIC 50 DOLLAR OCTAGONAL MS63

6157 1915-S Panama-Pacific 50 Dollar Octagonal MS63 PCGS. Designed by Robert Aitken, the 1915-S Panama-Pacific 50 Dollar commemorative "slugs" was produced in both round and octagonal format. Both types have an original mintage of 1,500 pieces plus several assay specimens, but only 645 octagonal examples were sold. These octagonal pieces add dolphins about the borders as a symbol of America's desire to keep the Panama Canal open throughout the term of the Great War. Always an impressive issue, this Select representative is appealing from both a technical and aesthetic standpoint. Both sides display vibrant matte-like luster and appealing golden coloration, with just a few wispy blemishes on the major devices that are nearly unavoidable on these massive strikings.
From The Barry Donnell Collection.(#7452)

EXTRAORDINARY QUALITY FIVE-PIECE 1915-S PANAMA-PACIFIC SET

6158 A magnificent Gem or better set of 1915-S Panama-Pacific Commemoratives, Half through Fifty Dollar.

Half Dollar MS66 NGC. Lovely amber and turquoise toning frames essentially brilliant centers. A solitary reeding mark to the left of the eagle precludes Superb status.

Gold Dollar MS66 PCGS. A satiny, ultra frosty Gem with delicate hints of pastel blue and lilac patina.

Quarter Eagle MS67 NGC. Impeccably preserved and boasting a bright, satiny sheen that far eclipses most examples seen.

Fifty Dollar Round MS65 ★ NGC. The Pan-Pac Fifty is one of the most beautiful coins ever minted and it is rife with symbolic meaning. Stuck on the eve of America's involvement in the First World War, the Greek helmet is pushed back on Liberty's head in a ready but not fully combative posture. The owl on the reverse signifies watchfulness. This is an absolutely splendid example with reddish-golden surfaces that are virtually unmarked and are endowed with satiny luster that is especially vibrant.

Fifty Dollar Octagonal MS65 NGC. The net mintage of the octagonal Fifty Dollar is slightly larger its round counterpart (645 vs. 483 pieces), probably because of the novelty of the eight-sided design. There is no disputing the effect of the dazzling luster or the appealing reddish-golden color of this Gem. While light facial marks are noticed under a glass, these positive qualities were obviously taken into consideration on the final grade.

Accompanying this lot is the original case, cardboard box, and card of issue. The black leatherette case opens to display a purple velvet-lined interior with slots for each of the five denominations. The box and case have substantial value of their own, as most holders (and nearly all the boxes) have been discarded or damaged over the years. (Total: 5 Coins)(#7452)

PRISTINE GEM 1851 GOLD DOLLAR MS66 PCGS

6159 1851 MS66 PCGS. For the first time since the inception of the denomination in 1849, Gold Dollar production at the Philadelphia Mint topped 1 million coins in 1851. A staggering total of 3.3 millions coins were produced, and, as one might surmise from this mintage figure, the 1851-P is a popular and readily obtainable coin for type purposes. Of course, at the MS66 level, this issue is a significant condition rarity. A simply breathtaking pristine Gem, the surfaces are overlaid in coruscating mint frost that exhibits a subtle green-gold color. We have no doubt about this coin's originality, and the razor sharp striking definition enhances the already memorable eye appeal. A tiny toning spot at the base of the first 1 of the date may be useful for future pedigree purposes.(#7513) (Registry values: N4719)

ALMOST PERFECT (MS68) 1851 GOLD DOLLAR

6160 1851 MS68 NGC. In our 2002 February Long Beach Sale we sold another MS68 example of this date (yes, not only is there another but the *Census Report* indicates a third has also been certified). That particular coin was noted as having "a tiny 'pimple' (an as struck feature) on Liberty's cheek." It was thought that this raised dot of metal might prove useful in tracing that coin's pedigree in the future. This is definitely a different coin from the one we offered two years ago, but what is interesting is this coin shows the same pimple-like dot on Liberty's cheek. This indicates to us that there may have been a small number of coins from this die set aside in the year of issue and preserved in optimal conditions—we know at least two were. The centers are just a bit softly struck on each side but the peripheral details are exceptionally strong with no hint of weakness. The thick, frosted mint luster has taken on a rich overlay of reddish patina and the surfaces are almost perfectly preserved.(#7513) (Registry values: N1)

SELECT UNCIRCULATED 1851-C GOLD DOLLAR

6161 1851-C MS63 NGC. Variety 4-D. The most "common" C-mint Gold Dollar in all grades, the 1851-C is still a deservedly rare coin whose original mintage is just 41,267 pieces. This is a pleasing Select Uncirculated example whose surfaces display rich golden overtones. The devices are fully struck, or as close to full as one could expect for a gold coin from the Charlotte Mint, and the surfaces are free of singularly bothersome abrasions. A nice coin for type purposes or an advanced date collection.(#7514) (Registry values: N2998)

RARE GEM UNCIRCULATED 1851-C GOLD DOLLAR, MS65 PCGS

6162 1851-C MS65 PCGS. Variety 4-D. A late die state, there is a reverse die break atop OF AM in the legend UNITED STATES OF AMERICA. This issue's original mintage of 41,267 pieces is greater than that of all other Type One Gold Dollars from the Charlotte Mint *combined.* Not surprisingly, the 1851-C is the most plentiful Gold Dollar from this popular Southern branch mint. When viewed in the wider context of U.S. numismatics, however, the mintage of the 1851-C seems low. What's more, Winter's estimate of 65-75 pieces extant in Mint State is the sign of a conditionally scarce, if not rare issue. This is one of the better produced C-mint gold coins that we can remember handling. The obverse is typically sharper than the reverse, but even the latter side is bold throughout. Both sides are attractively toned with rich copper-orange shades dominating selected protected areas. There are a few small identifying marks: a thin scratch bisects the two stars at the base of the obverse, and a small patch of marks is seen above the LA of DOLLAR in the reverse field. A conditionally rare offering for the C-mint gold specialist. Population: 6 in 65, 2 finer (3/04).(#7514) (Registry values: N7079)

RADIANT AND ORIGINAL 1851-D GOLD DOLLAR MS62 PCGS

6163 1851-D MS62 PCGS. Variety 3-E. Lemon and lilac color confirms the originality of this lustrous representative. The centers are not fully defined, but the strike is certainly above average for a Dahlonega Mint product. Liberty's cheek and chin each possess a tiny planchet flaw, but these do not affect the technical grade or the eye appeal. Only 9,882 pieces were produced. Population: 6 in 62, 2 finer (3/04).(#7515) (Registry values: N4719)

IMPORTANT 1854 TYPE TWO GOLD DOLLAR IN MINT STATE

6164 1854 Type Two MS62 PCGS. An orange-gold representative of this short-lived and conditionally challenging type, both sides are not excessively abraded for the designated grade. Well struck save for a little softness of detail in the center of the obverse. The often-seen clashmarks (as struck) in the central reverse field are barely perceptible. This is a coin that we are proud to offer to first-year type collectors and gold specialists alike.(#7531) (Registry values: N4719)

CONDITIONALLY RARE 1854 TYPE TWO GOLD DOLLAR MS66 NGC

6165 1854 Type Two MS66 NGC. Generally only located in AU or lower grades, any Mint State Type Two Gold Dollar is a significant coin, but in Gem condition it is also a major condition rarity and worthy of consideration by advanced collectors. The surfaces on this piece are smooth and unblemished with the only ripple in the fabric of the coin being the usually-seen die clash marks on each side. Thick, frosted mint luster rolls across each side and there is a considerable presence of reddish patina. Also fully struck throughout with complete definition on Liberty's hair curls, the coronet, and the date. An outstanding Type Two Gold Dollar. Population: 7 in 66, 3 finer (4/04).

Upon his appointment to the post of Mint Director in 1853, James Ross Snowden enacted plans to modify the Gold Dollar that James B. Longacre had executed in 1849. While Longacre faithfully increased the diameter of the denomination from 13 to 15 millimeters and reduced the thickness proportionately, he seized upon the opportunity to redesign both the obverse and reverse devices. The Treasury Department adopted the new design, coinage began on August 19, 1854. Unfortunately, the Mint soon realized the new design's ill-fated beauty. The relief of the obverse motif was too high and Longacre positioned it directly opposite the highest points of the reverse. This created poor metal flow into the die cavities and even the faultless Philadelphia mint could not produce fully struck examples. Most pieces emerged from the mint with weak devices and rapidly wore down to illegibility. The barely identifiable survivors retrieved from circulation were melted down as hastily as they had been designed. After two years of production at Philadelphia and token outputs at the branch mints that extended into 1856, Longacre completely reworked the denomination and created the Type Three Gold Dollar.(#7531) (Registry values: N10218)

DESIRABLE UNCIRCULATED TYPE TWO GOLD DOLLAR, 1855

6166 **1855 MS62 PCGS.** Even though there are quite a few survivors of this date in the lower grades, and even numerous examples in Mint condition, this date's status as a Type Two coin has greatly elevated its desirability, popularity, and price well beyond that of far scarcer issues of the Type One and Type Three designs. This piece has good mint luster and is well defined, even in the centers, and, of course, shows the ubiquitous die clash marks in the fields.(#7532) (Registry values: N4719)

SELECT UNCIRCULATED 1855 TYPE TWO GOLD DOLLAR

6167 1855 MS63 NGC. While always available for a price in lower (circulated) grades, the Type Two Gold Dollar is a rare and highly desirable type coin in Mint State. At the MS63 level it is very elusive and of the greatest importance to gold collectors. This piece is very well struck although some of the central softness shows at the center of the reverse. Bright orange-gold color with sparkling mint luster, there are only a few small abrasions scattered about, none of which are of individual importance. Notable typical die clashing is seen overall.(#7532) (Registry values: N4719)

MAGNIFICENT GEM 1855 GOLD DOLLAR

6168 1855 MS65 PCGS. Our last offering of a Gem 1855 Gold Dollar, a coin that realized over $35,000 in the 2003 FUN Sale, included the following introduction of the type: "Both the design and the production of the Type Two Gold Dollar suggest great haste on the part of the U.S. Mint. For the former, James Barton Longacre simply adapted the obverse of his Three Dollar gold design and mated it with a rendition of the Flying Eagle Cent reverse, also one of his recent creations. This design, coupled with a thinner, yet larger planchet, distinguishes the Type Two Gold Dollar from its Type One predecessor. Most examples of the former type are poorly produced. Clashmarks are virtually always seen, and the central highpoints are inadequately defined more often than not. This shoddy workmanship meant that the coins acquired wear at an unacceptably fast rate. Since it proved unsatisfactory for general circulation, the Type Two design yielded to Longacre's Type Three motif after only a few years." This carefully preserved representative does show the nearly inescapable die clashing, but the strength of strike is outstanding for the design and both sides are accented in lovely reddish-orange patina. Population: 34 in 65, 17 finer (3/04).(#7532) (Registry values: N7079)

ORIGINAL 1855-C GOLD DOLLAR, CHOICE AU58 NGC

6169 1855-C AU58 NGC. Variety 9-K, the only known die pairing. The 1855-C yields to only the 1849-C Open Wreath for high grade rarity honors among C-mint Gold Dollars. The typical survivor of this low mintage (9,803 pieces) issue in today's market is apt to grade no higher than VF. This one is just a bit weak at the centers but still a well preserved example of this popular one-year type. The amazingly smooth surfaces below subtle natural champagne-gold color. A curving die clash line (as struck) is noted from the final feather on the headdress down to Liberty's lowest haircurl. As nearly every known 1855-C Gold Dollar has been cleaned or dipped at one time, the collector who appreciates originality should pay careful attention to this coin.(#7533) (Registry values: N2998)

UNCIRCULATED 1855-O TYPE TWO GOLD DOLLAR

6170 1855-O MS62 NGC. The New Orleans Mint ceased production of Gold Dollars after a delivery of 55,000 coins in 1855. As the only O-mint issue in the Type Two series of 1854-1856, the 1855-O has long been popular among gold collectors. Although it is the most common branch mint Gold Dollar of the type, the '55-O is scarce in AU and quite elusive in Mint State. Relatively well struck throughout, the only mentionable incompleteness of detail is seen in the centers. The otherwise honey-gold color warms to medium gold hues at more direct angles. Moderately abraded, as befits the grade, yet free of individually sizeable distractions. An important bidding opportunity for the specialist, this is the first so graded '55-O Dollar that we have handled since 1999. *From The South Florida Collection.*(#7535) (Registry values: N4719)

ELUSIVE 1856-D GOLD DOLLAR UNC DETAILS

6171 1856-D Unc Details, Improperly Cleaned, NCS. Variety 8-K. A high grade survivor of this rare D-mint Gold Dollar, one of a scant 1,460 pieces struck. Of the 65-75 pieces estimated to be extant, precious few escaped circulation altogether. This lustrous yellow-gold example, while deemed to be cleaned, does not suffer from unnatural brightness. Typical for the issue, the U in UNITED is nearly invisible and there is additional bluntness on the hair curls, as well as in the date area.(#7543) (Registry values: N7079)

BU 1857-C GOLD DOLLAR RARITY

6172 1857-C MS61 NGC. Variety 10-L, the only known dies. In high grades (AU-Mint State), the 1857-C falls approximately in the middle of the scale as far as Charlotte Mint Gold Dollars are concerned. When viewed in the wider context of U.S. numismatics, nonetheless, any Uncirculated '57-C must be respected as a rare coin. Add to this the fact that this issue is the premier Type Three Gold Dollar from the fabled Southern branch mint and one can easily see the importance and desirability of the present offering. Typically impressed, both sides are generally bold with a few areas of striking softness here and there. The green-gold color is evenly distributed, and the eye appeal also benefits from a lack of individually mentionable abrasions. NGC and PCGS combined have seen only seven examples in MS61, and there are just two finer (3/04).(#7545) (Registry values: N4719)

ATTRACTIVE UNCIRCULATED 1859-C GOLD DOLLAR

6173 1859-C MS60 NGC. Variety 11-M, the only known dies. A nicely detailed yellow-gold example that is surprisingly free from detrimental contact. The central reverse is not fully struck, and there are interesting strike-thrus (as made) below the bust and on the reverse at 8 o'clock. The dies are rotated approximately 30 degrees counterclockwise. A mere 5,235 pieces were struck. Population: 3 in 60, 12 finer (4/04).(#7552) (Registry values: N4719)

UNSURPASSABLE 1859-C GOLD DOLLAR RARITY, MS63 PCGS

6174 1859-C MS63 PCGS. Variety 11-M, the only known dies. The final Gold Dollar issue produced in the Charlotte Mint, the 1859-C boasts a paltry original mintage of 5,235 pieces. It is one of the rarest C-mint Gold Dollars, although Winter's estimate of three or four Mint State coins extant is probably a bit on the low side. Nevertheless, it is an event of great importance when an Uncirculated '59-C appears in one of our auctions. This is one of the finest examples known to PCGS and NGC, and it is also among the finest 1859-C Dollars extant. As one might expect for a low mintage delivery, the surfaces exhibit a modest semi-prooflike finish. Winter does note that the 1859-C is equally as poorly made as the 1855-C, but the present example is actually quite bold over the obverse portrait and the reverse wreath. We do, however, note some softness of detail around the obverse periphery and in the center of the reverse, but all digits in the date are easily discernible. Rose-gold highlights decorate the otherwise green-gold surfaces. There are no singularly bothersome abrasions, but a pair of as-struck planchet flaws (on the obverse before Liberty's brow and in the reverse field at the LL in DOLLAR) are mentioned for pedigree purposes. In AU and Mint State grades, the 1859-C is surpassed in rarity by only the 1855-C and 1849-C Open Wreath among Charlotte Mint Gold Dollars. NGC and PCGS Population: 3 in 63, with none finer (3/04).(#7552) (Registry values: N7079)

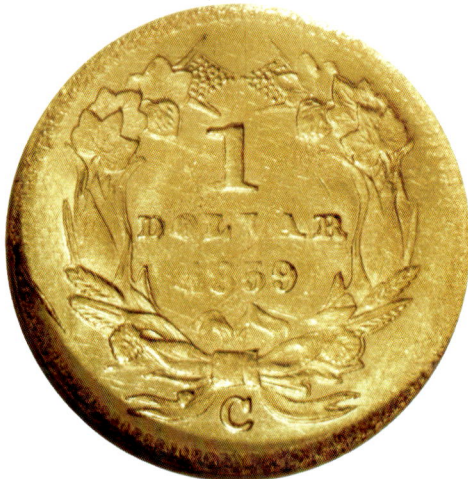

RARE 1860-D GOLD DOLLAR, AU55 NGC

6175 **1860-D AU55 NGC.** Variety 12-P, the only die variety. Recognized for decades as one of the great rarities of the series, a status that has been deflated slightly in recent years, although probably no more than 100-110 pieces are extant from a paltry mintage of 1,566 coins. In the upper reaches of AU and in Mint State, it is still considered to be of the utmost rarity. As always, the borders are weak and the U in UNITED is barely recognizable, these being diagnostic for the issue. Glowing, yellow-gold surfaces impart an almost semi-reflective sheen.(#7556) (Registry values: N4719)

RARE MINT STATE 1860-D GOLD DOLLAR MS60 NGC

6176 **1860-D MS60 NGC.** Ex: Browning Collection. Variety 12-P, the only die variety. Uncommonly vibrant for this usually lackluster issue with noticeably prooflike fields. Both the obverse and reverse present a bright, honey-golden appearance. The strike is typical with the UN in UNITED indistinct and some weakness noted at the left reverse border. The surfaces are clean for the assigned grade with a few small field marks on each side. One of the finest known 1860-D gold dollars. Population: 2 in 60, 6 finer (4/04).(#7556) (Registry values: N4719)

SUPERB GEM 1862 GOLD DOLLAR

6177 1862 MS67 NGC. This is an extraordinary representative of this otherwise easily obtainable P-mint issue. Both sides are crisply impressed with no areas of bothersome striking incompleteness. Billowy mint frost shimmers from richly colored, pinkish-gold surfaces. As befits the grade, neither the obverse nor the reverse exhibits a single abrasion of note. With solid technical quality and pleasing eye appeal, this coin would fit nicely into a stellar quality type set of U.S. gold. Population: 7 in 67, none are finer (4/04).(#7560) (Registry values: N1)

SPECTACULAR PROOFLIKE MS68 ★ 1864 GOLD DOLLAR

6178 1864 MS68 ★ NGC. After an enormous production of more than 1.3 million Gold Dollars in 1862, mintages of that denomination fell precipitously until the Silver Dollar denomination was temporarily abolished in 1873. Only 5,950 pieces were struck in 1864, the lowest mintage of any Philadelphia Mint issue up to that year. Unlike later low mintage issues, survivors were not widely saved as souvenirs. NGC has only encapsulated 56 pieces, several of which likely reflect resubmissions of the same coin. This is the second highest NGC-graded example, surpassed only by a solitary MS69 piece. This prooflike representative exhibits surprising cameo contrast for a business strike, and the surfaces are well preserved as befits the grade. Struck from a lightly clashed reverse die.(#7563) (Registry values: N1)

LOW MINTAGE 1865 GOLD DOLLAR MS66

6179 1865 MS66 NGC. A scarce Civil War era issue, the 1865 Gold Dollar combines a limited original mintage of a mere 3,700 business strikes with a similarly low survival rate. This premium Gem survivor is very well struck from striated dies and is accented in delicate reddish patina. Population: 4 in 66, 2 finer (4/04).(#7564) (Registry values: N4719)

RADIANT 1880 GOLD DOLLAR MS68

6180 1880 MS68 NGC. The 1880 Gold Dollar is a perennially popular issue from a tiny mintage of 1,600 business strikes. High quality production and extensive hoarding of the date have resulted in Gem examples being available to today's collector with some regularity. This Superb representative is certainly in the upper echelon of survivors, its peerless yellow-gold surfaces displaying radiant luster and needle sharp detail. Population: 12 in 68, 0 finer (4/04). *From The Garden State Collection.*(#7581) (Registry values: N4719)

GLITTERING GEM PROOF 1885 GOLD DOLLAR

6181 1885 PR65 PCGS. An exquisitely preserved specimen that derives it beauty from hairline-free fields that glimmer with mirrored brilliance. The only disturbance on this eye appealing little Gem is a tiny mint-produced blemish to the left of Liberty's ear. A barely noticeable alloy stain is situated directly above the D in DOLLAR. The 1885 is one of the more available proof gold dollars, having a generous mintage of 1,105 pieces, although its availability at the Gem level is far more limited. Population: 17 in 65, 24 finer (3/04).(#7635)

SCARCE 1802/1 CAPPED BUST QUARTER EAGLE AU50 NGC

6182 1802/1 AU50 NGC. Type of Bass-3007, R.4. Despite a stingy mintage of 3,035 pieces, three die marriages are known for the 1802, all of which share a common obverse. The present reverse marriage is noted for a bold die line from the upper left shield corner. The remaining luster is substantial and there are no obtrusive abrasions. Struck from lightly clashed dies. While all 1802 Quarter Eagles are traditionally referred to as overdates, no examples are known that display an irrefutable underdigit, and many numismatists regard the final digit as merely repunched.(#7650)

CONDITIONALLY RARE 1804 14 STAR REVERSE QUARTER EAGLE MS61 NGC

6183 1804 14 Star Reverse MS61 NGC. Breen-6119, Bass-3010, R.4. This early Quarter Eagle was produced to the extent of only 3,327 pieces. The coins were minted with both 13 and 14 stars on the reverse, the latter variety being the more common in today's hobby. Nevertheless, the 14 Star Reverse is still a rarity in all grades, and no more than 60-70 examples are now believed extant. One of the few certified Mint State survivors, the present example possesses bright, orange-gold surfaces with a tinge of milky-green color intermingled on the obverse. Well struck by the standards of the issue, the devices reveal only a few isolated areas of weakness, and a few adjustment marks are reported on the reverse rim. A lightly abraded, nicely lustrous survivor of this rare gold production. Population: 7 in 61, 2 finer (4/04).(#7652)

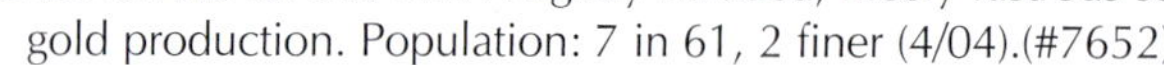

SCARCE UNCIRCULATED 1829 QUARTER EAGLE

6184 1829 MS62 NGC. Bass-3026, Breen-6132, R.4. An important type coin, not only because of the short life of the modified, small size Capped Head Left series, but also because the 1829's status as the first year of this type. Only 3,403 pieces were produced, and of the few survivors most are no better than XF—an Uncirculated coin such as this is certainly above average for both the issue and type. The bright green-gold surfaces show a glimmer of reflectivity in the fields, which is typical for coins of this issue. The striking details are uncommonly sharp for the series with only the slightest softness noted on the shield and adjoining eagle's wing. Only a few minor marks show on each side, none being worthy of singular mention.(#7669)

AU DETAILS 1831 QUARTER EAGLE

6185 1831—Cleaned—ANACS. AU Details, Net XF45. Bass-3028, Breen-6134, R.4. The 1831 is a more difficult issue in the Capped Head Left series, comparable to the 1830 and 1832, and considerably more difficult than the 1829. Only 4,520 pieces were struck, and most of these pieces were melted shortly after production as their bullion value exceeded face. Only one die marriage is known for 1831 Quarter Eagles, all of which have a widely recut U in UNITED. The eagle's shield is not fully struck, but the remaining design details are bold. Although the fields are hairlined, substantial bright luster aids the eye appeal.
From The Paulsboro Collection.(#7671)

SCARCE 1831 CAPPED BUST QUARTER EAGLE

6186 1831 AU53 PCGS.
The Capped Bust Quarter Eagle series is one of the most challenging group of coins in all of U.S. numismatics. Among the Reduced Size pieces from 1829 through 1834, the 1831 is a moderately difficult date to locate. This piece is fairly typical of others we have seen over the years with semi-reflective fields, bright yellow-gold color, and quite a strong strike on each side. There are numerous small field marks throughout, but none are large or distinctive enough to merit individual mention.(#7671)

PROOFLIKE GEM 1834 SMALL HEAD QUARTER EAGLE

6187 1834 MS65 PCGS. Breen-6138, Small Head, R.2. The Small and Large Heads are quite similar, but the curl above the L in LIBERTY is considerably less rounded on the Small Head subtype. Original bright lemon-gold color illuminates this rather prooflike Gem. The nicely preserved fields do not reveal any relevant handling marks, and the strike is crisp aside from a hint of softness on the initial vertical shield lines and the hair curls near Liberty's ear. A beautiful piece that would make an outstanding addition to the finest quality gold type set. Stored in a prior generation PCGS holder. Population: 7 in 65, 1 finer (3/04).

From The Greenwich Collection, Part One.(#7692)

CONDITIONALLY RARE GEM 1834 CLASSIC QUARTER EAGLE

6188 1834 MS65 NGC. Breen-6138, Small Head, R.2. As the premier issue in the Classic quarter eagle series, the 1834 is an immensely popular coin among type collectors. Mint records indicate that 112,234 pieces were produced; therefore, it is no wonder that the 1834 is also among the more available dates in this series. At the Gem level of preservation, however, it is anything but common. Well struck, this example displays rich yellow-gold surfaces that are free of most noticeable abrasions, save for some very slight scuffiness in the obverse field. A gorgeous Gem that would be hard to duplicate in any collection. Population: 11 in 65, 2 finer (4/04).(#7692)

FINEST 1839 QUARTER EAGLE CERTIFIED AT PCGS

6189 1839 MS62 PCGS. Breen-6148, R.3. The only dies. Recut 9 or 39/8, depending on one's point of view. A very scarce and underrated issue in the Classic series and a rarity at the Mint State level, every bit as difficult to locate as the higher priced C and D Mints of the Classic Head type. This is an exceptionally well struck example with a light coating of golden patina over each side. The underlying surfaces are particularly bright with a semi-reflective glimmer. Although fairly numerous, none of the contact marks are particularly unsightly. Currently, this is the finest example thus far certified by PCGS (3/04).(#7698)

COLLECTIBLE NEAR-MINT 1839-C QUARTER EAGLE WITH RECUT DATE

6190 1839-C AU58 NGC. Recut 39. Variety 3-C, McCloskey-C, R.3. Only 165-175 1839-C quarter eagles are believed extant today out of an original mintage of 18,140 pieces. Approximately 33-36 pieces are known in AU condition, and these pieces are very popular with collectors because of the Classic design and obverse mintmark. The devices on this piece are a bit softly defined but there are surprisingly few abrasions on either side, the only ones that bear individual mention are a tiny indention near star 6, and a couple of round abrasions under the E and R of AMERICA.(#7699)

BOLDLY STRUCK 1839-O QUARTER EAGLE, MS62 NGC

6191 1839-O MS62 NGC. High Date, Wide Fraction, Breen-6152, McCloskey-A, R.4. Only 17,781 pieces were produced for the sole New Orleans issue of the Classic Head type, which is further divided into two distinct die marriages. As is the case with the 1840-O issue, the mintmark is on the obverse above the date, unlike subsequent New Orleans dates of the denomination. This intricately struck Quarter Eagle has no shortage of shimmering luster across the olive-gold surfaces. There are a couple of faint marks on the neck and near the chin, and these are only observable under a glass. The fields are surprisingly free from distraction. A spindly die crack ventures through the olive branch, and faint mint-made clashmarks from the shield are present within Liberty's ear. The 1839-O is certainly a key to a type collection of New Orleans gold coins, particularly in Mint State.
From The Greenwich Collection, Part One.(#7701)

NEARLY UNCIRCULATED 1842-O LIBERTY QUARTER EAGLE CONDITION RARITY

6192 1842-O AU58 NGC. The '42-O entered numismatic history as a low mintage issue with just 19,800 pieces produced. Most of these coins saw heavy circulation, due at least in part to the absence of an 1841-O Quarter Eagle issue. As such, the 1842-O is the second rarest O-mint Two-and-a-Half after the 1845-O in terms of both total number of coins known and total number of examples surviving in high grade (per Doug Winter). This particular coin displays an above average strike for the issue with plenty of bold-to-sharp definition remaining despite a little bit of highpoint rub. Green-gold in color, the surfaces are expectantly abraded for a gold coin that spent actual time in the avenues of commerce. There are, however, relatively few distractions that are moderate in size, and the eye appeal also benefits from a modest semi-prooflike sheen that becomes evident as the coin rotates into the light. All-in-all, a pleasing near-Mint survivor of this conditionally challenging New Orleans Mint delivery.
From The South Florida Collection.(#7726)

LOWER CONDITION CENSUS 1842-O QUARTER EAGLE MS61

6193 1842-O MS61 NGC. The 1842-O began with a modest mintage of only 19,800 pieces, lowest among quarter eagles from the New Orleans mint. Only 65-70 coins are believed extant in all grades, the '42-O ranking second in overall rarity among O-mint quarter eagles, second only to the 1845-O. The '42-O is also a significant condition rarity, and Winter (1992) states that "the great majority of extant 1842-O Quarter Eagles grade Very Fine." Over the past several years a number of previously unrecorded Mint State coins have been certified, with a total of 20 pieces certified today in MS60-64 grades. Of course, this figure is somewhat inflated by inevitable resubmissions so the actual number of Uncirculated pieces is probably more on the order of 12-14 coins. This example is tied with several others at the lower end of the Condition Census. The 1842-O is a notoriously weakly struck issue, and this piece also shows soft details on most of the obverse stars, Liberty's hair, and the eagle's left (facing) leg. The surfaces are golden-orange in color with soft, satin-like mint luster. The only mark of note (for pedigree purposes) is a short, angling nick in the field below the O in OF on reverse. An impressive example of this widely recognized O-mint rarity. Population: 4 in 61, 5 finer (4/04).(#7726)

NEAR-MINT 1843-D QUARTER EAGLE AU58 PCGS

6194 1843-D Small D AU58 PCGS. Variety 4-F. This is the most common variety of the year and is distinguished by the die crack that passes through the F in OF and into the field. The 1843-D is the most frequently encountered D-mint Quarter Eagle with 36,209 pieces produced. Curiously, though, high grade pieces are very rare. Winter estimates that only 2-3 Uncirculated coins are extant although we believe the number to be somewhat higher. The surfaces on this piece are bright orange-gold and are lightly abraded. A vertical field mark is seen above Liberty's nose can serve as a future identifier of this attractive coin.(#7730)

ELUSIVE 1844-D QUARTER EAGLE MS62

6195 1844-D MS62 PCGS. Variety 5-H. As on many of examples of the conditionally challenging 1844-D, one of a mere 17,332 pieces struck, this piece shows noticeable weakness of strike at the centers. That deficiency aside, the pleasing green-gold surfaces display more than adequate luster and only modest scuffiness in the fields. Although certification figures list seven representatives in higher Mint State grades (including 5 at NGC), we feel reasonably certain that resubmissions cause this number to be somewhat inflated and that the present examples qualifies at the low end of Condition Census. Population: 10 in 62, 2 finer (3/04).(#7736)

IMPORTANT 1846-C QUARTER EAGLE, MS61 A LOWER CONDITION CENSUS EXAMPLE

6196 1846-C MS61 NGC. Variety 7-F. The '46-C is one of the premier rarities in the Charlotte series of quarter eagles, ranking fourth of the 20 issues in overall rarity and second in high grade rarity. Only 4,808 pieces were struck and it is reliably estimated that today only 65-75 coins are known, three-quarters of which are VF or lower. This is one of the few Uncirculated coins known and it is a lower Condition Census example, being tied with at least two other pieces at the MS61 grade level. Better struck on the obverse than the average '46-C, the reverse is soft, as usual. The green-gold surfaces show just the slightest hint of reddish patina on each side and there are no mentionable abrasions present. There are, however, two areas of what appear to be either planchet roughness or die clashing on the reverse above the eagle's wings.(#7741)

BORDERLINE UNCIRCULATED 1849-D QUARTER EAGLE

6197 1849-D AU58 NGC. Variety 12-M. The date is entered lower and further left than its Variety 11-M counterpart. Sharply struck aside from the fletchings and claws, and the only marks remotely worthy of individual mention are near the A in STATES. A mere 10,945 pieces were struck. The dies are rotated clockwise approximately 35 degrees. Population: 41 in 58, 9 finer (4/04).(#7754)

UNCIRCULATED 1851-C QUARTER EAGLE RARITY

6198 1851-C MS61 NGC. Variety 13-G, the only known dies. Although Winter's estimate of 5-6 extant Mint State '51-C Quarter Eagles is probably a tad on the low side for today's market, the present BU representative still appears to qualify for low end Condition Census standing. The striking detail is above average for the issue with emerging definition over and around the central highpoints. Both sides display dominant medium gold color, although we also note some mottled reddish-orange tinting in the left obverse field. A smattering of light abrasions is consistent with the assigned grade.

The 1851-C was produced to the extent of 14,923 pieces. In terms of overall rarity, this issue ranks 12th out of the 20 Quarter Eagle deliveries from the Charlotte Mint. In AU and Mint State grades, a '51-C Two-and-a-Half should be considered rarer than a similarly graded 1840-C, 1843-C Large Date, 1850-C, and 1856-C, among others.(#7760)

DESIRABLE 1852-D QUARTER EAGLE, AU53 NGC

6199 1852-D AU53 NGC. Variety 15-M, the only die pairing. The '52-D is a very scarce issue with only 4,078 pieces originally produced. Sharply defined excepting the eagle's leg and claw, the surfaces are generally clean except for a small scratch under the eagle's beak. This is mentioned only as an aid for future identification. Bright golden color is seen over both sides.(#7765)

IMPORTANT, SECOND FINEST KNOWN 1854-D QUARTER EAGLE, MS62 PCGS

6200 1854-D MS62 PCGS. Variety 17-M, the only known die pairing. The 1854-D Quarter Eagle is a very desirable issue in any condition and has been for many decades, giving it the status of a "classic rarity" among Dahlonega quarter eagles. Just 1,760 pieces were originally minted, the prime motivating factor in its numismatic fame, and while perhaps not waving the great rarity banner as it once did, the '54-D is nevertheless among the scarcest and most sought-after of all Quarter Eagle issues. It is also a monumental condition rarity, with pieces grading as high as AU50 being the finest most collectors could ever hope to acquire.

Only eight Mint State examples of the '54-D are presently known to exist at both services combined, this piece being the second finest, and bettered by a lone MS64 at NGC. None are higher at PCGS. The strike is exceptionally well executed for the issue, with typical softness showing on the eagle's left leg. All other details, including the denticles, are quite sharp. A hint of yellow-gold patina lends originality to the lustrous surfaces. An area of diagnostic die scratches is seen above star 12, and some (also diagnostic) die polish lines are seen at the rim from star 1 under the date to star 12. Three barely visible milling marks are noted on Liberty's lower jaw, these being the only identifiers worthy of note. Of paramount importance to the gold specialist and near the top of the list of Platinum Night highlights.(#7771)

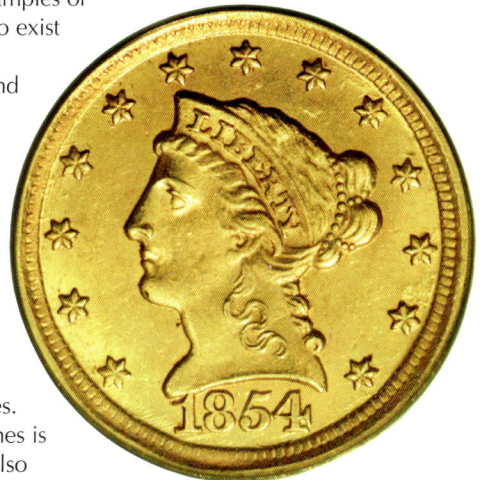

APPEALING 1857-D QUARTER EAGLE CONDITION CENSUS MS62 QUALITY

6201 1857-D MS62 PCGS. Variety 20-M, the only known dies. In the second edition of his book on Dahlonega Mint gold coinage, Doug Winter speculates that a small hoard of high grade 1857-D Quarter Eagles may have existed at one time. This is not to suggest that the '57-D is common in Mint State, for no D-mint gold issue can rightly be described as such. In reality, the 1857-D Two-and-a-Half is rare in grades above the AU level with Winter estimating that a mere 8-10 coins are extant in the various Uncirculated grades.

Typically well struck for the issue, both the obverse and the reverse abound in boldly delineated features. There is also quite a bit of sharp detail in evidence, perhaps most noticeably over the obverse star centrils. Green-gold and orange-gold hues compete for dominance as the coin rotates under a light, with none of the angles revealing any abrasions of singular note. Pedigree concerns compel us to mention a short scrape in the reverse field below the D mintmark. Winter lists four MS62 PCGS examples in his Condition Census listing for this issue, one of which may be the present example.(#7783)

FINEST KNOWN OLD STYLE REVERSE 1861 QUARTER EAGLE

6202 1861 Old Reverse, Type One MS66 PCGS. While important as a high grade type coin and as one of the handful of finest known examples for the date, this piece is the single highest certified example of this rare hubbing variety. This enigmatic issue was produced when someone at the Philadelphia mint, perhaps under pressure to increase production, pressed the old reverse hub for this design, which was discontinued in 1859, back into service. This variety can be distinguished by the lowest arrowhead almost touching the CA in AMERICA. The arrowheads are also closer together than on the new hub, the lettering is larger, and the period after the D is more distant. This particular example has all the characteristics of a Gem, with a bold, crisp strike, superb luster that shimmers from each side, and lovely surfaces that display only a few scattered, tiny abrasions that are consistent with the MS66 grade. Clash marks, as produced and as are often seen on high grade survivors of this variety, are visible on the reverse. A stunning coin and an important specimen for the gold specialist. Population: 1 in 66, 0 finer (3/04).(#97794)

VERY RARE, CONDITION CENSUS 1872 QUARTER EAGLE MS63 NGC

6203 1872 MS63 NGC. Scarce in all grades, with an original mintage of just 3,000 business strikes and 30 proofs, the 1872 Quarter Eagle is extremely rare in Uncirculated grades and, according to Akers, is more often found as a nice proof than in BU. This example is one of only two pieces graded MS63 by the two major services, and it is perhaps the second finest known, as there is a lone coin graded higher (as of 3/04), a PCGS MS64. In fact, it is the finest example of this issue that we have ever handled. The surfaces are bright yellow-gold with reflective fields and a few scattered abrasions that define the Select Uncirculated grade. Well struck, this piece is a true miracle of survival, and the gold specialist will be hard pressed to locate another in similar condition.(#7815)

THE LEGENDARY
"LITTLE PRINCESS"
1841
QUARTER EAGLE
LIBERTY
1841
2½D.

FINEST CERTIFIED 1841 "LITTLE PRINCESS" QUARTER EAGLE PR65 DEEP CAMEO

6204 **1841 PR65 Deep Cameo NGC.** The mysterious "Little Princess" is, simply put, one of the rarest issues in over two centuries of United States gold coinage. Its unknown, but obviously tiny mintage was not recorded in the *Annual Report of the Director of the Mint* and, according to many specialists, is comprised entirely of proof strikings in various states of preservation that were originally intended for inclusion in specimen sets. Others, such as David Akers, have written that the population of 15 to 17 survivors is too high in comparison to other proof Quarter Eagles from the decade as well as similarly dated gold proofs of other denominations, and that a few of the lower grade pieces may have been struck from the same dies, but under different circumstances. Writing in 1999, Mark Borckardt suggested that a portion of the known pieces were issued for specimen sets intended for collectors and dignitaries while others could have been produced for "presentation or some other purpose, perhaps for some long-forgotten ceremony. In 1841 the quarter eagle was the smallest gold coin produced by the United States (the gold dollar did not make its debut until 1849). Thus, a civic, political, commercial, or other ceremony requiring gold coins as an honorarium or gift would find the quarter eagle to be convenient." Perhaps also, Mint officials wished to have a continuation of dates in the Quarter Eagle series and so a few clandestine pieces may have been struck strictly to serve this purpose.

Although there were several offerings of this important rarity during the 19th century and a brief notation in Snowden's 1860 work *A Description of Ancient and Modern Coins in the Cabinet Collection at the Mint of the United States,* the numismatic community was relatively unaware of the 1841 Quarter Eagle until the Edgar H. Adams publication, first released in 1909, entitled *Official Premium List of United States, Private, and Territorial Gold Coins,* where the author noted that just two pieces were known. The first recorded use of the term "Little Princess" was 50 years ago in Stack's Davis/Graves Sale. A roster of known 1841 Quarter Eagles, largely the result of research by Walter Breen in *Walter Breen's Complete Encyclopedia of U.S. and Colonial Coins,* first published in 1988, is as follows:

1) **Smithsonian Collection.** Placed in the Mint Cabinet in the year of issue.

2) **Eliasberg/Bass Collection.** Formerly in such noted numismatic hands as Raymond, Newcomer, Green, and Boyd. The coin was sold in a PR64 PCGS holder for $178,250 as lot 105 in the Harry W. Bass, Jr. Collection - Part III.

3) **Bass Collection.** Acquired by Harry W. Bass, Jr. from World Wide Coins in 1974. Certified PR60 by PCGS, this piece realized $115,000 as lot 335 of the Harry W. Bass Collection, Jr. Sale - Part II.

4) Mitchelson/Connecticut State Library Collection. An impaired proof.

5) Menjou Collection. Formerly belonging to Schermerhorn, Friedberg, Graves, and Pierce. Only a handful of rarities, including a set of $4 Stellas, was withheld from the Grant Pierce Collection sold by Stack's in 1965 and later offered in the 1976 ANA Sale. The 1841 Quarter Eagle appeared as lot 2787 where it fetched what was then a very impressive price of $41,000.

6) Norweb Collection. An impaired specimen that realized $30,800 in 1988.

7) Wolfson Collection. Later in the cabinets of Shuford and Herstal.

8) Peters Auction. Sold by dealer Jess Peters at the 1973 ANA.

9) Mid-American Auction. Later sold by Superior as part of the Heifetz Collection.

10) Superior Auction. An XF specimen sold as lot 1345 of Auction '86.

11) Stack Collection. Part of an important cabinet formed by James A. Stack, Sr. which was sold in 1994.

12) Fairfield Collection. An XF specimen that has the distinction of being the Breen *Encyclopedia* plate coin.

13) Dunham Collection. The publicity generated by this coin when it was sold by B. Max Mehl in 1941 secured the numismatic importance of the 1841.

14) Herdman Collection. There is some speculation, provided by Breen, that this and the following Empire coin are actually the same.

15) Empire Inventory. A "walk in" purchase in the heyday (early 1960's) of the Empire Coin Company.

16) Robison Collection. Earlier in the Terrell Collection.

17) Hydemann Collection. The lowest grade piece on the registry, just a Very Good.

The dazzling 1841 Quarter Eagle we are now privileged to offer comes to us without the advantage of a pedigree, but it is our opinion that this finest certified representative is almost certainly number 5 on the roster, the coin tracing back to the Adolphe Menjou Collection, fittingly the first specimen that was actually dubbed the "Little Princess" in print. The brightly mirrored yellow-gold surfaces have dramatic "two-toned" effect. A few wispy contact marks can be detected in the fields surrounding the major design elements, but the fragile mirrors are refreshing hairline-free. These enviable qualities of extreme rarity, numismatic fame, and finest certified status combine to make the Gem Deep Cameo 1841 Quarter Eagle in this sale one of the most memorable gold coin offerings of the decade. Population: 1 in 65 Deep Cameo, 0 finer (4/04). (#97867)

BEAUTIFUL, DEEPLY CAMEOED 1882 PROOF TWO-AND-A-HALF

6205 1882 PR64 Deep Cameo PCGS. The Philadelphia Mint's delivery of 4,067 Quarter Eagles in 1882 included 67 examples struck in proof format. Although some high grade survivors of the business strike issue display markedly prooflike surfaces, the present coin is readily identifiable as a genuine specimen by the position of the 1 in the date relative to the dentil below the left base. That diagnostic notwithstanding, the pinpoint striking detail, richly frosted texture to the devices, and unfathomably deep fields could only be the result of proof production methods. Aglow in yellow-gold hues, both sides are smooth and nearly in the Gem category. There is a small lintmark (as struck) in the right obverse field that should be of obvious importance for pedigree purposes. Population: 1 in 64 Deep Cameo, with just one additional DCAM example finer (3/04).(#97908)

SPARKLING 1900 QUARTER EAGLE PR64 DEEP CAMEO

6206 1900 PR64 Deep Cameo PCGS. The 1900 proof Quarter Eagle has a mintage of 205 pieces, one of the larger production figures for the series, and it has been estimated that up to 130 pieces remain of this popular turn-of-the-century date. Although just shy of Gem quality, this dazzling specimen has heavily frosted devices that lend a stark white-on-black effect. Population: 2 in 64 Deep Cameo, 8 finer (3/04).(#97926)

PR66 ULTRA CAMEO 1904 QUARTER EAGLE

6207 **1904 PR66 Ultra Cameo NGC.** This magnificently struck premium Gem has unimprovable Ultra Cameo contrast on the reverse, while the obverse also exhibits imposing gold on black contrast. Essentially pristine from a technical perspective, a faint mint-made planchet streak below the A in STATES provides a pedigree marker for any future auction appearances. Just 170 proofs were struck, less than in any of the four preceding years, and few survivors can match the exceptional contrast and preservation of the present piece. Population: 1 in 66 Ultra Cameo, 2 finer (4/04).(#97930)

1909 QUARTER EAGLE, GEM BU MS65 NGC

6208 **1909 MS65 NGC.** A very attractive specimen that is fully struck in all areas and exhibits a rich yellow-gold color, and surfaces that resemble the rare Roman Gold proofs of this year. A high-end, Gem specimen. Population: 74 in 65, 9 finer (4/04).(#7940) (Registry values: N2998)

GEM MINT STATE 1910 INDIAN HEAD QUARTER EAGLE

6209 **1910 MS65 PCGS.** While lower grade Mint State Indian Quarter Eagles are readily available for this and nearly all the other dates in this highly collectible series, Gem survivors are not at all common for any issue. The 1910 mintage is particularly elusive in Gem grades, and PCGS has to date graded only a half-dozen pieces any finer than MS65. The present example displays rich honey-gold luster with satiny surfaces that are unmarred by any singularly mentionable abrasions. The strike is above average for the issue, particularly in the feather details of the Indian's headdress. A lovely Gem example that is fit for the very finest of collections.(#7941) (Registry values: N4719)

NGC MS65 1911 QUARTER EAGLE

6210 **1911 MS65 NGC.** This issue saw the second highest mintage in the series (next to the 1913), as more than 700,000 examples were produced. Gem examples are, however, very scarce, and specimens grading better than MS65 are virtually unobtainable as NGC and PCGS have combined graded only two finer examples (both NGC MS66s). This piece possesses spectacular orange-gold luster and well-preserved surfaces that display very few noticeable marks or blemishes, and the strike is as sharp as any we've seen on a business strike example of this design. Population: 65 in 65, 2 finer (4/04).(#7942) (Registry values: N2998)

BRILLIANT UNCIRCULATED 1911-D INDIAN QUARTER EAGLE

6211 1911-D MS62 NGC. We are pleased to be offering several examples of this important 20th century gold issue in the present sale. The BU representative in this lot possesses dominant honey-gold coloration over bold-to-sharp features. The relatively few abrasions that seem to account for the BU designation are neither sizeable nor individually distracting. The all-important D mintmark is fully formed and readily evident. Accuracy alone compels us to mention a tiny, well concealed alloy spot in the Indian's feathered headdress.(#7943) (Registry values: N4719)

NGC MS63 1911-D TWO AND A HALF

6212 1911-D MS63 NGC. Scarce in all grades and especially so in Mint State grades, this popular D-mint issue commands eager attention from collectors when found in Select BU condition. Frosty yellow-gold luster is evident on both sides, and the fields and devices are relatively clean for the grade, displaying only light, scattered abrasions that are typical at the MS63 grade level. Well-struck and with a bold, pronounced mintmark.(#7943) (Registry values: N4719)

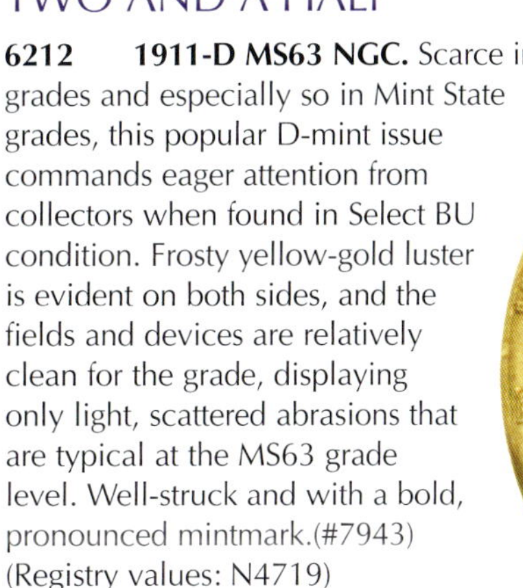

KEY DATE 1911-D INDIAN QUARTER EAGLE IN PCGS MS64

6213 1911-D MS64 PCGS. The premier branch mint Quarter Eagle in United States coinage history, the 1911-D also boasts the lowest mintage in the Indian Two-and-a-Half series with just 55,680 pieces produced. Perhaps needless to say, this is the rarest issue of this short-lived and eminently collectible type. Satiny-to-frosty in texture, the surfaces are fully original with a rich endowment of orange-gold color. We have no criticisms about the strike, all features displaying razor sharp delineation. With few abrasions of any size and none that would call into question the validity of the near-Gem assessment, we wholeheartedly recommend this coin to 20th century gold specialists.(#7943) (Registry values: N7079)

LOVELY NEAR-GEM KEY ISSUE 1911-D QUARTER EAGLE

6214 1911-D MS64 NGC. The undisputed key to this series, the 1911-D Indian Head Quarter Eagle has long been a favorite among collectors both because of its remarkably low mintage of just 55,680 pieces and its rarity in high grades. Most often seen in EF and AU grades, this issue is very scarce in the higher Mint State grades and is seldom offered above the MS64 grade. This example shows the diagnostic wire rim on the right side of the obverse, and the mint mark is bold and well formed. It is sharply struck on both sides, clearly showing all of the feather details on both the Indian's headdress and on the eagle, and displays only a few light, scattered abrasions that are consistent with the near-Gem grade. One tiny spot is noticed just in front of the Indian's mouth, and is mentioned for accuracy and as a potential aid for pedigree information.(#7943) (Registry values: N7079)

LUSTROUS GEM 1912 INDIAN QUARTER EAGLE

6215 1912 MS65 PCGS. Whenever this late-date type is encountered in MS65 or better condition it is an occasion to pause and take a closer look. Because of the incuse design on Indian Quarter Eagles and Half Eagles, the highpoints are especially vulnerable to abrasions and the slightest hint of friction. This is a lovely, highly lustrous example that has rich reddish patina and is strongly struck throughout with an absolute minimum of contact marks. Population: 37 in 65, 4 finer (3/04).(#7944) (Registry values: N4719)

LUSTROUS 1913 QUARTER EAGLE, MS65 NGC

6216 1913 MS65 NGC. A shimmering Gem example, this lovely piece has terrific bright, golden luster that is far above average for the date or series. It is well struck, and the luster is so intense that it emits a mild reflectivity on both sides. A couple of tiny abrasions are noticed just to the left of the Indian's face, but these are easily overlooked when this gorgeous piece is viewed as a whole. A very scarce issue in Gem Mint State, with no pieces graded any finer to date by NGC. Population: 27 in 65, 0 finer (4/04).(#7945) (Registry values: N4719)

MAGNIFICENT AND ORIGINALLY TONED 1915 QUARTER EAGLE

6217 **1915 MS65 PCGS.** This beautiful Gem example is one of the more striking 1915 Quarter Eagles that we have handled in some time. It is wonderfully preserved of course, the surfaces virtually pristine as one should expect for the MS65 grade, but the tremendous originality of color immediately grabs the viewer's attention with variegated iridescent tints of yellow, orange, and pink. Terrific luster adds to the overall appeal. Rare any finer, as PCGS has graded a mere two examples finer to date, with MS65 being the highest grade so far awarded by NGC.(#7948) (Registry values: N2998)

EXQUISITE GEM QUALITY 1911 INDIAN QUARTER EAGLE IN PROOF

6218 **1911 PR65 NGC.** Like the 1908, but unlike the 1909 and 1910, the 1911 proof Quarter Eagle displays a dark matte texture. Rich honey-gold color envelops both sides, the devices displaying needle sharp delineation in all areas. There are hardly any disruptions to the finish, as one should expect for the Gem designation, and the eye appeal is extraordinary in all regards. Clearly, this is one of the most important 20th century gold offerings in this sale.

Proof Indian Quarter Eagle production amounted to a mere 191 pieces in 1911. This total is commensurate with that of most other issues in this series, but some sources have overstated the rarity of the 1911 by estimating that only 24 pieces were extant. Writing in 2001, Mike Fuljenz and Doug Winter (*A Collector's Guide to Indian Head Quarter Eagles*) opine that 85-95 specimens remain in collectors' hands, a range that we credit as accurate.(#7960) (Registry values: N4719)

POPULAR FIRST-YEAR 1854 THREE DOLLAR GOLD AWE-INSPIRING MS68 PCGS QUALITY

6219 **1854 MS68 PCGS.** The Three Dollar gold series of 1854-1889 is among the more curious in U.S. numismatics. If we are to believe Breen, Congress authorized this denomination for ease of exchanging Three Cent Silvers and purchasing sheets of three cent stamps. The initial Philadelphia Mint delivery occurred on May 8 of 1854 with the final coins of this date emerging from the presses on November 10. Although not widely recognized as such, the 1854 represents a one-year type—the letters in DOLLAR on the reverse are significantly smaller than on coins dated 1855-1889.

As a first-year issue, the 1854 appears to have been saved in not insignificant numbers. As such, it should come as no surprise that this issue is the most plentiful Three Dollar gold piece in today's market after the 1878. The certified population of the 1854, however, dwindles rapidly as one reaches and then surpasses the MS65 level. Only one coin has received an MS68 designation at the major grading services (3/04), and it is the extraordinary PCGS example that we are offering in the present lot.

There is much to recommend this coin to discerning collectors, first and foremost of which is the exceptional technical quality. The strike is as close to full as one should expect for the type, and the surfaces are overlaid in warm satin-to-softly frosted luster. There are virtually no abrasions, and a very shallow planchet flaw (as struck) in the obverse field before the point of Liberty's neck is the only worthwhile pedigree marker. Of course, the eye appeal is also worthy of praise, both sides being awash in orange-gold color with a few blushes of soft rose-gold tinting intermingled here and there. One of, if not *the* finest Three Dollar gold coin of any issue that we have ever offered.

Most certainly Ex: Sotheby's sale of 11/1999, lot 74.(#7969) (Registry values: N1)

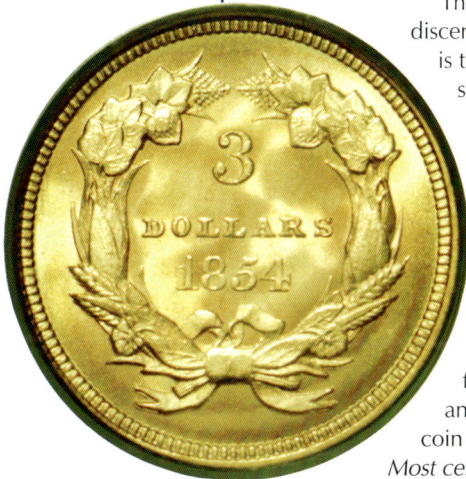

FAMOUS 1854-D THREE DOLLAR, AU DETAILS

6220 **1854-D AU50 Details, Repaired, NCS.** Variety 1-A. As with all genuine '54-D Threes, this piece shows distinct weakness on the obverse and the TED in UNITED is doubled. A famous Dahlonega rarity, this being the only D-mint of the denomination and one of just 1,120 pieces struck, making the 1854-D the object of competition from both collectors of the Three Dollar series as well as Southern gold enthusiasts. The repairs about the rims of lustrous example are skillfully executed and even less visible within the confines of the holder.(#7970) (Registry values: N7079)

1854 DAHLONEGA THREE DOLLAR GOLD RARITY IN CHOICE AU

6221 **1854-D AU55 NGC.** Variety 1-A, the only known dies. As the only Three Dollar gold delivery produced in the Dahlonega Mint, the 1854-D holds a place of honor in the annals of numismatic history. This issue is also a significant gold rarity with Winter estimating that only 100-125 coins are extant in all grades from a paltry original mintage of fewer than 1,500 pieces. The author further states that no more than 27 of these examples grade at the various levels of AU. Hallmark striking softness is seen around much of the obverse rim, and the highpoints of Liberty's hair curls are a bit soft. We stress, however, that the latter feature is due as much to light rub as it is to striking incompleteness, and the reverse wreath is quite bold. Rich olive-gold and orange-gold colors intermingle over surfaces that are remarkably free of sizeable abrasions for a circulated gold coin from the Georgia branch mint. An ever-popular issue at a desirable and scarce level of preservation.(#7970) (Registry values: N7079)

NEAR-MINT 1854-O THREE DOLLAR GOLD PIECE

6222 **1854-O AU58 NGC.** While not in the same rarity class as the other branch mint Three Dollar issue produced this year, the 1854-O is equally as popular as the only O-mint delivery of this type. While well circulated '54-O Threes can usually be found with a little bit of searching, AU50-53 examples are elusive and Choice About Uncirculated survivors are rare. This is a medium gold representative whose surfaces reveal remnants of a semi-prooflike finish at more direct angles. Overall sharp in strike with minimum highpoint rub and scattered abrasions that are well within the context of the assigned grade. Worthy of inclusion in a high grade circulated date set of 19th century gold, or a better date type set that highlights branch mint coinage. *From The South Florida Collection.*(#7971) (Registry values: N2998)

ONE OF THE FINEST KNOWN 1856 THREE DOLLAR GOLD PIECES MS64 PCGS

6223 **1856 MS64 PCGS.** Even though the Philadelphia Mint coined 26,010 three dollar gold pieces this year, the 1856 is markedly scarcer than the 1854 and 1855 in all Mint State grades. This piece has an above average strike, although we do note slight weakness on the U in UNITED. The surfaces are radiantly lustrous, with a hint of orange patina over medium yellow-golden color. A notable opportunity for the gold specialist, and a lightly marked, seemingly high-end example, at the near-Gem level of preservation. Tied for the highest-graded, at PCGS. Population: 9 in 64, 0 finer (3/04).(#7974) (Registry values: N4719)

IMPORTANT MS64 1856-S THREE DOLLAR GOLD PIECE

6224 **1856-S MS64 NGC.** Breen-6355. Medium S, with a minor die break from the base of the second L in DOLLARS leaning down to the left. While the 1856-S was a relatively high production issue with 34,500 pieces produced, attrition took a great toll on that number, and today even problem-free AU coins are a challenge to locate. Strict Mint State examples are very scarce with fewer than two dozen pieces believed known today. This is one of the finest known with two others graded MS64 and none finer. This is an exceptionally pleasing and lustrous coin that displays rich reddish patina on each side and strong striking details throughout, the only exception being the bow knot on the lower reverse, as usually seen on three dollar gold pieces.(#7975) (Registry values: N7079)

RARE HIGH GRADE 1868 THREE DOLLAR GOLD

6225 1868 MS65 NGC. While the 1868 is hardly a scarce issue in average condition, it is a significant coin in Mint State and rare as a Gem. The average example of this date is only XF, and of the few Uncirculated coins extant, this is at the upper end of the Condition Census. This is a splendid coin that exhibits bright, frosted mint luster that is virtually undisturbed by contact marks of any importance. Sharply defined, except on the bow knot at the bottom of the wreath, as often found, the coin possesses a considerable overlay of pinkish-rose patina. Population: 3 in 65, 1 finer (4/04).(#7989) (Registry values: N7079)

CONDITIONALLY RARE 1871 THREE DOLLAR MS64 PCGS

6226 1871 MS64 PCGS. A rare Three Dollar issue with the vast majority of known survivors are XF and AU with Mint State examples very rare. Unlike many 1871s, this piece is not wholly prooflike, but does display a moderate semi-reflectivity in the fields that enlivens the subtle champagne-golden patination that covers each side. Fairly well struck, as usually found, with only slight abrasions to account for the grade, there is only the slightest reported weakness on the hair curls and the bow knot. Bright and highly desirable. Population: 10 in 64, 2 finer (3/04). *From The Greenwich Collection, Part One.*(#7993) (Registry values: N4719)

FROSTY GEM 1878 THREE DOLLAR GOLD, MS65 PCGS

6227 1878 MS65 PCGS. By far the most frequently seen date in the Three Dollar series, the 1878 is a natural for type purposes. In MS65 condition, it is one of the most enchanting gold type coins from the 19th century. The surfaces on this piece exude thick mint frost, the type of frost that swirls around each side as only seen on 1878 Threes. The nearly flawless coin shows a slight overlay of reddish patina on each side. One milling mark is seen in the reverse field over DOLLARS. An exemplary Three Dollar Gold Piece.(#8000) (Registry values: N4719)

LUSTROUS 1878 THREE DOLLAR MS65 PCGS

6228 1878 MS65 PCGS. An unquestionably attractive coin, thick frosty luster ripples across both sides. Liberty's hair and headdress are free of noticeable striking incompleteness, and the reverse is equally well struck. After the first-year 1854 (138,618 pieces produced), the 1878 boasts the largest mintage (82,324 coins) in this series. As such, Gem quality representatives are considered "common" by Three Dollar gold standards. Nevertheless, such coins are rare in an absolute sense and fewer in number than high quality type collectors in today's hobby. Population: 130 in 65, 66 finer (3/04). *From The Greenwich Collection, Part One.*(#8000) (Registry values: N4719)

STUNNING 1878 THREE DOLLAR GOLD, NGC MS67

6229 1878 MS67 NGC. A tremendous example for the date and type, one of the finest Three Dollar Gold Pieces that this cataloger has ever seen. The surfaces are virtually pristine, with only a couple of tiny, trivial abrasions noticed under even the closest scrutiny, and the luster is frosty and as bright as can be. The natural contours of the dies produced a magnificent halo effect with the luster shining at slightly different angles around the head of Miss Liberty, giving this piece wonderful visual appeal. Sharply struck, with only a couple of insignificant areas of isolated weakness noticed after much searching under magnification. Unobtainable any finer, a beautiful example that combines the best of technical merit and aesthetic appeal and a coin that is destined for the finest of type sets or specialized collections. Population: 12 in 67, 0 finer (4/04).(#8000) (Registry values: N7079)

NGC MS64 THREE DOLLAR, 1888

6230 1888 MS64 NGC. Even though only 5,000 business strikes of this issue were originally produced, this is one of the more available dates in the series because by the late 1880s this denomination hardly ever circulated and most examples were saved in relatively high grades. At the MS64 level, however, survivors are scarce and are usually found only after patient searching. The present example will provide the collector with a brilliant, yellow-gold appearance and minimal abrasions for the grade, an overall pleasing specimen to represent the date or type.(#8010) (Registry values: N2998)

VISUALLY APPEALING GEM 1888 THREE DOLLAR

6231 1888 MS65 PCGS. Unlike most other late-date Three Dollar gold issues, the 1888 rarely shows prooflike fields or prooflikeness combined with mint frost. This Gem example, one of just 5,000 business strikes produced, is fully frosted and has swirling cartwheel luster that is hardly affected by even the slightest signs of coin-to-coin contact. The strike is short of full, but quite strong overall and a delicate orange patina frames each side.

From The Greenwich Collection, Part One.(#8010) (Registry values: N4719)

REFLECTIVE GEM MINT STATE 1888 THREE DOLLAR GOLD

6232 1888 MS65 PCGS. A beautiful Gem example with reflective surfaces, rich orange-gold luster, and a sharp strike, one of a mere 5,000 business strikes minted in the next-to-last year of production for this series. While most examples of this date were not likely put into circulation and many were saved in Mint State grades, at the MS65 level this issue is anything but common. A couple of tiny abrasions are present on the cheek, and are mentioned not because they are distracting (which they are certainly not, as they are relatively tiny) but because of the fact that without them this piece would challenge a grade or two higher. A beautiful example for the type collector or specialist in the series, and certain to attract many bidders.(#8010) (Registry values: N4719)

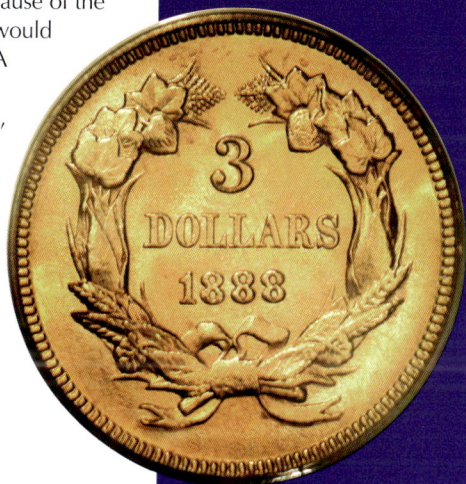

GEM PROOF 1888 THREE DOLLAR GOLD

6233 1888 PR65 PCGS. As the most commonly encountered proof of the three dollar series, the 1888 is the usual choice for type purposes. The official proof output for the year is 291 pieces, a somewhat optimistic mintage that likely resulted in up to 100 coins being destroyed after going unsold. This date is usually seen with porosity in the fields or a "halo" effect as it is more commonly known, only faintly visible on this specimen. The surfaces display even, rich, reddish tinted patina, and the devices are moderately frosted against the strongly mirrored proof finish seen in the fields. Definitely a must-see specimen. Population: 30 in 65, 17 finer (3/04).
From The Greenwich Collection, Part One.(#8052) (Registry values: N7079)

REMARKABLY PRESERVED CAMEO PROOF 66 1879 STELLA

6234 1879 Flowing Hair, Judd-1635, Pollock-1832, R.3, PR66 Cameo NGC. The Stella, or Four Dollar gold piece, was proposed by John Kasson as an international coin whose value would be roughly equivalent to that of an Austrian 8-florin. The coin was designed by Chief Engraver Charles Barber in 1879 prepared an obverse design that depicted a portrait of Liberty facing left with long, flowing hair. The date appeared at the bottom and the inscription 6 G .3 S .7 C 7 G R A M S around the central portrait. With stars in between each character, this inscription advertised the coins' weight as 7 grams and gave the proportionate composition of gold, silver, and copper. The reverse depicted ONE STELLA 400 CENTS superimposed atop a five pointed star with the inscriptions UNITED STATES OF AMERICA, E PLURIBUS UNUM, DEO EST GLORIA (God is glorious), and FOUR DOL. in the surrounding field. Using these dies, the Philadelphia Mint struck approximately 15 examples in the specified (metric alloy) in December 1879. Early the following year, a further 400 or so (90% gold alloy) pieces followed, also dated 1879, although careless Mint employees improperly spaced the dies with the result that these later examples display weak definition on the hair over Liberty's ear. These were widely distributed around Washington to popularize the proposed new denomination, but were soon forgotten when the international gold coin was rejected by Congress.

The present example displays deeply mirrored fields and thickly frosted devices. With slightly soft central hair features and planchet striations that were not obliterated through striking, this specimen is an unmistakable survivor of the 1880 delivery. The metric gold alloy inscribed on the obverse probably describes this coin's composition, although, as stated earlier, the Philadelphia Mint did strike an undetermined number (probably 400) coins on standard gold planchets. We cannot, therefore, say for certain whether this coin contains a metric or standard gold alloy. There is, however, little doubt surrounding the rarity and desirability of Charles E. Barber's Flowing Hair Stella among advanced gold type collectors. The memorable eye appeal of the honey-gold surfaces is hardly diminished by a slight overlay of milky patina. For pedigree purposes, an inconspicuous dark toning spot over the second U of UNUM is visible on the reverse. Still, this is one of the finest Stellas available in today's market and is destined for the collection of an advanced gold enthusiast.(#8057)

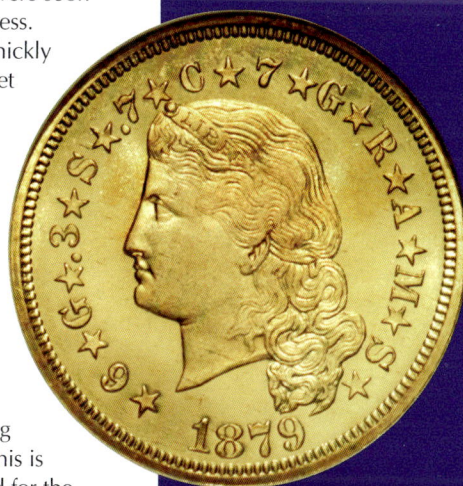

MORE AFFORDABLE 1879 FLOWING HAIR FOUR DOLLAR ANACS-CERTIFIED

6235 1879 Flowing Hair, Judd-1635, Pollock-1833, R.3—Scratched, Cleaned—ANACS. Net PR55. The attribution, as well as the striking characteristics, identify this coin as one of the 1879 Flowing Hair Stellas struck in standard gold alloy early in 1880. The otherwise sharp definition wanes a little in the centers, particularly on the obverse, and one can even see some Mint-made striations in these areas. Despite some mishandling, the surfaces retain much of the original proof finish. The fields are appreciably reflective and the devices are suitably frosted in finish. The interplay between this reflectivity and frosted texture provide a relatively pleasing cameo effect that is more-or-less evident depending upon the light angle. Both sides exhibit green-gold coloration with scattered hairlines from a cleaning. A few moderate distractions are noted on the obverse around Liberty's neckline and before the brow, and there is a reverse pinscratch from the left border.

We are pleased to be offering more than one representative of the fabled Flowing Hair Stella in this sale. While the present specimen is not perfect, it does offer plenty of crisp striking definition, much of the original finish, and pleasing coloration for a more modest sum. A respectable candidate for inclusion in a gold type set.

From the Virgil Farstad Collection, Part Two.(#88057)

HIGHLY COLLECTIBLE 1795 SMALL EAGLE FIVE DOLLAR GOLD

6236 1795 Small Eagle AU58 NGC. B. 6-E, Miller-8, R.5. A very scarce die pairing, often seen cleaned and/or damaged. The obverse displays a closely spaced date with the 9 and 5 almost touching, and the star at the lower right is farther from the bust than any other 1795 obverse. A thin die crack is seen on the reverse from the rim through the N of UNITED to the eagle. Offered here is an exceptionally fine example of this popular, first year Half Eagle. The striking details are strong throughout and much of the original luster remains in the more protected areas of the design. The basic yellow-gold color of the coin is sharply accented by deep reddish patina that surrounds the devices and also lies within the recesses of the design elements.(#8066)

1795 SMALL EAGLE FIVE DOLLAR UNC DETAILS

6237 1795 Small Eagle Unc Details, Obverse Repaired, NCS. Breen-6412, B. 1-B, Miller-2, R.4. The obverse is distinguished by the crowded stars below the Y in LIBERTY, while on the reverse the final S in STATES is low and touches the wreath. The obverse of this bright yellow-gold gold representative has been tooled and whizzed, our guess would be to remove graffiti in the fields. While faintly hairlined, much of the coin's inherent luster survives on the reverse.(#8066)

HIGHLY SOUGHT AFTER 1796/5 FIVE DOLLAR GOLD AU53 PCGS

6238 1796/5 Small Eagle AU53 PCGS. Breen-6418, B. 9-I, Miller-16, R.5. The lone die pairing used in the second year of Half Eagle production, and a very scarce item in any grade. Even though the mintage of 6,196 pieces is not substantially less than the 1795, the 1796/5 Five Dollar is a much more elusive issue. This example is well struck through the centers and retains much semi-reflective luster about the devices. The surfaces are a mixture of green-gold and pale orange. For future identification, a small, lateral post-striking mark is seen between the 1 and 7 of the date. Population: 6 in 53, 15 finer (3/04).(#8067)

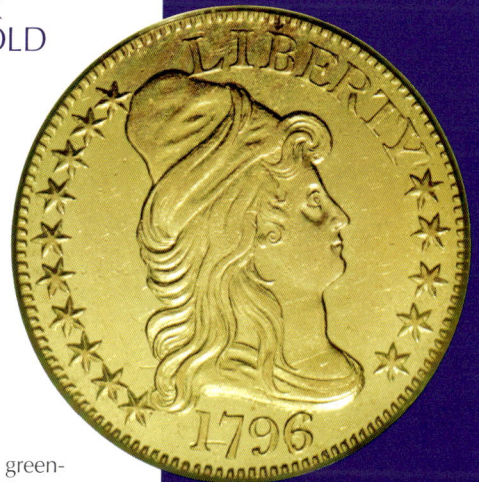

VERY RARE 1797 16 STARS HALF EAGLE
POSSIBLY THE FINEST KNOWN IN PRIVATE HANDS

6239 1797 Small Eagle, 16 Stars MS60 NGC. Breen-6420, B. 12-K, Miller-19, R.6. The 16 Stars 1797 Small Eagle five is one of the major rarities in the half eagle series. The obverse die has 11 stars on the left and five on the right. This is not an altered 15-Star die, but it is distinctive with differently placed devices. It is believed that both varieties were made in late 1795 or early 1796 with the final digit in the date omitted—a common practice in the early Mint when it was uncertain in which year a die would actually be used. Breen stated that the 16-Star coins constituted the delivery of 1,390 half eagles struck sometime after Tennessee was admitted to the Union (as the 16th state) on June 1. Probably no more than 35 examples survive today of all four Small Eagle varieties dated 1797, which include two varieties of 15-Star coins and two 16-Star half eagle varieties.

While several Mint State pieces are believed known of the 16-Stars, it is actually a much rarer coin than it appears as several of the higher graded pieces are impounded in museums. In fact, this is the only Uncirculated coin certified by either of the major services to date (3/04). The surfaces show the usual green-gold coloration one expects from early gold with almost none of the reddish patina often seen. Close examination shows considerable prooflikeness around the stars and legends, this reflective quality only being interrupted by numerous small abrasions that are peppered over each side, none of which are large enough to merit individual mention. A heavy pie-shaped pair of die cracks are seen on the lower reverse, as seen on later die states. Well struck around the margins, there is slight softness noted in the centers over Liberty's hair and the eagle's breast. A very rare opportunity to acquire one of the key issues in the half eagle series.

Ex: Stanley Kesselman (7/16/73); Harry Bass II (Bowers and Merena, 10/99), lot 721. (#8068)

RARE AND IMPRESSIVE 1795 CAPPED BUST RIGHT FIVE WITH HERALDIC EAGLE REVERSE MS63 PROOFLIKE NGC

6240 1795 Large Eagle MS63 Prooflike NGC. B. 5-W, Miller-13, R.7. Despite the presence of the date on the obverse, the 1795 Capped Bust Right, Heraldic Eagle Fives were not produced in 1795. Rather, these coins were produced in 1797 at the earliest, but more likely in 1798, perhaps as part of the 3,226 pieces delivered on December 5 of the latter year. Breen notes that extant 1795 Heraldic Eagle Fives display significant evidence of hasty workmanship, namely die rust on the obverse and generally poor striking quality. While the obverse portrait of the present example does reveal some rust pits, as one should expect for a leftover die that probably received very little attention prior to being pressed back into service, the overall impression is quite pleasing. There is plenty of bold, and even some sharp definition in evidence, the only noteworthy softness of detail being confined to the central highpoints. The color of this coin is pleasingly original with a deeply set, green-gold sheen throughout. One can also discern some isolated blushes of rose tinting in a few areas over and around the central reverse. Perhaps the most significant feature of this coin is the markedly prooflike finish. The fields are mirrored, suggesting an early impression from this press run, while the devices are more frosty in texture. Also, and interestingly for a business strike, an identifying lintmark (as struck) is seen on Liberty's cheek. The presence of this lintmark, as well as the prooflike finish, could mean that this coin was either the Menjou or Kern specimen, both of which were erroneously offered as proofs in 1950 (per David W. Akers, 1979). This issue is the third rarest in the Capped Bust Right, Heraldic Eagle Five Dollar series of 1795-1807. NGC and PCGS combined have seen just six examples in MS63 (resubmissions?), with a mere four finer (3/04).(#8075)

IMPORTANT MINT STATE 1804 HALF EAGLE, MS61 NGC

6241 1804 Small 8 MS61 NGC. B. 2-E, Miller-64, R.5. All Half Eagles from 1795 through 1804 are rare, and in mint condition extremely so. In the late 1700s Secretary of the Treasury Alexander Hamilton pegged the ratio of silver to gold at 15 to 1. However, silver was being mined and imported from Mexico, Central and South America in ever increasing quantities, while gold production was growing more slowly. The U.S. Mint did not adjust the standard, and by the turn of the century the true value ratio had shifted to 15 3/4 to 1, so it was advantageous to melt and/or export gold coins and then sell the bullion at a profit relative to silver. For this reason, early gold coins are now quite elusive in any condition.

The green-gold color of this coin shows off mint luster that is exceptional, being bright and disturbed by only a few obverse abrasions. A couple of die cracks are noted, one vertical that bisects the obverse, the other horizontal the bisects the right half of the reverse. A noteworthy specimen destined for the gold specialist.(#8085)

ORIGINAL 1805 HALF EAGLE MS63 PCGS

6242 1805 MS63 PCGS. Close Date, Breen-6445, B. 3-B, Miller-74, R.5. The scarcer of the two Close Date die pairings of this date. This impressive example possesses pale yellow-gold color and extensive shimmering luster. The strike is bold, since only the left (facing) border of the shield and the fletchings lack intricate definition. A small planchet flaw (as made) on the bust truncation does not distract. The surfaces are devoid of relevant marks. Struck from boldly clashed dies, and the obverse features a network of slender, mint-made die cracks that intersect below Liberty's ear. Population: 34 in 63, 15 finer (3/04).
From The Greenwich Collection, Part One.(#8088)

DESIRABLE 1806 FIVE DOLLAR, 7x6 STARS OBVERSE, MS60 NGC

6243 1806 Round Top 6, 7x6 Stars MS60 NGC. B. 5-E, Miller-84, R.2. This is the only variety of this date to show seven stars on the left and six on the right. 1806 Half Eagles are available in almost all grades (except MS65), and as such, they are widely used by collectors as representatives of the Capped Bust Right type of 1795-1807. This subtle green-gold example has soft, slightly muted mint luster and typically abraded surfaces for the assigned grade.

From The Greenwich Collection, Part One.(#8089)

DESIRABLE UNCIRCULATED 1806 ROUND TOP 6 HALF EAGLE

6244 1806 Round Top 6, 7x6 Stars MS62 PCGS. Breen-6448, B. 5-E, Miller-84, R.3. There are six die marriages of 1806-dated Eagles, but Breen 5-E is differentiated from the other varieties in two important ways. The 6 in the date ends with a knob instead of a point, and the stars are arranged seven left and six right instead of the usual eight by five arrangement. As a result, the right side stars are crowded when compared with their left side counterparts, since the right periphery is also shared with the legend LIBERTY. Both sides of this coin exhibit a frosty, amber-gold sheen that is suggestive of originality. Although lightly abraded, as befits the grade, the surfaces are especially attractive with nicely defined features save for normal softness on the obverse stars.(#8089)

SELECT UNCIRCULATED 1806 FIVE DOLLAR, MS63 PCGS

6245 1806 Round Top 6, 7x6 Stars MS63 PCGS. B. 5-E, Miller-84, R.3. An unusual variety that crowds six stars between LIBERTY and the bust, while the first star is distant from the hair curls. The reverse variety is distinguished by an incomplete lowest olive leaf, which has an outline but no inner veins. This bright Mint State example with frosty, yellow-gold surfaces and a hint of reflectivity in the fields. A few handling marks are seen in the obverse field, but the number of distracting abrasions is minimal for an early gold coin at the Select BU level of preservation. The only distinguishing feature on either side is a faint mark in the obverse field near Liberty's nose and a tiny toning spot at the midpoint of the eagle's Left wing. Well struck in most areas.
From The Greenwich Collection, Part One.(#8089)

SELECT UNCIRCULATED 1806 ROUND TOP 6 HALF EAGLE

6246 1806 Round Top 6, 7x6 Stars MS63 NGC. Breen-6448, B. 5-E, Miller-84, R.3. Although a decent number of B. 5-E examples exist in Mint State, they are rare coins when viewed in the wider context of U.S. numismatics. Only 64,093 Half Eagles of all types were produced in 1806, and those of the Round Top 6 variety are the most easily obtainable half eagles produced prior to 1807. A lovely Select quality survivor, both sides are colored in orange-gold and green-gold hues. This issue is generally not well defined, but the present example displays crisp definition over most features. Modest brightness is noted in the fields, the surfaces are free of most abrasions. For pedigree purposes, a thin scratch is seen from the upper left tip of the shield to the E of UNITED.(#8089)

1807 BUST RIGHT HALF EAGLE, MS63 PCGS

6247 1807 Bust Right MS63 PCGS. Small Date, Small Obverse Stars, Small Reverse Stars, Breen-6449, B. 1-A, Miller-85, R.5. The only Small Reverse Stars variety for the year, although the incomplete details on the olive branch are also of numismatic interest: two berries have no stem, and two leaves lack veins. Although the 1807 Bust Left is common for an early gold issue, all six Bust Right varieties of this date are rare. An exquisitely struck and shimmering example that has faint slide marks in the fields, but there are no individually relevant abrasions. A few faint adjustment marks are noted on the obverse border near 9 o'clock, these are strictly of mint origin and are completely inconspicuous. Housed in a green label PCGS holder.
From The Greenwich Collection, Part One.(#8092)

AMAZINGLY PRESERVED 1807 CAPPED BUST LEFT HALF EAGLE, MS65 NGC

6248 1807 Bust Left MS65 NGC. B. 5-D, Miller-101, R.3. Although his Capped Bust motif has achieved its greatest popularity on the Half Dollar of 1807-1834, John Reich also designed the Half Eagle that made its debut in 1807. While Liberty's portrait is nearly identical on both denominations, particularly in 1807-1808, the placement of the eagle's wings sets the two designs apart. Mint records indicate that 51,065 Capped Bust Left Half Eagles were produced in 1807. While many of these pieces have since been lost to the meltings of early 19th century America, the fact that the denomination served its greatest purpose as backing for bank transactions explains why most survivors are minimally worn. This is not to suggest that the 1807 is a common issue in XF-AU grades, and Mint State coins are of the utmost rarity. The example that we have the honor of offering here is tied with the finest 1807 Capped Bust Left Half Eagle that we have ever handled. It is interesting to speculate how this coin survived. Perhaps it was obtained directly from the mint shortly after striking as a souvenir from the first year of this design. Nevertheless, there is no doubt that this coin was well cared for since the day of production. Both sides display a richly frosted texture with warm green-gold overtones. The razor sharp striking definition would do justice to a Liberty Half Eagle from the 1890s. Distraction-free with not even the most inconspicuous pedigree marker in evidence. Population: 2 in 65, 2 finer (4/04).(#8101)

SCARCE 1808/7 HALF EAGLE AU58

6249 1808/7 AU58 NGC. Close Date, Breen-6455, B. 2-A, Miller-104, R.5. This lesser-seen die marriage can be identified by an incomplete lower curl on the portrait and relatively close spacing between the 5 and D in the denomination. Well detailed in the centers with ample evidence of frosty luster over green-gold and reddish surfaces. Population: 8 in 58, 24 finer (4/04).(#8103)

DESIRABLE MINT STATE 1809/8 HALF EAGLE

6250 1809/8 MS62 NGC. B. 1-A, Miller-108, the only known dies, R.3. Third year of the modified design, the 1809 Half Eagles were produced during a period when the Mint was undergoing significant changes in its production processes as well as personnel. Struck from an earlier die state, the underdigit is quite clear within the lower loop of the 9. The striking details are exceptionally strong on each side with pinpoint definition on Liberty's hair curls, the peripheral stars, and the eagle's plumage. The surfaces are sparkling and highly lustrous with an even layer of reddish patina on each side.(#8104)

1810 SMALL DATE, LARGE 5 HALF EAGLE, MS62 PCGS

6251 1810 Small Date, Large 5 MS62 PCGS. B. 2-D, Miller-113, High R.5. Well frosted for the grade, the surfaces are pleasingly colored in green-gold shades. This is a well produced coin, and there are no areas of mentionable striking softness. A few light, shallow abrasions seem to account for the MS62 designation, but the eye appeal alone would do justice to a higher grade. Among Capped Bust Left Half Eagles, the 1810 B. 2-D is more difficult to locate than the 1807, 1808, 1809/8, 1811, and 1812. Only 100,287 Half Eagles of all varieties were produced with this date.(#8106)

SELECT UNCIRCULATED 1810 HALF EAGLE, MS63 NGC

6252 1810 Large Date, Large 5 MS63 NGC. B. 1-A, Miller-109, R.2. This die marriage constitutes the majority of extant Capped Bust Left Half Eagles. In general, this is a well struck coin that typifies how this issue is usually found. Sharply struck, with any weakness limited to the left (facing) wing and the eagle's lower neck as they approach the shield, neither side has any individually mentionable abrasions. As a pedigree identifier a small dark toning spot shows between the 8 and 1 of the date. The MS63 grade is perhaps ideal for this desirable gold type, as the cost climbs substantially any finer. *From The Greenwich Collection, Part One.*(#8108)

SCARCE 1811 HALF EAGLE WITH TALL 5, MS62 NGC

6253 **1811 Tall 5 MS62 NGC.** B. 1-A, Miller-115, R.4. Only two die varieties exist for the 1811 issue, which are readily distinguished by the size of the 5 in the denomination. The Tall 5 variety is considered to be slightly scarcer. The present example is from a sharp strike and has satiny pastel-yellow color. The luster, although a bit subdued, is quite extensive for the grade. There are no singularly mentionable abrasions. There is a hint of die clash showing on each side. A pleasing Mint State example of this scarce variety.
From The Greenwich Collection, Part One.(#8110)

ATTRACTIVE 1812 HALF EAGLE SCARCE BREEN 1-A VARIETY

6254 **1812 MS63 PCGS.** Narrow 5D, Breen-6465, B. 1-A, Miller-117, R.4. The scarcer of the two die marriages known for the year, which are promptly distinguished by the space between the 5 and D of the denomination. A canary-gold piece with extensive satiny luster and a nearly undisturbed obverse. A couple of unimportant luster grazes are observed in the reverse field below the scroll. Well struck except for the upper right corner of the shield. The central hair curls are unusually bold, and the obverse exhibits faint clash marks, as made. Encapsulated in a green label PCGS holder.
From The Greenwich Collection, Part One.(#8112)

ELUSIVE NEAR-GEM 1812 CAPPED BUST HALF EAGLE

6255 1812 MS64 PCGS. Wide 5 D. B. 1-B, Miller-118, R.3. A lovely near-Gem that has extensive frosty luster and pleasing surfaces. Well struck except for the eagle's neck and left wing, there is a raised curved die line (as struck) on the shield, which is present on all known examples. A moderate die crack reaches the reverse border below the right wingtip. The obverse dies are perfect, and the cheek is quite smooth. The final star has a jagged lower right point, which is widely believed to be the signature of Mint engraver John Reich.(#8112)

COLLECTIBLE MINT STATE 62 1813 FIVE DOLLAR GOLD

6256 1813 MS62 NGC. B. 1-A, Miller-119, R.3. The two reverse dies for 1813 are very similar, but Miller-119 has the S in STATES is slightly further from the left edge of the scroll. The Capped Head Left design made its debut in 1813, and type set collectors are thankful that a few examples from the first year of production were saved for subsequent generations. The vast majority of the mintages of this type were melted by speculators, since the bullion value exceeded face. Offered here is a particularly well preserved example, with frosty reddish-golden surfaces that are equally sharp from side to side. Only the presence of a few wispy field marks keeps this splendid 1813 Five from an even loftier rating.(#8116)

SCARCE 1818 FIVE DOLLAR GOLD, MS60 NGC

6257 **1818 MS60 NGC.** B. 1-A, Miller-123, R.5. Scarcer than the STATESOF variety, the 1818 date is definitely rarer than the 1813 but not quite as difficult as other dates in the series. This piece has excellent mint luster, presenting a pronounced green-gold appearance with subtle reddish highlights. The surfaces are peppered with small abrasions but none are singularly distracting. A bit softly struck in the centers, one identifiable small mark shows under the M of AMERICA. Still a lovely example of this scarce early gold type.(#8119)

RARE 1818 HALF EAGLE, 5D OVER 50 VARIETY MS63 NGC

6258 **1818 5D Over 50 MS63 NGC.** B. 3-C, Miller-125, R.6. Discovered by H.P. Smith in 1906, this variety was soon forgotten until rediscovered in the 1950s at New Netherlands. The reverse die was used again the next year, but there is little difference in rarity or demand for this or the "Normal Dies" variety. The features are very well defined with strong definition on the hair curls of Liberty, the peripheral stars, and eagle's plumage. A clear 0 is seen under the D of 5 D on the reverse. Pronounced green-gold color over each side with subtle reddish peripheral accents, a few small abrasions are scattered about accounting for the grade. A lustrous and attractive, high grade early Five Dollar coin. Population: 4 in 63, 1 finer (4/04).(#8120)

EXTREMELY RARE 1831 SMALL 5D HALF EAGLE XF DETAILS

6259 1831 XF Details, Damaged, NCS. Small 5D, Breen-6493, B. 1-A, Miller-160, R.6. The Small 5 D variant is estimated to be three to four times scarcer than its Large 5 D counterpart, although both are rarely encountered. Considered as a separate, collectible variety, the Small 5 D 1831 is actually rarer than the 1830 Large 5 D, the 1834 Crosslet 4, and even the 1832 Square Base 2, 13 Stars. The example now offered suffers from an old cleaning and has a cluster of scratches to the right of the eagle. A depressed swath to the left of the portrait between stars 4 and 5 is perhaps the result of a planchet lamination.(#8153)

EXCEEDINGLY RARE 1833 HALF EAGLE, MS62 PCGS

6260 1833 Large Date MS62 PCGS. B. 2-B, Miller-168, R.5. Very rare, as are both date variants, with the Large Date variety the more "common" of the two, representing perhaps 60-70% of the surviving examples. The date is widely spaced with the period distant to the right of the D on the reverse.

The fields are bright with a strong semi-prooflike gleam. The devices are somewhat irregularly struck with some areas absolutely full, and others noticeably soft. A curving die crack is seen from the rim through star 1 down through the 1 of the date and back to the rim. This can be used as a future identifier. The rich green-gold color of the coin has taken on a light accent of reddish patina, and there are only small abrasions scattered across each side. Population: 3 in 62, 6 finer (3/04).(#8157)

CONDITIONALLY CHALLENGING 1834 CLASSIC HEAD HALF EAGLE MS63 PCGS

6261 1834 Plain 4 MS63 PCGS. Second Head, Breen-6502, McCloskey 2-B, R.3. This Block 8 example has a triple punched 4 and no tongue within the eagle's beak. A very impressive, high grade example of this always-popular first-year issue in the Classic series. A little strike softness shows at the central regions. The lustrous surfaces show a few minor abrasions and luster grazes, but none are worthy of individual mention. Each side exhibits a bright, honey-gold appearance. A conditionally challenging type.(#8171)

SCARCE 1838-C REPUNCHED 5 HALF EAGLE AU53

6262 1838-C AU53 NGC. Breen-6516, Repunched 5, McCloskey 1-B, R.4. The 1838-C is the second rarest issue in the series of Classic Fives (second only to the Crosslet 4), and is particularly elusive in AU and better condition. Additionally, it is the only Classic Half Eagle struck in the Charlotte mint, and as such is a very popular coin with collectors. As a later state of the Repunched 5 variety, this piece shows the rim-to-rim diagonal die crack and faint evidence of repunching on the 5. Excessive die polishing has removed portions of the eagle's feathers on the left side. While a bit softly struck on Liberty's curls, tinges of orange patina about the peripheral devices tend to make this still-lustrous example more attractive than the typical AU survivor. Population: 2 in 53, 12 finer (4/04).(#8177)

POPULAR 1839-D HALF EAGLE, AU55 NGC

6263 1839-D AU55 NGC. Variety 2-A. On this variety, the mintmark is over the 39 of the date and centered in the field with the left edge of the D over the center of the 3. Lower in mintage than the Classic Head design by William Kneass struck the year before, the 18,939 examples struck in Dahlonega are largely lost to collectors today, with only 125 to 150 examples still thought to exist. This is an attractive survivor with light evidence of circulation, Winter estimates that this piece is one of only 25 to 30 pieces known in About Uncirculated condition today. The pleasing, satiny surfaces have good overall visual characteristics and a typical amount of scattered contact marks. Pleasing golden color with reddish accents at the border areas. Population: 12 in 55, 18 finer (4/04).(#8193)

RARE MINT STATE 1840 CHARLOTTE HALF EAGLE

6264 1840-C MS60 NGC. Ex: Ashland City. Variety 2-B. Die State I. The 1840-C is very rare in all grades with only 70-80 pieces known today. In terms of overall rarity among C-mint half eagles, the 1840-C ranks second after the 1842-C Small Date. Until the appearance of this piece, the only other unquestionably Uncirculated '40-C fives were the Pittman coin (later graded MS64 by NGC) and the Elrod/Milas MS60. Well struck throughout with strong definition on the central devices as well as the peripheries. The surfaces are a bit lackluster, as expected for this issue, and the fields are lightly marked on each side. The only mentionable abrasions are a shallow horizontal scrape in the left obverse field between stars 4 and 5, and a nick in the upper reverse field between the eagle's head and the TE of STATES. Rich olive-golden color. Population: 1 in 60, 2 finer (4/04).(#8196)

ORIGINAL MINT STATE 1841-C FIVE DOLLAR, MS61 NGC

6265 **1841-C MS61 NGC.** Variety 3-C. The 1841-C is one of the more frequently offered C-mint Fives, especially in VF and XF grades. However, in strict Mint State there are only 5-6 pieces believed known. This piece is tied as fifth finest known on the Condition Census with the Elrod specimen (which we sold in our February 1999 Long Beach Sale for $18,400). As with most high grade survivors of this issue, this piece shows sharp detailing on each side, which explains one reason why these coins are so popular for type purposes. The surfaces show numerous small abrasions, which is expected from both the grade and the issue, and the fields have a semi-reflective sheen that is most appealing. Population: 4 in 61, 1 finer (4/04).(#8203)

CONDITIONALLY RARE 1847 HALF EAGLE, MS64 PCGS

6266 **1847 MS64 PCGS.** The 1847 is one of the more commonly encountered half eagles from the 1840s, even in lesser Uncirculated grades, but its importance as a No Motto type coin far outweighs the difficulty of the individual issue. This noteworthy example puts most of the Mint State pieces we have seen to shame. Both sides display remarkable strength of detail and shimmering mint luster beneath an even layer of orange patina. There is tiny planchet streak in front of Liberty's neck that is not necessarily distracting, but might be useful for pedigree purposes. Population: 2 in 64, 2 finer (3/04).(#8231)

FLASHY NEAR-MINT 1849-C HALF EAGLE

6267 1849-C AU58 PCGS. The 1849-C is one of the more frequently available C-mint Fives and it is also one of the better produced ones, as a general rule. There are some noticeable scuffmarks in the fields but the amount of actual circulation on this well stuck example is minimal. The surfaces have retained considerable luster below a dash of light green-gold color. Population: 4 in 58, 10 finer (3/04).(#8241)

SCARCE 1852 HALF EAGLE MS63

6268 1852 MS63 NGC. One of the more available issues among No Motto Fives, but elusive both as a date and as a type coin at the Select level of preservation. This lustrous example is well defined on the obverse, but shows the usual softness on the neck of the eagle. Population: 20 in 63, 12 finer (4/04).(#8250)

NEAR-MINT 1852-D HALF EAGLE

6269 1852-D AU58 NGC. Variety 27-S (per Doug Winter's second edition and revised attribution system). The '52-D is one of the more frequently encountered D-mint fives, and as such it is commonly used as a type coin. This near-Mint example has bright yellow-gold coloration and shows slightly soft striking definition over the highpoints of the design. A few abrasions are scattered over each side, the most notable being a couple of diagonal marks on the back of Liberty's cheek.(#8252)

ELUSIVE 1854-O HALF EAGLE MS61

6270 1854-O MS61 PCGS. A near-twin to the similarly certified 1854-O Half Eagle sold in our July 2003 Baltimore for $6,325, this elusive Mint State representative is also mildly prooflike and is struck with uncommon sharpness. The '54-O is a scarce and somewhat overlooked New Orleans Five in all grades, with fewer than 150 pieces believed to be extant from a mintage of 46,000 pieces. Survivors qualifying at the Uncirculated level are extremely scarce, probably numbering less than 10 pieces. Population: 3 in 61, 2 finer (3/04).
From The South Florida Collection.(#8259)

IMPORTANT MINT STATE 1856-D HALF EAGLE

6271 1856-D MS61 PCGS. Variety 33-BB, the only currently known variety. The 1856-D was produced to the extent of only 19,786 coins, and this issue is one of the rarest Dahlonega Half Eagles from the standpoint of total number of coins known. In fact, the '56-D ranks third in this regard after only the 1861-D and the 1842-D Large Date. Writing in 1997, Doug Winter noted that the 1856-D is among the more sharply defined D-mint half eagles from the 1850s, this despite chronic bluntness of detail over the central features. This coin is softly impressed over Liberty's hair curls and the eagle's neck and leg feathers, but the peripheral areas are crisp and include full radial lines on the obverse stars. The surfaces are a bright orange-gold color with a moderately frosted sheen. As identifiers, close examination reveals a series of diagonal pinscratches across the obverse and Liberty's cheek. Minimally abraded for the grade, this coin is should be of obvious importance to Southern gold specialists.(#8268)

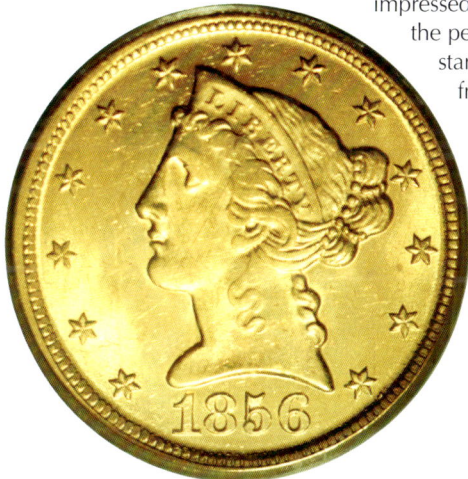

BEAUTIFUL MINT STATE 1859 CHARLOTTE HALF EAGLE, PCGS MS62

6272 1859-C MS62 PCGS. Ex: Ashland City. Variety 27-M. Die State II. Tied for second finest known with the MS62 in the Michigan Collection, and only bettered by the fabulous MS66 coin formerly in the Elrod and Eliasberg Collections. Sharply defined on the obverse, the reverse shows the usual softness from an improperly annealed reverse die. The obverse fields are bright and glitter with sparkling prooflike reflectivity, a result of heavy die striations on that side. Even reddish-golden toning is overlaid on both obverse and reverse. Distinguished by a tiny dark spot of color in the lower left obverse field just above the end of Liberty's bust. Population: 2 in 62, 2 finer (3/04).(#8281)

COLLECTIBLE HIGH GRADE 1860-C FIVE DOLLAR

6273 1860-C AU55 NGC. Variety 28-M. A very scarce Charlotte Half Eagle that has the third lowest mintage of the series with only 14,813 coins struck. This piece is rather typical for the issue with minimal wear and a bright, overall appearance. The obverse has myriad small abrasions that are commensurate with the grade, while the reverse is slightly cleaner. The reverse is, of course, ill-defined having been struck from the improperly annealed die first used in 1859.(#8285)

UNHERALDED 1863-S HALF EAGLE AU53

6274 1863-S AU53 NGC. Even though 17,000 pieces were struck of the 1863-S, most of the surviving examples (of which there are surprisingly few) are well circulated. Akers said this issue is comparable to the P-mint from 1863, which has a business strike mintage of just 2,442 pieces, and is even scarcer in high grades. Only a single Mint State example has been certified by both NGC and PCGS combined. This moderately abraded example displays above-average definition in the centers and small portions of luster in the areas surrounding the devices. Population: 3 in 53, 17 finer (4/04).(#8295)

DESIRABLE HIGH GRADE 1863-S HALF EAGLE

6275 1863-S AU55 PCGS. The few '63-S Fives we have offered have invariably been well circulated, as is the typical survivor of this long underappreciated issue. A total of 17,000 pieces were originally struck, but fewer coins are extant from this somewhat unimpressive figure (for the era and denomination), than on issues with mintage of one half or even one tenth that of the 1863-S. Any coin grading AU or higher can be considered an extreme rarity, so the importance of this piece is unquestionable. The highpoint definition is virtually complete, save for the radials on the first two stars. A number of scattered marks are present, but the yellow-golden surfaces still offer much of the original luster.(#8295)

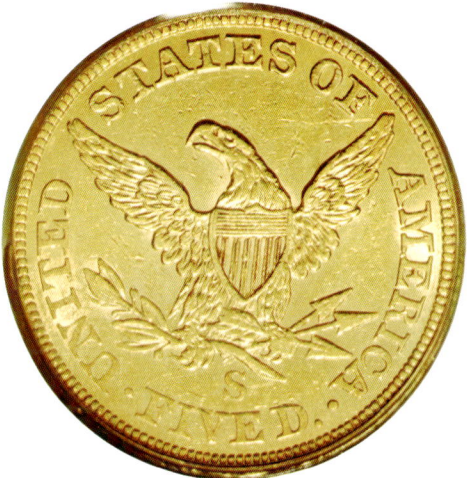

SCARCE NEAR-MINT 1866 MOTTO HALF EAGLE

6276 1866 AU58 NGC. The first year of the With Motto design for Half Eagles and an extremely scarce issue from a mintage of just 6,700 business strikes. The majority of survivors grade XF at best and pieces nearing Mint State qualify as Condition Census. This sharply struck example has tinges of pinkish-gold color at the margins and numerous choppy abrasions in the fields are responsible for the slightest break in luster. Population: 12 in 58, 4 finer (4/04).(#8311)

CONDITIONALLY RARE, CHOICE AU58 1868 $5

6277 **1868 AU58 NGC.** Like most issues from this decade, the 1868 Half Eagle was minted in limited quantities and it is by mere chance that any high grade pieces survived for today's collectors. Only a faint hint of wear shows on the highest portions of the design of this piece, and the surfaces display bright golden luster. Moderate abrasions are present on each side, as are often seen on issues from this era. This specimen is undoubtedly among the finest known examples. PCGS has yet to grade any coin above this grade, and NGC has graded only two pieces higher. Rare in any grade, we expect spirited bidding on this high grade specimen.(#8315)

PREMIER 1870-CC FIVE DOLLAR XF40

6278 **1870-CC XF40 PCGS.** Variety 1-A. Where else but a Heritage Signature Sale can a serious collector of Western Mint gold choose between more than one example of this elusive inaugural year Carson City issue? This evenly worn representative displays prominent green-gold coloration with tinges of coppery color picked up about the rims and devices. An old pinscratch between TA in STATES near the reverse border is useful for attribution. *From The Barry Donnell Collection.*(#8320)

DESIRABLE 1870-CC HALF EAGLE XF40

6279 **1870-CC XF40 PCGS.** Variety 1-A. The 1870-CC is an extremely challenging issue from an original mintage of only 7,675 pieces, and enjoys added popularity as the premier date from the Carson City facility. The example offered here is at least on par with the average survivor, of which there are perhaps 50-60 pieces known, being well detailed with relatively unabraded yellow-gold surfaces.
Ex: 1982 ANA Mid-Year Sale (Krueger, 2/82), lot 1636.
From The Barry Donnell Collection.(#8320)

EXTREMELY SCARCE 1871 HALF EAGLE MS61

6280 **1871 MS61 NGC.** This P-mint half eagle is considered very rare, rarer in fact than the two branch mint issues from this abbreviated production year. It boasts a tiny mintage of only 3,230 business strikes, most of which grade only VF or XF. Mint State pieces are virtually unknown. Well struck with bright, semi-reflective fields and peppered with small field marks on each side which limit the grade. Identifiable by a light copper stain at the point of the truncation of the bust and a darker spot between the second and third stripes on the shield. Population: 2 in 61, 0 finer (4/04).(#8322)

NEARLY MINT STATE 1874 CARSON CITY HALF EAGLE

6281 1874-CC AU58 NGC. The production records report that the 1874-CC half eagle had the highest mintage of any issue of this denomination from the Carson City mint for the decade of the 1870s, and indeed survivors from this issue are among the more commonly found from this era. Common here is a relative term however, as even heavily worn examples are desired by collectors, and high grade pieces are virtually non-existent. In fact, the two major grading services have to date certified just two examples in Mint State grades (a pair of PCGS MS62s). This example shows just a touch of light rub on the highest points of the design, and in fact looks fully Uncirculated on the reverse. A few scattered marks are present, consistent with the short stint this piece spent in the channels of commerce, the only readily noticeable abrasions being a thin scuff in the left obverse field and a few minor abrasions between the fifth and sixth stars and the eighth and ninth stars. A pleasing coin overall, especially considering the condition rarity that this piece represents. Population: 9 in 58, 0 finer (4/04).(#8334)

OUTSTANDING 1876-CC HALF EAGLE AU55

6282 1876-CC AU55 PCGS. Variety 1-A. Generally well defined for this uncommon Carson City Five, with surfaces that retain significant original luster. Two horizontal, paper-thin marks above the right side of the date are the only blemishes worthy of mention. The diagnostic die lump on Liberty's throat, present on all genuine '76-CC Half Eagles is easily visible to the unaided eye. With the lowest mintage of all CC's of this denomination, just 6,887 pieces, this issue is elusive in all grades and is comparable in scarcity to the more highly regarded 1873-CC. Population: 5 in 55, 4 finer (3/04).
From The Barry Donnell Collection.(#8340)

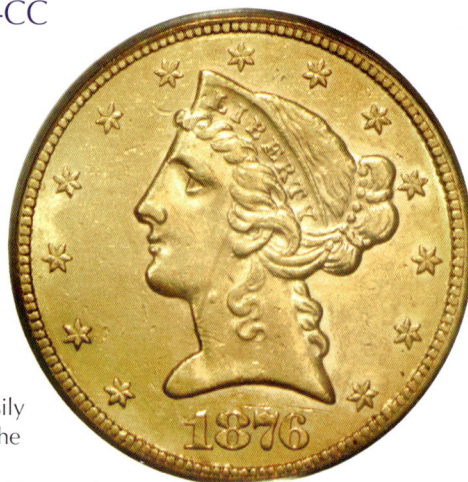

CHALLENGING 1878-CC FIVE DOLLAR XF45

6283 1878-CC XF45 PCGS. Variety 1-A. A muted green-gold example with subtle traces of coppery patina in the recesses. Two small facial marks and a more lengthy diagonal blemish at the back of Liberty's neck are not particularly offensive when one considers the rarity and importance of this Carson City issue.
From The Barry Donnell Collection.(#8346)

HIGH QUALITY 1878-CC LIBERTY HALF EAGLE

6284 1878-CC AU50 PCGS. Variety 1-A. The odds of choosing from several XF or better 1878-CC Half Eagles in the same sale are extremely long, although we were surprised to notice that three VF or better pieces appeared in our 2003 FUN Sale. This thoroughly original example shows minimal wear over the highpoints and has a light overlay of reddish-orange patina on the obverse. Clusters of tiny contact marks can be seen under Liberty's chin and in the vicinity of the mintmark.
From The Barry Donnell Collection.(#8346)

CONDITION CENSUS 1878-CC FIVE DOLLAR AU53

6285 1878-CC AU53 PCGS. Variety 1-A. The 1878-CC is an extreme condition rarity among Carson City Half Eagles, being even more elusive in grades above XF than its already brief production of 9,054 pieces would suggest. There is much to recommend about this solid AU representative. The strike is reasonably sharp for the issue and lustrous yellow-gold surfaces are only sparingly abraded. Only a few small contact marks in the vicinity of the 1 in the date are of the slightest consequence. Most likely Condition Census quality for this challenging, often overlooked CC Five. Population: 1 in 53, 4 finer (3/04).
From The Barry Donnell Collection.(#8346)

INCREDIBLE 1890 LIBERTY HALF EAGLE MS68

6286 1890 MS68 NGC. Phenomenal quality for this or any other issue in the Liberty Half Eagle series. The sheer eye appeal of this coin helps secure the lofty MS68 designation. Sharply defined in all areas, the fields are bright and shimmer with prooflike reflectivity, as one might expect of an issue of just 4,240 business strikes. The surfaces are not completely free from post-striking marks, but are temptingly close and certainly none are obvious to the unaided eye. To state that this coin is the finest known of the few pieces that are known is to state the obvious. It is likely that a wealthy collector acquired this piece directly from the Philadelphia Mint. But who really knows for sure? Perhaps someone noticed the low mintage at the time of issue, celebrated a 50th anniversary, or marked the arrival of a first-born child. For the entire With Motto type, only nine other pieces have been so graded by NGC, while two are certified finer (3/04). Just six others are certified as such by PCGS (4/04).(#8375)

PLATINUM NIGHT

SCARCE 1892-O HALF EAGLE MS62

6287 1892-O MS62 PCGS. A difficult New Orleans Half Eagle at any grade level and the first issue of its denomination struck at the historic facility since 1857. Just 10,000 pieces were issued. Only a few dozen Mint State pieces are believed to survive, and only one coin has certified above MS63. This sharply detailed example displays tinges of orange patina at the margins and is separated from the Select level by a smattering of choppy field marks.
Ex: Stack's Public Auction Sale (10/97), lot 1105, where it realized $3,300.

From The Barry Donnell Collection.(#8381)

CONDITION CENSUS 1895 HALF EAGLE, MS67 NGC

6288 1895 MS67 NGC. A Condition Census example, the surfaces are as smooth as we have ever seen on an 1895 Half Eagle. Both sides are also free of bothersome alloy spots, and the strike is needle sharp over all features. This frosty, orange-gold example would make an attractive addition to any gold collection that goes beyond the normal pale. Population: 2 in 67, none finer at either service (4/04).(#8390)

UNSURPASSABLE 1899 LIBERTY HALF EAGLE, MS67 PCGS

6289 1899 MS67 PCGS. A truly remarkable specimen! One might wonder how this coin has been saved for over 100 years in such a careful state of preservation. Boldly struck throughout with rich yellow-golden luster equally coating each side. Close examination with a loupe fails to detect any meaningful abrasions or alloy spots. For future identification, a tiny diagonal line is seen in the left obverse field that is parallel to Liberty's nose. A fortunate opportunity for the gold specialist or the astute type coin collector. This is currently the single finest example thus far certified by PCGS (3/04).(#8398)

FABULOUS ELIASBERG PEDIGREED 1899-S HALF EAGLE, NGC MS69

6290 1899-S MS69 NGC. Ex: Eliasberg. Like many of the late nineteenth and early twentieth century coins from the famed Eliasberg Collection, this piece was obtained at face value by John H. Clapp directly from the San Francisco mint. It is perhaps the most pristine example of the type that this cataloger has ever seen, and is certainly the finest example of the date that we have ever seen or handled. It is the finest certified by either service (the only close competition is a PCGS MS68, with no other examples graded by either service above MS66), and is among the finest known specimens *for the type*. The surfaces display intense luster with a reflective quality that is highly unusual for the issue, indicating that this piece was indeed a "special" coin set aside for an important collector. The strike is impeccable, sharp enough that it compares to many proofs of the era in this respect. A long, hard look at the surfaces under magnification does reveal a couple (literally, only a couple) of tiny, nearly insignificant abrasions—but then MS70 is supposed to be only a theoretical grade of perfection, right? One tiny toning spot just in front of Liberty's upper lip is mentioned for accuracy, and provides an easy pedigree marker for this important numismatic treasure. A stunning coin that is equal in importance alongside the other denominations of this year and mint also offered in this sale, and is certainly the most important 1899-S half eagle that we have ever had the pleasure to offer. Population: 1 in 69, 0 finer (4/04).(#8399)

SCARCE MS64 1909 INDIAN HALF EAGLE

6291 1909 MS64 PCGS. Even though more than 600,000 pieces were struck of this issue, the 1909 is not a common coin in the preferred grades of Mint State. This is an especially pleasing example that has bright, softly frosted mint luster that rolls around each side virtually unimpeded by abrasions. Fully struck also, the surfaces have a lovely orange-gold coloration that deepens slightly around the margins.
Ex: September Long Beach Sale (Heritage, 9/98), lot 7142, where it realized $9,430.(#8513) (Registry values: N2998)

ELUSIVE GEM 1909-D INDIAN HALF EAGLE, MS65 NGC

6292 1909-D MS65 NGC. With uncommonly smooth surfaces, this colorful Gem would do justice to any high quality type set. Swirls of tan-gold patina are draped over the otherwise smooth surfaces of this well frosted example. Boldly struck and extremely scarce in this high grade. Population: 56 in 65, 0 finer (4/04).(#8514) (Registry values: N4719)

CONDITIONALLY SCARCE 1909-D FIVE, MS65 PCGS

6293 **1909-D MS65 PCGS.** The '09-D is by far the most available $5 Indian issue in Mint State, but the vast majority of survivors fall into the MS60 to MS63 grade range. This sharply defined Gem example is very well struck and shows only minimal surface marks. Population: 49 in 65, 5 finer (3/04). *From The Greenwich Collection, Part One.*(#8514) (Registry values: N4719)

CONDITIONALLY CHALLENGING 1909-O FIVE DOLLAR

6294 **1909-O MS62 SEGS (MS60 Cleaned).** A lightly cleaned but certainly presentable example of this low mintage key. Sharply struck devices, a few marks are noticed in the reverse field.(#8515) (Registry values: N4719)

ELUSIVE MINT STATE 1909-O FIVE DOLLAR GOLD

6295 1909-O MS61 NGC. With the lowest mintage in the series (34,200 pieces), the 1909-O is the premier rarity among Indian half eagles. It is conditionally rare as an uncirculated piece, such as this one. As always, the striking details are a bit soft, but curiously the mintmark is quite bold with even the left side of the O strongly defined. The most obvious surface marks are a few on the reverse, and subdued, satiny luster still remains overall.

From The South Florida Collection.(#8515) (Registry values: N4719)

ELUSIVE GEM 1910 INDIAN HALF EAGLE, MS65 NGC

6296 1910 MS65 NGC. The 1910 is generally categorized as one of the more available issues in the Indian Half Eagle series, but even it becomes difficult to obtain at the Choice level, and is very elusive in such a superior state of preservation as this one. This remarkable Gem exhibits soft, matte-like luster with subtle reddish-golden overtones. Not only is the strike almost fully executed, but both sides are nearly free from post-minting blemishes. Population: 17 in 65, 1 finer (4/04).

From The Greenwich Collection, Part One.(#8517) (Registry values: N7079)

GEM UNCIRCULATED 1911 INDIAN HALF EAGLE

6297 **1911 MS65 PCGS.** This is a bight, lustrous coin with a little light granularity that is not uncommon for the series. The color is medium gold on the obverse with some orange-gold tinting evident on the reverse. A couple of marks are seen at the top of the obverse, a couple are also present near IN GOD WE TRUST. A well preserved, overall bold representative of this, a popular type date for this conditionally challenging series. Population: 31 in 65, 1 finer (3/04).(#8520) (Registry values: N7079)

VERY SCARCE 1911-S HALF EAGLE, MS64

6298 **1911-S MS64 PCGS.** The 1911-S is very scarce in MS63 and better grades, and in fact, high quality examples are equally as elusive as the two previous S-mint issues. This is a very attractive example that has the usual soft, frosted mint luster with a deep overlay of reddish-orange and lilac coloration. Lightly abraded.(#8522) (Registry values: N7079)

PLATINUM NIGHT

RARE GEM 1911-S INDIAN HALF EAGLE

6299 1911-S MS65 NGC. Astonishing quality for this conditionally elusive Five Dollar Indian. The 1911-S is very scarce in all grades of Mint State despite its mintage of 1.4 million pieces. In Gem condition, Akers rates it as an R.8 issue although today, this is slightly overstated. This is a splendid coin whose surfaces are covered with frosted, champagne-gold mint luster. Well defined throughout, there are virtually no impairments on either side. The only noticeable marks are a tiny planchet indention immediately to the left of the eagle's leg, and a diagonal mark from the M of UNUM also to the eagle's leg. Population: 3 in 65, 0 finer (4/04).(#8522) (Registry values: N7079)

CONDITIONALLY RARE 1914 INDIAN FIVE DOLLAR GOLD

6300 1914 MS65 NGC. A quaint and delicately frosted Gem example of Pratt's curious incuse design. This specimen typifies the effulgent reddish-gold color that collectors often see on this P-mint issue. As one would expect, the mint used powerful striking pressure on this example to draw forth even the smallest particular. The fields and devices are placid but it is possible to isolate a few small abrasions that are only visible under close examination. A scarce, though available, gold piece that type collectors strongly favor. Population: 8 in 65, 1 finer (4/04).

From The Greenwich Collection, Part One.(#8527) (Registry values: N4719)

HEAVILY MELTED 1929 HALF EAGLE MS63

6301 1929 MS63 PCGS. A typically lustrous yellow-gold representative. The 1929 Half Eagle is a well documented scarcity that was extensively melted in the 1930s. Most of the normally Mint State survivors that are available to today's collector surfaced from European holdings. The present example displays immediate eye appeal, but is kept at the Select level by a few small facial marks on the Native American. *From The Barry Donnell Collection.*(#8533) (Registry values: N4719)

GEM MATTE PROOF 66 1911 HALF EAGLE

6302 1911 PR66 NGC. As with the 1908 proof issue of this design, the mint returned to a dark matte finish for the proof issues of 1911. The lemon-yellow surfaces on this specimen display no faults worthy of mention, and the strike is as sharp as any we have seen for the date or type. Just 139 examples were originally produced, and survivors are more often seen in lower grades than this nearly pristine Proof 66 example. Only a handful of pieces have received a higher grade from either major grading service, and the relatively high figure published by NGC of 20 certified in this grade undoubtedly reflects at least a few repeat submissions of the same coin or coins. Population: 20 in 66, 6 finer (4/04).(#8542) (Registry values: N7079)

UNSURPASSABLE SUPERB 1913 MATTE PROOF HALF EAGLE

6303 1913 PR67 NGC. Only 99 proofs were reportedly struck in this year, and of course, far fewer survive today. Most authorities assert that some two dozen pieces of this date are still extant, but we believe the actual number may be somewhere in the range of 30-45 coins. It is worth noting that when Akers compiled the data for his *magnum opus* on the Half Eagle series he only recorded 18 appearances over a 37-year period, and when Breen published his 1977 book on proof coinage he was unable to find any recent auction records.

The sandblast or matte finish of this coin is undisturbed by even the smallest imperfections and there are no "shiny spots" on either side. The coin has a pronounced olive-green caste—one is tempted to compare it to the 1908 proof issues—but this is a brighter shade of green than seen proofs from that earlier year. An exquisite piece of proof gold and obviously very rare. Population: 6 in 67, none finer at either service (4/04).(#8544) (Registry values: N10218)

AU DETAILS 1795 13 LEAVES EAGLE

6304 1795 13 Leaves—Repaired, Whizzed—ANACS. AU Details, Net VF30. Breen-6830, B. 1-A, Taraszka-1, R.3. A lightly whizzed representative that has numerous faint pinscratches on the reverse field. The lower right obverse field has been smoothed, affecting the outline of Liberty's neck. Nonetheless, sharply detailed, and both sides retain considerable luster. *From The Paulsboro Collection.*(#8551)

HIGHLY DESIRABLE, FIRST YEAR 1795 TEN DOLLAR

6305 1795 13 Leaves AU Details, Improperly Cleaned, NCS. B. 3-B, Taraszka-4, R.5. A heavy die lump between OF and AMERICA attributes the reverse, while the obverse is identified by a series of tiny die lumps below the tip of the bust. A better variety that is seen much less often than the Breen 1-A die pairing. A lightly hairlined example of this rare and historic issue. A couple of crisscrossing adjustment marks are seen at the center of the reverse. The eagle's wings have sharply detailed plumage and the upper obverse has a light die crack from 11 o'clock to 1 o'clock. From the first year of the denomination, and also from the inaugural year of gold coinage at the Philadelphia mint.(#8551)

1795 13 LEAVES TEN DOLLAR AU DETAILS

6306 1795 13 Leaves, AU Details, Improperly Cleaned, NCS. Breen-6830, B. 2-A, Taraszka-2, R.4. The tip of a palm leaf nearly touches the lower left base of the U in UNITED, and the star after the Y in LIBERTY is comparatively distant from that letter. Although minimally worn and rather well detailed, the rich golden surfaces are somewhat dulled by an abrasive cleaning that leaves wispy hairlines throughout. Contact marks are scattered across the obverse, the deepest of which is located just beneath the portrait and above the first two digits of the date.(#8551)

IMPORTANT 1795 EAGLE, CHOICE AU55 NGC

6307 1795 13 Leaves AU55 NGC. B. 1-A, Taraszka-1, R.3.Despite its status as the nation's gold monetary unit, the Eagle enjoyed less popularity within financial circles than the smaller Half Eagle. As the Five Dollar coin had a similar value to foreign gold coins of the period, the Philadelphia mint concentrated its earliest gold coinage efforts on that denomination. When the government finally initiated Eagle production on September 22, 1795, only 5,583 1795-dated pieces were produced between that date and March 30, 1796. In stark contrast, the Mint's initial production of 8,707 Half Eagles was achieved in a much shorter time frame between July 31 and September 16, 1795. Regardless of its limited appeal to banks and merchants, the size of the eagle made it an impressive coin. As a result, curious American citizens saved many examples as first-year souvenirs, but numismatic scholars stress that fewer than 3% of the original mintage survives today in all levels of preservation.

An attractive example of our nation's first Eagle, with only a trace of wear on the highest points and in the fields. The surfaces display a few scattered abrasions, and the bright yellow-gold color does not inhibit the traces of original luster. For pedigree purposes, a thin curving scratch is seen from star 7 down to Liberty's throat.(#8551)

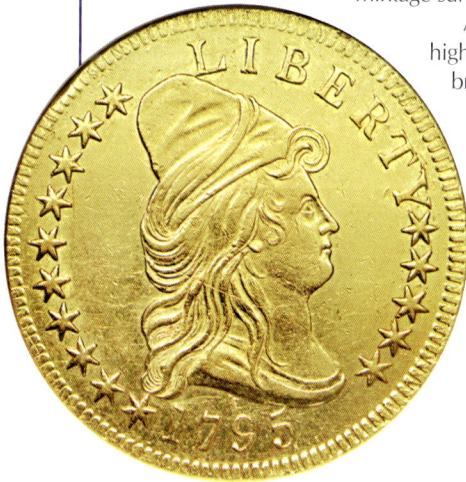

IMPRESSIVE NEAR-MINT 1795 TEN DOLLAR GOLD

6308 1795 13 Leaves AU58 NGC. B. 1-A, Taraszka-1, R.3. The most frequently seen variety of the year, which is distinguished by a minute extension at the top left of the upper left of the serif of the Y in LIBERTY. The 1795 Capped Bust Right, Small Eagle Ten was produced with five known die marriages between September 27, 1795 and March 30, 1796. It seems highly likely that representatives of the B. 1-A variety were the first delivered because they were preserved in greater numbers than examples of the other four die marriages. The novelty of these large, impressive gold coins and their resultant popularity among the public at the time also explains why most survivors grade XF-AU; i.e., many examples were retrieved after a short stint in circulation and preserved for posterity. With a pleasing, green-gold sheen and ample remaining definition over the main design elements, this coin would do wonders for a high grade circulated type set. There is a smattering of light abrasions on both sides, most of which are not individually distracting, and none of which are out of context with the Choice AU grade level. One of numerous important gold offerings in this memorable Heritage sale.(#8551)

EXTREMELY SCARCE 1795 NINE LEAVES EAGLE

6309 1795 9 Leaves AU Details, Burnished, NCS. Breen-6831, B. 4-C, Taraszka-3, R.6. Only 116 pieces are theorized by Breen to have been struck of this rare variety, all in March of 1796. The extreme rarity of the 1795 Nine Leaves can best be understood when one views the reverse of this coin. A ragged V-shaped die crack is seen below the leaves and another irregular break is seen through the first T in STATES. These are apparently common to most, if not all Nine Leaves coins, and their presence, which is less obvious on this piece than most examples seen by this cataloger, indicates early failure of the reverse die. Clusters of tiny digs and scratches are seen on the obverse, mostly at 2 o'clock and 8 o'clock, although a few others are noticed to the right of the date.(#8552)

EXCEEDINGLY DIFFICULT 1798/7 CAPPED BUST EAGLE

6310 1798/7 9x4 Stars AU Details, Damaged, Burnished NCS. B. 1-A, Taraszka-9, R.4. A very rare early Ten that is seldom offered by anyone in any grade. Breen estimates that perhaps only 18-20 pieces are known out of the original mintage of 900 coins. Of that tiny number of survivors, three are known to be mutilated, 9-12 are in Mint State, and the remainder are in the VF to AU grade range. Although both sides have been noticeably cleaned and are slightly porous as a result, this coin appears well balanced and is an excellent value for the early gold specialist.(#8560)

ELUSIVE MINT STATE 62 1799 EAGLE LARGE STARS OBVERSE

6311 1799 Large Stars Obverse MS62 PCGS. B. 5-G, Taraszka-22, R.3. The Philadelphia mint struck 37,449 Capped Bust Right, Heraldic Eagle Tens between May 14, 1799 and September 4, 1800. Breen (1988) believes that all of these coins were dated 1799, an opinion also advanced by, among other editions, the 2004 *Guide Book*. Although the 1799 rivals the 1801 for the distinction of the most readily obtainable date of the type, only approximately 2% of the original mintage is believed extant in all grades. The B. 4-E and B. 5-G die marriages seem to be the most common in today's market, and they include a not insignificant number of Mint State coins.

Virtually all of the central design elements on both sides of the present example are crisply detailed. Even the peripheries are uncommonly well impressed for the type. Some die polish lines (as produced) show up particularly in the reverse field. Both sides are awash in green-gold color that lightens to reddish-gold shades as the surfaces dip into the light. Semi-reflective in texture with a number of tiny field marks confined mostly to the obverse side.(#8562)

ATTRACTIVE 1799 SMALL STARS EAGLE XF40

6312 1799 Small Stars Obverse XF40 NGC. Irregular Date, Breen-6840, B. 4-D, Taraszka-20, R.5. One of the two "Irregular Dates" of 1799, this scarcer die pairing is most easily distinguished by the die defect within the C in AMERICA. The example offered here displays balanced wear and is tinged in attractive orange patina. A few relatively minor marks are scattered about, including an old diagonal scratch on the portrait that we suspect is not Mint produced.(#98562)

SCARCE 1800 TEN DOLLAR XF45

6313 **1800 XF45 PCGS.** Breen-6842, B. 1-A, Taraszka-23, R.4. The only die pairing for the year and a difficult coin to locate in any grade, being a frequently overlooked early Eagle from a reduced mintage of 5,999 pieces. A prominent die crack along the top of LIBERTY is seen on virtually all pieces seen and perhaps explains the brief production of the 1800. Tinges of coppery-red patina are noticed here and there over well struck, but moderately scuffy surfaces.(#8563)

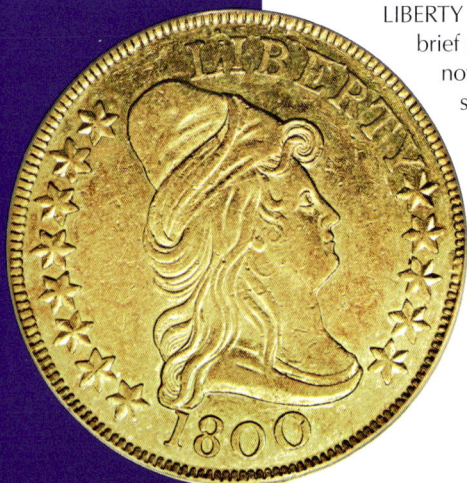

DESIRABLE 1801 TEN DOLLAR GOLD

6314 **1801 Unc Details, Burnished, NCS.** B. 2-B, Taraszka 25, R.3. The surfaces have been obviously cleaned at one time and are now retoned a deep red color overall. That being said, the coin has extraordinary detail with sharp hair detail, strong definition on the stars, and fine feather detail on the eagle. An exceptionally smooth, high grade example.(#8564)

SPLENDID AND WELL STRUCK 1801 EAGLE, MS63 PCGS

6315 1801 MS63 PCGS. Breen-6843, B. 2-B, Taraszka-25, R.3. One of only two die varieties for the year, Breen 2-B has the first star further from the curl than on its Breen 1-A counterpart. The original honey-gold color and the exquisite strike on the major devices ensure the eye appeal of this impressive early Eagle. Some faint and completely unobtrusive adjustment marks (as produced) are found on the obverse at 5 and 11 o'clock; these do not extend past the borders and cannot be seen except under a lens.

Unlike the Half Eagle denomination, the mintage of Eagles ceased in 1804. The Heraldic Eagle type was struck in small quantities, and the vast majority of these pieces were melted to reclaim the bullion during the first half of the 19th century. Many survivors were used in jewelry or are otherwise impaired. The present piece is a noteworthy exception. Housed in an earlier generation, green label PCGS holder.

From The Greenwich Collection, Part One.(#8564)

COLLECTIBLE MINT STATE 1803 EAGLE SMALL STARS REVERSE

6316 1803 Small Stars Reverse MS61 NGC. B. 1-D, Taraszka-26, R.6. A scarce variety that is identifiable by the star size as already noted and by the placement of the space between the two center clouds below the upright of the E in STATES. The fields are bright and semi-reflective, giving this piece eye appeal that transcends the assigned MS61 grade. The rich, yellow-gold surfaces show a few tiny field marks but the striking details are sharply defined in all areas. An important and attractive Mint State example of this popular, early Eagle.(#8565)

SCARCE HIGH GRADE 1845-O LIBERTY EAGLE CHOICE AU58 NGC

6317 **1845-O AU58 NGC.** The 4 in the date is clearly repunched with remnants of the initial digit far to the left. Similar in rarity to the 1846-O, the 1845-O is more difficult to locate in all grades than the 1842-O, 1843-O, and 1844-O. While the typically offered example grades either VF or XF, this lightly circulated survivor boasts considerable remaining definition. The surfaces are noticeably abraded, yet bright with green-gold coloration. Population: 9 in 58, 5 finer (4/04).
From The South Florida Collection.(#8593) (Registry values: N2998)

IMPORTANT, ELUSIVE 1860-S EAGLE AU50 PCGS

6318 **1860-S AU50 PCGS.** A couple of nice AU 1860-S tens have surfaced over the past decade. Still, this is an important condition rarity with only 20-25 pieces believed to exist in all grades. The original mintage was a paltry 5,000 pieces, and of the few survivors known today, almost all are clustered in the VF-XF grade range. Well struck, this piece shows rich reddish-gold color and slightly subdued surfaces overall with no more than the usual amount of bagging marks from a coin of this grade. Population: 2 in 50, 6 finer (3/04).(#8632) (Registry values: N7079)

RARE 1860-S TEN DOLLAR UNC DETAILS

6319 1860-S Unc Details, Burnished, NCS. Four obverse dies arrived in San Francisco for the production of 1860-S Eagles. Some, if not all of these dies were combined with two holdover reverses to produce a scant 5,000 pieces. In a series replete with scarce issues, this S-mint delivery ranks near the top of the list in terms of both overall and high grade rarity. This minimally abraded representative is one of just a handful of pieces that were spared from circulation, and although rather pleasing in appearance, a few wispy hairlines are an indication of an old cleaning. (#8632) (Registry values: N7079)

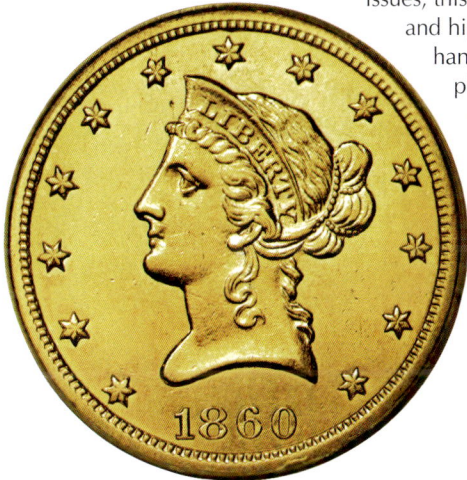

ELUSIVE FIRST YEAR 1870-CC EAGLE XF45

6320 1870-CC XF45 PCGS. Variety 1-A. Simply stated, the 1870-CC Ten Dollar is the key issue among Carson City Eagles and, indeed, a profound rarity in the entire run of CC-mint gold issues. Struck from a tiny mintage of 5,908 pieces, the small number of survivors (25-30 pieces in all) is almost invariably low grade, Fine or Very Fine, topping out with a precious few AUs. Akers states that "only the famous Double Eagle of the same date surpasses the 1870-CC Eagle as the rarest of all Carson City gold coins." This still-lustrous example falls just outside Condition Census for the issue, being generally well detailed and tinged in attractive reddish patina. Abrasions are about on par with what is expected of gold issues from this historic Western Mint.
Population: 5 in 45, 6 finer (3/04).
From The Barry Donnell Collection.(#8658) (Registry values: N7079)

CHALLENGING 1871-CC TEN DOLLAR VF35

6321 1871-CC VF35 PCGS. Struck in the second year of Carson City gold production and from a paltry mintage of 8,085 coins, the number of 1871-CC Eagles extant in all grades is probably fewer than 75 pieces. This borderline-XF example is light in color with the normal severity of surface marks for the grade. A bit of the coin's deficiency in detail originates from strike and not from the moderate amount of wear received by this challenging CC Ten.
From The Barry Donnell Collection.(#8661) (Registry values: N1793)

CHOICE XF 1871-CC EAGLE

6322 1871-CC XF45 PCGS. Considered the second most available Carson City eagle from the 1870s, the 1870-CC is still a significant coin in a collectible grade such as this. Conditionally challenging, the Condition Census for this issue ranges from AU53 to MS62. The striking details are somewhat weak over the highpoints, as one would expect, with numerous small abrasions scattered over each side. Medium orange-gold coloration.(#8661) (Registry values: N2998)

UNHERALDED 1872-CC EAGLE XF45

6323 1872-CC XF45 PCGS. Variety 1-A. The 1872-CC ranks high on the list of Carson City Tens as both a condition and absolute rarity. Only 4,600 pieces were struck, and the median survivor is fails to reach an XF rating. This attractive example has average or better sharpness and is notable for originality and modest surface marks. Population: 5 in 45, 9 finer (3/04).

From The Barry Donnell Collection.(#8664) (Registry values: N4719)

NOTEWORTHY EXTREMELY FINE 1873-CC LIBERTY TEN

6324 1873-CC XF40 NGC. Variety 2-A. The first of two XF 1873-CC Eagles in this sale, the present example is attractively patinated in olive-copper hues. There is light overall rub on both sides, but one can still discern subdued traces of original luster in the more protected peripheral areas. True to form for the issue, this piece displays slightly bolder detail on the reverse than on the obverse, but we stress that no areas reveal detracting lack of definition. The only singularly mentionable abrasions are concentrated in the reverse field before the eagle's beak, and a strike through (as produced) is seen on the same side at the second T in STATES. The 1873-CC is similar in terms of both overall and high grade rarity to the 1872-CC. Survivors of the former delivery are infrequently offered in grades above the Choice VF level.(#8667) (Registry values: N4719)

EXTREMELY SCARCE 1873-CC EAGLE XF45

6325 1873-CC XF45 PCGS. Variety 2-A.The 1873-CC is a seldom encountered Carson City eagle whose rarity carries far beyond its already tiny mintage of 4,453 coins. Additionally, it is one of the great condition rarities in the series, being rated by specialists as third scarcest in the series according to grade. This lustrous example easily qualifies in the top half of pieces extant, being moderately abraded and having the slightest tinge of reddish patina. The central devices are somewhat blunt on the highpoints, but much of the lack of detail can probably be attributed to the soft strike always seen on this issue. Population: 11 in 45, 8 finer (3/04).
From The Barry Donnell Collection.(#8667) (Registry values: N4719)

CHALLENGING 1877-CC EAGLE XF45

6326 1877-CC XF45 PCGS. Another difficult Coronet Eagle from the Carson City facility, with an original mintage of only 3,332 pieces. This piece is somewhat finer than the average example known of this scarce issue and, aside from the normal softness of detail on the hair curls, the strike is well executed. Numerous small abrasions are clustered about the date and there is a touch of prooflike luster still in evidence in the areas surrounding the devices. *From The Barry Donnell Collection.*(#8678) (Registry values: N2998)

HIGHLY DESIRABLE 1878-CC TEN DOLLAR GOLD, AU50 NGC

6327 1878-CC AU50 NGC. Variety 1-A. Tiny die lumps below the E in TEN and a die line above the bust truncation are diagnostic of this issue. A mere 3,244 pieces were struck, a mintage so low that among all Carson City gold issues of all denominations, only the 1879-CC Eagle has a smaller production. AU is about as high a grade as can be obtained for this date, since just one 1878-CC is certified in Mint State by either service. The present coin has pronounced reddish-golden surfaces, as well as some central softness as is often seen. A couple of noticeable abrasions are reported on Liberty's cheek and neck, otherwise the fields are remarkable clean for this typically abraded CC issue. Population: 2 in 50, 11 finer (4/04).(#8681) (Registry values: N7079)

VERY SCARCE 1878-CC TEN DOLLAR AU53

6328 1878-CC AU53 PCGS. Variety 1-A. Tiny die lumps between the EN of TEN and the lower reverse border are seen on all known examples. With the second lowest mintage in the series of a mere 3,244 pieces, the 1878-CC is not surprisingly one of the rarest Carson City Eagles. Like many of its predecessors, it is also known for poor striking details. Aside from this diagnostic deficiency, the present example is particularly nice for the issue. Yellow-gold surfaces retain significant portions of luster and the only abrasion worthy of note is a teardrop mark in the left reverse field. Population: 2 in 53, 4 finer (3/04). *From The Barry Donnell Collection.*(#8681) (Registry values: N7079)

FINEST KNOWN 1878-S TEN DOLLAR MS64

6329 1878-S MS64 PCGS. The 1878-S Ten Dollar was struck just a year before an explosive increase in S-mint production of Eagles. Just 26,100 pieces were minted, and it is scarce in any condition, being seldom available better than a low-end AU. This remarkably preserved and produced example is assuredly one of the finest pieces known, being at the very least tied for that honor (there is a distinct possibility that the NGC census represents a resubmission of this exact coin) with a similarly graded 1878-S at NGC, and will undoubtedly be of great interest to many collectors of this series.

The surfaces are a rich golden color with prooflike fields and uncommonly bold design elements. As for identifying marks, the most obvious one is a small dig in the upper reverse field between the S and O in STATES OF. There is also a shallow scratch in the field below TRUST. On the obverse there is a reeding mark that runs roughly parallel to the front of the coronet. Population: 1 in 64, 0 finer (3/04).(#8682) (Registry values: N7079)

LOW MINTAGE 1879-CC TEN DOLLAR XF45

6330 1879-CC XF45 PCGS. Variety 1-A. The '79-CC Ten Dollar has an impressively low mintage of only 1,762 pieces, the lowest output of any gold coin ever produced in the Carson City Mint. Of that tiny number, it is believed that a mere 40-50 pieces are extant today in all grades, making it the second rarest Eagle behind only the extremely rare 1870-CC. This bright, well balanced example has the expected quota of light to medium sized abrasions on each side. Population: 4 in 45, 14 finer (3/04). *From The Barry Donnell Collection.*(#8684) (Registry values: N4719)

PRIZED 1879-O TEN DOLLAR AU50

6331 1879-O AU50 PCGS. The 1879-O is one of the most popular scarcities in the Ten Dollar series. It is also a significant coin in that it is the first O-mint Eagle struck after an 18-year lapse in production occasioned by the Civil War and its aftermath. A mere 1,500 pieces were produced, the second lowest mintage of any Eagle from the New Orleans facility. This is a moderately abraded reddish-golden example with flashes of prooflike luster in evidence when the coin is held at a slight angle. Population: 7 in 50, 14 finer (3/04).
From The South Florida Collection.(#8685) (Registry values: N4719)

CHALLENGING 1879-O EAGLE AU53

6332 1879-O AU53 NGC. A marginally finer representative of this low mintage New Orleans issue. Both sides of the rich golden example now offered retain glimpses of prooflike luster that are most noticeable on the reverse. Parallel pinscratches extend from the back of Liberty's hair to the obverse border just below 3 o'clock.(#8685) (Registry values: N4719)

UNDERAPPRECIATED 1882-CC EAGLE AU58

6333 1882-CC AU58 PCGS. This is a frosty textured example with almost no perceptible wear. Abrasions are generally very light and the strike is well executed in all areas .The 1882-CC Ten Dollar, one of 6,764 pieces produced, is the rarest CC-mint Eagle produced after 1879, with survivors being equally as elusive as those of the 1871-CC and 1874-CC deliveries. Population: 6 in 58, 0 finer, NGC reporting only a single Mint State coin (3/04).

From The Barry Donnell Collection.(#8696) (Registry values: N2998)

UNBELIEVABLE MS69 EAGLE Ex: CLAPP, ELIASBERG

6334 1899-S MS69 NGC. Ex: Eliasberg. Stunning. Awe-Inspiring. Breathtaking. These are only a few of the words that one could use to describe the beauty of this spectacular piece, perhaps *the finest* Liberty Eagle that we have ever had the pleasure to behold. Like most of the other S-mint coins obtained by Eliasberg from the John H. Clapp collection in 1942, this piece was purchased directly from the United States branch mint in San Francisco for face value at the time of issue. While not a proof, it is described by Bowers & Ruddy in their 1982 sale of the gold portion of Eliasberg's collection as a "specimen." While this term was obviously there used in a loose sense of the word, this coin is certainly a special piece that was set aside at the time of striking because of its nearly pristine attributes. Alas, it isn't perfect, as very close inspection indicates a couple of tiny abrasions that are seen only after close inspection, but we won't cast the first stone to fault this piece, as any collector of this denomination knows that bagmarks are the rule rather than the exception on this big, heavy gold coin (we have seen many Gem graded examples that, quite honestly, weren't all that pretty because of a number of noticeable abrasions). It is sharply struck, beautifully lustrous, and is as close to perfect as one could ever expect to find. One of the finest graded examples of the type in existence, and the finest certified for the date by NGC by a full *four* points. A stunning beauty that could be the ultimate type example for the Liberty Eagle series.
Population: 1 in 69, 0 finer (4/04).
(#8744) (Registry values: N1)

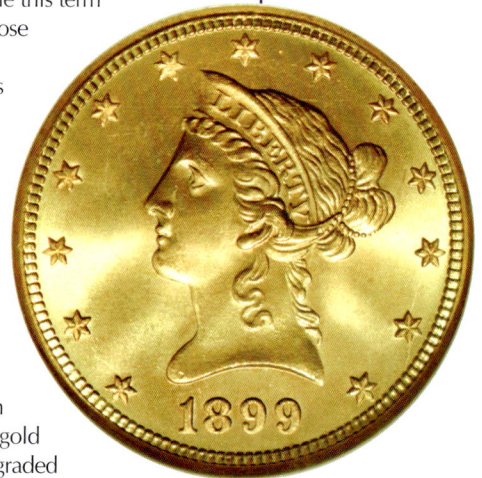

AFFORDABLE SELECT PROOF 1889 EAGLE

6335 1889 PR63 PCGS. The 1889 is a very rare issue in proof format. It is the rarest proof Liberty Eagle of the 1885-1907 era with an extant population (per Akers, 1980 and Breen, 1988) of approximately 12 coins. If this estimate is correct, then a decent number of proof 1889 Eagles in today's market may be impaired because NGC and PCGS combined have certified just ten pieces in all grades. The present example is not without its problems, but, nonetheless, it represents an important bidding opportunity for the advanced gold specialist. Both sides are sharply struck with rich orange-gold color. The proof finish is readily evident, both sides being lightly cameoed. There are scattered hairlines in the fields, and a large scratch is in the obverse field between stars 1 and 3.
From The Greenwich Collection, Part One.(#8829)

NEAR-GEM PROOF 1899 LIBERTY EAGLE

6336 1899 PR64 PCGS. The Philadelphia Mint delivered only 86 proof Liberty eagles in 1899, fewer than 30 of which are believed extant. Writing in 1977, Breen opines that the 1899 is "much rarer than commonly believed..." Nicely cameoed, the surfaces are yellow-gold in color with modest olive accents that appear as the coin rotates beneath a light. We can find no singularly mentionable distractions, but a small curly lintmark (as struck) is visible on Liberty's lower jaw should serve as a useful pedigree marker. A bright and flashy specimen, we recommend this coin for inclusion in either an advanced gold collection or a proof type set.
From The Greenwich Collection, Part One.(#8839)

BRIGHT, SATINY MS64 1907 WIRE RIM INDIAN TEN

6337 **1907 Wire Rim MS64 PCGS.** After Mint officials determined the Wire Rim ten to be impractical as a regular production coin (because of the wire rim itself), the design was then modified by Charles Barber, resulting in the very scarce Rolled Edge variety and eventually the standard No Periods type. The Wire Rim Ten is widely recognized as a pattern, but it is also collected as a part of the regular series, with a status that is analogous to the 1856 Flying Eagle cent. This is a bright, satiny example that shows the usual die polishing marks in the fields that give the coin its satiny glow. There is one notable abrasion: a horizontal abrasion across the face of the Indian.(#8850) (Registry values: N7079)

IMPORTANT 1907 WIRE RIM SAINT-GAUDENS TEN DOLLAR

6338 **1907 Wire Rim MS64 PCGS.** In the opinion of this cataloger (and a great many other numismatists, we suspect), the Indian Eagle is one of the most beautiful coins ever produced by the U.S. Mint. The work of Augustus Saint-Gaudens, this design made its debut in 1907. The original coins produced (500 examples, according to a letter that Henry Chapman wrote to John Garrett in 1908) are the only coins of this type that display Saint-Gaudens's design in its original form. The name of this issue stems from the delicate, knife-like rim that both sides display. This feature is the result of metal being forced between the collar and the dies during striking; the coins were not originally designed with a rim. The wire rim on both sides had the potential to interfere with the ejection process, and it also caused stacking problems. What's more, the lack of a traditional rim made the surfaces very susceptible to abrasions. These considerations explain why the Mint did not adopt Saint-Gaudens' original design for circulation. Debate still rages over whether or not these coins were produced as proofs or business strikes. Either way, they were not intended for general circulation, but rather to demonstrate the design and striking characteristics of the new Indian Eagle.

The present coin is satiny in finish with an original, deep orange-gold sheen. The surfaces are partially veiled in hazy overtones, but the diagnostic striations (as struck) in the reverse field are readily evident. There are a couple of thin vertical abrasions in the left reverse field, but otherwise both sides are distraction-free.(#8850) (Registry values: N7079)

SHARPLY STRUCK GEM 1907 INDIAN TEN

6339 1907 No Motto MS65 NGC. While not rare in an absolute sense, the 1907 is one of only three No Motto issues in the Indian Eagle series, and as such it remains a favorite issue among gold type collectors. This is an unusually well struck example, with soft definition in the centers being the norm for this issue. The luster is frosted and there are virtually no surface interruptions as the luster races around each side when it is slowly tilted beneath a light. For identification purposes, one microscopic indention is noted at the center of the reverse on the eagle's lower wing.

From The Greenwich Collection, Part One.(#8852) (Registry values: N2998)

COLLECTIBLE, HIGH GRADE 1907 INDIAN TEN MS66 NGC

6340 1907 No Motto MS66 NGC. After the pattern Wire Rim strikings and the failed Rolled Edge Tens of 1907, Saint-Gaudens' design was modified a third time this year and more than a quarter million regular production Tens were struck. The overall quality of these coins is quite high, most likely a combination of both careful production and the fact that quite a few pieces were set aside as novelties. This piece has rich orange-gold color overall and thick, frosted mint luster. Sharply struck, there are no singularly mentionable abrasions on either side. Population: 88 in 66, 12 finer (4/04).(#8852) (Registry values: N4719)

SATINY, PROBLEM-FREE MS66 1907 TEN DOLLAR INDIAN

6341 1907 No Motto MS66 NGC. Close examination reveals a very fine granularity on each side of this piece, but this does not inhibit the outstanding, thick satiny luster that rolls over each side as the coin is slowly tilted beneath a light. Subtle rose and lilac coloration is overlaid on the otherwise yellow-gold surfaces, and as one might expect from the grade, there are no obvious marks on either side.(#8852)

(Registry values: N4719)

LOW MINTAGE 1908-S TEN DOLLAR MS66

6342 1908-S MS66 NGC. A desirable Indian Ten Dollar that is a favorite of collectors not only because of the low mintage of only 59,850 pieces, but also because of the considerable eye appeal these coins possess in the better grades of Uncirculated. This premium Gem displays ample detail and luxuriant mint frost over fine-grain, matte-like surfaces.(#8861) (Registry values: N7079)

REMARKABLE GEM 1908-S SAINT-GAUDENS EAGLE MS66 NGC

6343 1908-S MS66 NGC. The Congressional mandate of 1908 that returned the motto IN GOD WE TRUST to the ten dollar gold piece provided an excuse for Charles E. Barber to once again vent his frustrations over the Mint's adoption of an outsider's superior design. In actuality, Barber's influence over the Indian Head eagle's motif predates Congress' assertion a year. The initial relief of Saint-Gaudens' design, like that of his double eagle, was too bold for its own good. While the breathtaking features stand out in unparalleled beauty on the early high relief patterns of 1907, the accompanying die wastage and production time would never suffice for regular issue coinage. Accordingly, the first 239,406 business strikes to emerge from the Philadelphia Mint in 1907 incorporated Barber's crude modifications. In addition to lowering the relief, the Chief Engraver omitted the triangular periods that once delineated E PLURIBUS UNUM, redesigned the branch, reshaped several of the letters in the legends, strengthened the feathers in the headdress, and reworked some of Liberty's hair curls. In 1908, in addition to adding the motto in the reverse field before the eagle, Barber continued to tinker with minor design elements in a vain effort to improve the striking quality of the denomination. While these inconspicuous alterations did strengthen certain key features, they failed to achieve the Chief Engraver's original goal, and poor impressions would continue to be the norm until the denomination's demise in 1933.

The present Gem possesses all of the qualities that never fail to excite eager bidders. It is the first S-mint installment in this popular series and among the first With Motto issues. While the eagle's shoulder and talon, as well as Liberty's highest hair curls, exhibit characteristic incompleteness of definition, the balance of this coin is smartly impressed and quite crisply defined for the series. Although many of the 59,850 pieces that the west coast branch mint delivered in 1908 saw circulation, this gorgeous specimen was delicately preserved over the past ten decades. The frosty, orange-gold surfaces are smooth, although, for accuracy, we mention a somewhat distracting abrasion in the left obverse field that joins the bottom of star 1 to the tip of Liberty's nose. An important piece, we anticipate stiff competition for this specimen from the numerous gold specialists who will accept only the best for their prized collections. Population: 5 in 66, 2 finer (4/04).(#8861) (Registry values: N7079)

GEM 1910-D INDIAN TEN
UNSURPASSABLE IN GRADE AT PCGS

6344 1910-D MS66 PCGS. While the 1910-D ranks as one of the more plentiful Indian Eagles in terms of total number of coins known, the present Gem is rare from the standpoint of surface preservation. The luster is not only full, but vibrant with a shimmering, satin-to-frosty texture. Both sides are predominantly reddish-gold in color, although there are some softer powder-blue hues in a few field areas. With sharply struck devices and none but the most trivial of bagmarks, this coin is a lovely representative of one of the United States' most attractive coinage designs. Population: 23 in 66, none are finer (3/04).(#8866) (Registry values: N4719)

CONDITIONALLY RARE
1911-D EAGLE MS64 NGC

6345 1911-D MS64 NGC. Perhaps the most recognizable combination of date and mintmark in the various series of Indian U.S. gold, being a key issue both as a Quarter Eagle and Half Eagle, in addition to its notoriety as an Eagle. Just 30,100 pieces were originally struck and a large majority did manage to circulate, thus creating one of the outstanding condition rarities in the series of Indian Tens. This high grade specimen exhibits bright, satiny luster with a uniform overlay of orange patina. A few trivial blemishes are noticed in the fields, but these are only discernible after close examination. Other than a few mass-melted rarities among 20th century gold, this Choice Mint State 1911-D certainly ranks among the most valuable and prestigious gold coins from the past 100 years. Population: 11 in 64, 0 finer (4/04).(#8869) (Registry values: N7079)

ELUSIVE NEAR-GEM 1911-S TEN DOLLAR, MS64 PCGS

6346 1911-S MS64 PCGS. In the series of Ten Dollar Indians, the 1911-S is considered one of the premier rarities. Even after the appearance of a small hoard of 40-50 pieces in the late 1970s, this did not materially affect the availability of high grade examples. This is one of only 23 pieces to have been so graded by PCGS with only 27 finer (3/04). The granular surfaces show thick mint frost and rich, deep reddish-gold color. A few shallow marks are noted on the primary obverse device, but the reverse is remarkably free from disturbances.

From The Greenwich Collection, Part One.(#8870) (Registry values: N2998)

ELUSIVE GEM UNCIRCULATED 1914-D EAGLE

6347 1914-D MS65 NGC. The second most common branch mint Indian Head Eagle after the 1910-D, the '14-D is, nevertheless, an undeniably rare coin above the MS64 level. The present Gem numbers itself among the nicest representatives in today's market. The finely granular surfaces show thick, swirling frost and pleasing orange-gold coloration. There are only a few small contact marks and the devices display razor sharp definition throughout.(#8876) (Registry values: N4719)

MAGNIFICENT GEM 1914-S INDIAN TEN, MS65 NGC

6348 1914-S MS65 NGC. While Saint-Gaudens' Double Eagle was produced primarily for use by the banking system, his beautiful eagle fulfilled its duty to the United States Treasury as a circulating medium of exchange. When one stops to consider the purchasing power that Ten Dollars possessed in the early part of this century, it is little wonder that few Americans could afford to set aside an Indian Head Eagle for future posterity regardless of how pristine it looked. While this grim reality hit many Indian Head issues hard, the San Francisco mint's production of 1914 suffered one of the worst attrition rates of them all. Although About Uncirculated and lower Mint State specimens are obtainable for a price, true Gems, such as the coin offered here, are of the utmost rarity and desirability. This is a stunning representation with a crisp, essentially complete strike (save for minimal softness on the eagle's upper wingtip) that is quite foreign to the series. The vivid orange-gold surfaces exhibit swirling mint frost and slight underlying granularity. There are no single abrasions that are worthy of concern and the surfaces do full justice to the vaunted grade designation. For future identification, a tiny black spot is seen about midpoint on the last feather. It is difficult for us to imagine a more attractive example of this conditionally challenging issue for an advanced gold collection. Population: 6 in 65, 3 finer (4/04).(#8877) (Registry values: N7079)

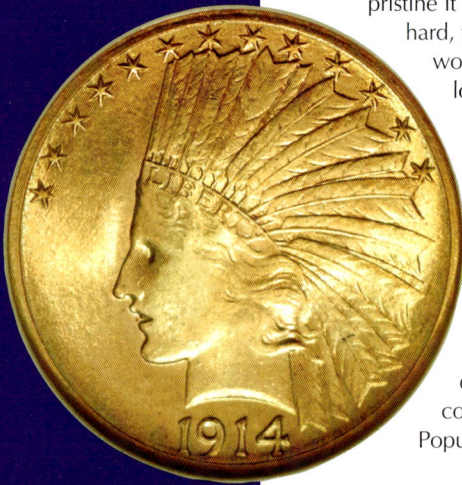

EXTRAORDINARY 1908 MOTTO INDIAN TEN DOLLAR PR66

6349 1908 Motto PR66 NGC. Of the 116 proof Tens struck in this year, all but two have the distinctive dark finish this issue is known for, somewhere between a khaki and olive color. While it is widely recognized that the 1908 is the most "common" date among matte proofs of the classic Indian Eagle design, the number of survivors is not as large as its mintage might suggest. In addition, widespread distribution among non-collectors caused many of the surviving proofs of this date to be impaired, showing nicks, scratches, or shiny spots. Traditional sources state that somewhere between two and three dozen pieces exist today. However, we believe a larger number are extant, somewhere in the range of 45 to 55 coins. One has to closely scrutinize this specimen to find even the most inconsequential blemishes. Population: 8 in 66, 6 finer (4/04).(#8890) (Registry values: N7079)

CHOICE BU 1854-S DOUBLE EAGLE

6350 1854-S MS64 NGC. This is a conditionally scarce survivor of the premier Liberty Double Eagle from the San Francisco branch mint. The strike is expectantly sharp for a Type One Twenty with virtually full definition throughout. Warm orange-gold color flows over frosty textured, slightly granular surfaces. There are remarkably few abrasions for the MS64 level of preservation. There are several interesting die cracks around the peripheries. All in all, this coin presents uncommonly well for the Choice grade. Population: 9 in 64, 1 finer (4/04).

From The Greenwich Collection, Part One.(#8913) (Registry values: N7079)

ELUSIVE MINT STATE 1855 TWENTY MS61 NGC

6351 1855 MS61 NGC. The 1855 begins a five-year run of underrated, overlooked Double Eagles from the Philadelphia Mint. This is the eighth rarest of 17 Type One issues from this mint. Approximately 100-150 pieces are known in the various About Uncirculated grades with most in the AU50-55 range. Solid AU58s are very scarce and Uncirculated pieces are quite rare with just 13 to 16 pieces believed extant today. The surfaces are exceptionally smooth for the grade and exhibit a bold strike throughout. Although slightly subdued, the luster presents a soft reddish-golden appearance. Definitely a premium coin for the grade and worth a close look.(#8914) (Registry values: N4719)

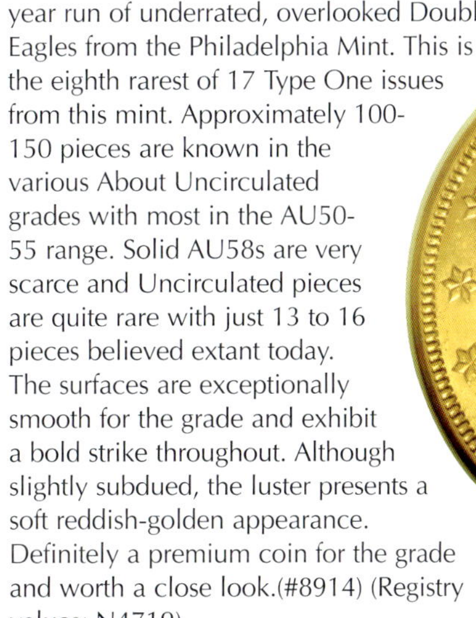

CHOICE 1857-S DOUBLE EAGLE, Ex: *S.S. CENTRAL AMERICA*

6352 1857-S Broken A MS64 PCGS. Ex: *S.S. CENTRAL AMERICA.* A lovely survivor from the "Ship of Gold," this coin displays lustrous, satiny surfaces that are free of all but a few small abrasions in the left obverse field. Both sides are crisply struck and there is no distracting haziness. The box and all the paperwork are included.(#70004)

GEM 1857-S TWENTY DOLLAR Ex: *S.S. CENTRAL AMERICA*

6353 1857-S MS65 PCGS. 20A. Spiked Shield. Ex: *S.S. CENTRAL AMERICA.* A razor sharp strike nicely defines the features of this spectacular Gem. The frosty luster has not diminished during the extended period of time that this piece spent at the bottom of the ocean. Both sides are exquisitely framed in coppery-orange patina. A few trivial luster grazes are noticed on the cheek, but these do not affect the splendid eye appeal of this dazzling Gem. The box and all the original paperwork is included(#8922) (Registry values: N4719)

OUTSTANDING 1857-S TWENTY DOLLAR MS66 Ex: *S.S. CENTRAL AMERICA*

6354 1857-S MS66 NGC. Ex: *S.S. CENTRAL AMERICA.* An essentially blemish-free representative of this famous shipwreck issue. More information on this fascinating hoard can be found in the Q. David Bowers book entitled *A California Gold Rush History featuring the Treasure from the S.S. CENTRAL AMERICA.* For pedigree purposes, we note an inconsequential reeding mark between star 13 and the portrait. Both sides radiate a frosty, golden-rose sheen with captivating cartwheel effects. There is not a single ill-defined feature, and the eye appeal is commensurate with the assigned grade. The box and all the original paperwork is included. Population: 11 in 66, 0 finer (4/04).(#8922) (Registry values: N7079)

RARE 1858-O TWENTY, AU55 NGC Ex: EAGLE COLLECTION

6355 1858-O AU55 NGC. Ex: Eagle Collection. This coin represents above average quality for the issue. There are approximately 150-175 1858-O Double Eagles known with 45-55 of these grading About Uncirculated. Most of the About Uncirculated 1858-Os are in the AU50 to AU53 range. This issue is very scarce in properly graded AU55, very rare in AU58, and extremely rare in Uncirculated. There are only three encapsulated Uncirculated examples currently known, two of which are: an NGC MS60 (which is very high end for the grade, by the way) in an Illinois collection, and the incredible Bass III: 795 example, graded MS62 by PCGS, that sold to a prominent Midwestern collector for $50,600.

This is a particularly pleasing example that is better struck than most pieces known. The first four stars are well defined, as is the rest of the coin. There are no mentionable abrasions on either side, and the coin has bright green-gold coloration.

From The South Florida Collection.(#8924) (Registry values: N2998)

LEGENDARY 1870-CC DOUBLE EAGLE XF DETAILS

6356 1870-CC XF Details, Improperly Cleaned, NCS. The 1870-CC is the first Double Eagle issue struck at the Carson City facility and a legendary rarity that is among the most prized issues in the entire series of Liberty Twenties. It is surpassed in overall rarity only by the ultra-rare 1861 Paquet, the 1856-O, and the business strikes of 1882 and 1886, but none of these important issues garner more attention than is generated by the appearance of a '70-CC. Only 3,789 pieces were originally produced and reliable estimates place the number of survivors in the neighborhood of 45 pieces. From the standpoint of condition rarity, the '70-CC ranks number one in the Liberty Double Eagle series, with most known examples being only Very Fine or Extremely Fine, with heavily abraded surfaces. The median grade example offered here actually displays less abrasions than the typical survivor and the strike is more than adequate for this premier CC issue. A paper thin disturbance down the portrait and a few ill-placed marks to the left of Liberty's ear lobe are really mentioned primarily for attribution. While the cleaning qualifier on the NCS insert could hardly be disputed, it fails to be a major distraction on this important Carson City rarity. *From The Barry Donnell Collection.*(#8958) (Registry values: N10218)

CHALLENGING KEY 1871-CC TWENTY XF40

6357 1871-CC XF40 PCGS. As the second rarest Carson City Double Eagle, the 1871-CC is always in demand by collectors of this popular series. Only 17,387 pieces were produced and it is reliably estimated that fewer than 150 coins are extant in all grades. Offered here is a smooth yellow-gold example that represents a median grade for the issue. *From The Barry Donnell Collection.*(#8961) (Registry values: N1793)

HIGHLY COLLECTIBLE 1871-CC LIBERTY DOUBLE EAGLE

6358 **1871-CC AU55 PCGS.** A scarce early CC-mint double eagle. The small original mintage of 17,387 pieces only partially explains the rarity of this issue today as most examples undoubtedly saw heavy circulation on the frontier. As one would expect from a Carson City gold coin, the surfaces are heavily abraded but still display abundant traces of mint luster that evidence modest reflectivity. All of the important details are readily visible with light wear confined to the highpoints of the devices. A golden opportunity for the numerous collectors who specialize in the coinage of the Nevada branch mint. Population: 7 in 55, 0 finer (3/04).(#8961) (Registry values: N1793)

SHIMMERING 1871-S DOUBLE EAGLE MS62

6359 **1871-S MS62 NGC.** Although located with some regularity in AU grades, this Type Two S-mint emerges as a very difficult issue in anything finer than an entry level Unc. This nearly Select example displays bright, shimmering luster and appealing golden-orange overtones. Population: 14 in 62, 1 finer (3/04).(#8962) (Registry values: N4719)

SATINY 1873-CC DOUBLE EAGLE AU50

6360 **1873-CC AU50 PCGS.** Variety 1-A. A moderately scarce Carson City issue whose overall rating is eighth out of 19 issues, but also one that is often seen well circulated. Just 22,410 pieces were struck. The obverse of this bright, satiny representative has taken the brunt of the numerous small to medium sized abrasions, as is typical for the design.

From The Barry Donnell Collection.(#8968) (Registry values: N2998)

SCARCE AND POPULAR 1875-CC DOUBLE EAGLE, MS62

6361 **1875-CC MS62 PCGS.** The combination of the scarce Type Two design and the Carson City mintmark make this an irresistible coin for advanced 19th century gold type collectors. The fields are semi-reflective, as often seen, and most of each side has deep golden-orange coloration with a slight accent of lilac in the upper left obverse field. Well defined in the centers, the only notable area of weakness is on the obverse stars.(#8974) (Registry values: N4719)

RARE HIGH GRADE 1879-O LIBERTY TWENTY, AU53 PCGS

6362 **1879-O AU53 PCGS.** A nice, strong strike, as often seen; on this piece, the borders are sharper than usual with full denticles on the obverse and reverse. Nearly full mint luster is visible beneath even, medium yellow-gold color. There are a few stray abrasions here or there, but the overall quality of the surfaces is far above average for the issue. Also, there are none of the severe spots or mint-made planchet faults that are commonly seen on 1879-O double eagles.

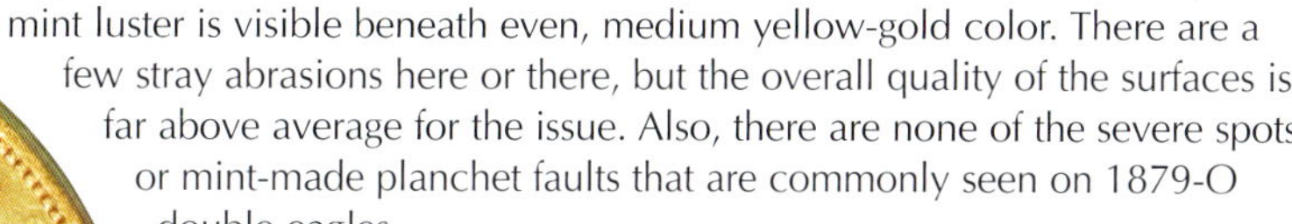

Its tiny mintage figure of 2,325 coins and its status as the only Type Three New Orleans Double Eagle make the 1879-O an especially popular issue. There are around 75-85 pieces known but many of these are in low grades and the majority of the choice, higher grade examples are in tightly-held collections. This date currently appears on more want lists than almost any other Liberty Head Double Eagle. Population: 5 in 53, 12 finer (3/04). *From The South Florida Collection.*(#8990) (Registry values: N4719)

FINEST KNOWN, EXCEEDINGLY RARE 1881 TWENTY DOLLAR COIN

6363 **1881 MS61 PCGS.** Only 2,220 circulation strike 1881 double eagles were produced. Approximately 25-35 pieces are known today with most of these grading XF40 to AU50. In the middle to higher AU grades, the 1881 is extremely rare and the only pieces to have been encapsulated as Uncirculated (as of March 2004) are the PCGS MS60 that we auctioned for $29,235 in our 1997 ANA Sale and this specimen, the finest known to either service.

Recent sales records include an example cataloged as "Brilliant Uncirculated" in the October 2001 Dallas Bank Collection Sale which brought $21,850, a PCGS AU50 that realized $14,950 in our February 2001 Long Beach Sale, and a PCGS AU55 that garnered $14,950 in the October 1999 Bass II Sale. Considering the unquestioned rarity of this issue (and the great popularity of this series), it remains extremely undervalued in our opinion.

The surfaces of this piece are unquestionably original with a bit of the "dirty gold" appearance seen on so many Double Eagles from this era. Probably struck from a later state of the dies, there is little evidence of the original prooflike finish in the fields—a trait seen on all Twenties of this issue to one degree or another. Well struck, numerous small and medium sized contact marks litter the surfaces, these being the grade-limiting factors. A very special opportunity for the advanced U.S. gold enthusiast.(#8994) (Registry values: N1)

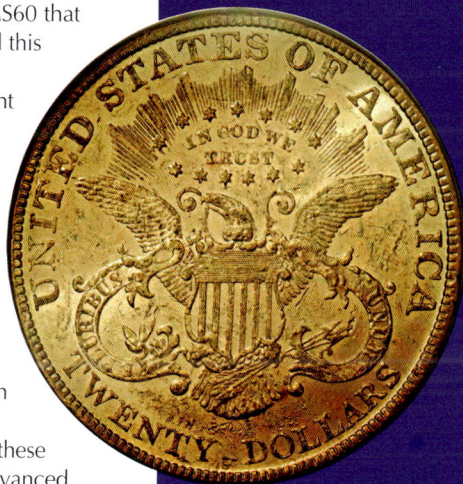

EXCEEDINGLY RARE 1885 LIBERTY TWENTY DOLLAR AU58 PCGS

6364 1885 AU58 PCGS. It is, indeed, a very unusual and pleasant opportunity to be able to offer one of the most elusive Liberty Double Eagles in the entire series. The 1885 has the second lowest business strike mintage—751 pieces—of any Liberty Twenty Dollar coin, next only to the 1882. From this tiny mintage, a total of 71 pieces have been certified by both services in all grades, undoubtedly, some of which are the same coins, and only 16 pieces have been certified higher than AU58 by both major grading services (03/04). The strike is sharp and the surfaces show considerable prooflike reflectivity. Numerous marks and abrasions are noted overall, the most prominent being on the eye, cheek, and neck of Liberty.(#9003) (Registry values: N4719)

CHALLENGING 1889 DOUBLE EAGLE MS63

6365 1889 MS63 NGC. A well frosted, satiny representative with far fewer abrasions that is normally encountered for the issue. With a small mintage of only 44,070 business strikes, the number of surviving Mint State examples is limited and pieces that qualify at the Select level are legitimately rare. Population: 6 in 63, 0 finer (4/04).(#9010) (Registry values: N4719)

LOW MINTAGE 1891-CC TWENTY AU50

6366 1891-CC AU50 PCGS. Variety 1-A. Judging by its paltry original mintage of 5,000 pieces, the Carson City Mint seems to have spent the majority of its time for gold delivery in 1891 on the Half Eagle and Eagle at the expense of the Double Eagle. Only the ultra scarce 1870-CC sports a lower production figure among CC-mint Twenties. This lightly circulated example displays delicate reddish accents and a modest degree of prooflike luster in the areas surrounding the devices. Abrasions are fairly numerous, but not overbearing.
From The Barry Donnell Collection.(#9017) (Registry values: N2998)

PRIZED 1891-CC TWENTY DOLLAR MS62

6367 1891-CC MS62 NGC. Although the 1891-CC Half Eagle and Eagle are the most heavily produced Carson City issues of their respective denominations, the same cannot be said for the 1891-CC Double Eagle. In fact, it is among the rarest Carson City Twenties. The typical survivor grades XF or AU, and Uncirculated survivors are rare. Since few if any numismatists were interested in high denomination branch mint gold coins in 1891, it is not surprising that only a solitary PCGS MS63 has been certified finer than the present coin. This boldly struck piece has crisp star centrils and rich definition within the folds of Liberty's hair. Although the surfaces show evidence of past bag storage, as do all Mint State examples, the only abrasion remotely worthy of individual mention is a short scratch below the final A in AMERICA.(#9017) (Registry values: N7079)

WELL PRESERVED 1892-S TWENTY MS64

6368 1892-S MS64 PCGS. This issue is one of the more challenging S-mints from the decade, yet still can be obtained without too much difficulty in average Mint State grades. The situation abruptly changes at the MS64 level, this piece being one of just a handful we have offered over the years. Creamy, well struck surfaces are notable for their originality and are limited in grade by a series of small facial marks to the left of Liberty's ear. Population: 35 in 64, 0 finer (3/04). *From The Garden State Collection.*(#9021) (Registry values: N4719)

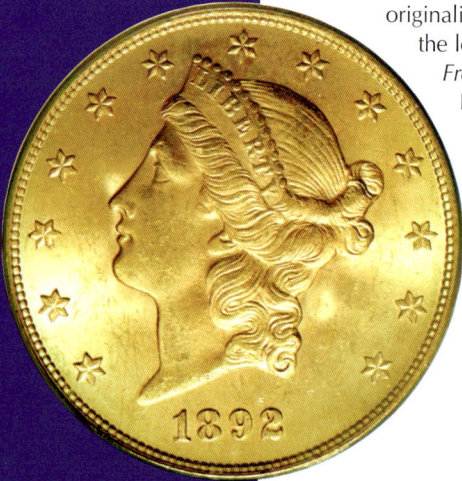

SATINY 1898 DOUBLE EAGLE MS63

6369 1898 MS63 NGC. A satiny, Select quality example that is sharply struck throughout with warmly colored, orange-gold features. Modest abrasions are primarily found on the facial area and in the field to the left.(#9033) (Registry values: N2998)

ESSENTIALLY PERFECT MS68 1899-S DOUBLE EAGLE PURCHASED DIRECTLY FROM THE MINT BY GEORGE CLAPP IN 1899

6370 **1899-S MS68 NGC.** Ex: Eliasberg. Aside from coins struck in the past fifty years, it is rare that one finds a 100+ year old coin, especially a high denomination gold coin, that can trace its pedigree directly back to the Mint. The great copper collector and general U.S. coin enthusiast George Clapp visited the Mint in 1899 and purchased at least one complete set of all the denominations struck in San Francisco that year. This is one of those coins, and to our knowledge it has only been in two major collections since that time with an unknown number of owners since 1982. George Clapp sold his collection of gold coins to Louis Eliasberg in July 1942 via Stack's for more than $100,000. It was this transaction between Clapp and Eliasberg that formed the foundation of what was to be the only complete set of United States coins ever assembled.

We will never be certain what compelled George Clapp to visit the Mint in 1899 and purchase coins of that year at face value, but one thing that may have figured into his purchases is the uniformly high visual appeal of the coins produced in that Mint in that particular year. Excellent luster characteristics are known through all the denominations; however, what is also an unfortunate characteristic are the heavily abraded surfaces usually seen on 1899-S coins. This, of course, is not a factor on this particular piece as it shows only the slightest luster graze on the obverse. There is also an abrasion on the obverse rim between stars 1 and 2. The reverse is essentially perfect. The striking details are fully defined in all areas with complete obverse and reverse star radials and full hair detail. The mint luster is softly frosted and close examination shows evidence of very light die striations on the obverse. These have almost faded out on this particular coin but can still be seen above the coronet. Which brings up another interesting point. Even though the Bowers catalog of the Eliasberg gold coins (1982) states that this coin was "a 'specimen' piece saved at the time of issue," there is no evidence that anything special or out of the ordinary was done to produce this coin, except perhaps double striking it. A magnifier reveals that this piece was struck from a later state of the dies as there are several minute die cracks around the obverse rim. Curiously, there is also a P-shaped bit of thread that was struck into the coin just above Liberty's eye. The coin also displays a subtle intermingling of rose and lilac coloration, which is not apparent to the casual viewer but is immediately visible with a magnifier.

In the entire series of Liberty double eagles, including all three types, there are only two coins that have been certified as MS68, and both are 1899-S. It is certainly tempting to say this second piece represents a resubmission of this particular coin, but we are not sure that is the case. Another Superb Gem 1899-S double eagle is also known, from the Dallas Bank Collection. That coin is nearly perfect also and may well have been certified as MS68 as well. Nevertheless, one is unlikely to ever encounter another Liberty double eagle that is as perfectly preserved, has the mint luster, and overall eye appeal of this amazing coin.

Purchased directly from the San Francisco Mint by John Clapp, November, 1899 at face value; John H. Clapp Collection, 1942, to Louis Eliasberg; Eliasberg Collection (Bowers and Ruddy, 10/82), lot 1002.(#9036)
(Registry values: N1)

GEM BU 1901 $20, MS65 PCGS

6371 1901 MS65 PCGS. A boldly struck Gem that has blazing cartwheel luster and impressively undisturbed surfaces. Only 111,430 pieces were struck, which is only a fraction of the majority of the 20th Century issues in the series. Population: 216 in 65, only 3 are finer (3/04).(#9039) (Registry values: N2998)

SPECIMEN 63 1856-O DOUBLE EAGLE—A UNIQUE EXAMPLE OF THIS LEGENDARY DOUBLE EAGLE RARITY

6372 1856-O SP63 NGC. Many specialists believe that this is the single most important New Orleans double eagle in existence. It is also one of the most important coins from this mint regardless of denomination. This 1856-O double eagle is the finest example known by a wide margin. It is also a specimen striking and certified as such by NGC. As an issue, the 1856-O needs little introduction. It remains one of the few transcendent rarities among 19th century U.S. gold, recognized as such even by non-gold collectors.

The original mintage for this issue was a paltry 2,250 pieces, making the 1856-O one of the classic rarities in U.S. gold coinage. It is both the rarest gold coin struck by the New Orleans mint, and the rarest regular issue Liberty Head double eagle. The estimated number of survivors ranges from 10-12 (Breen) to as high as 15-20 (Winter). A mere 3-5 pieces are believed extant in the various AU grades, and this is the only Uncirculated example known.

This coin has an appearance unlike any other 1856-O double eagle. While weakness is generally found on O-mint double eagles from this era, including the 1856-O, this coin shows an amazing full strike in all areas and fully reflective fields, quite unlike the finish seen on other New Orleans twenties from this period. Each star has satiny luster and shows shadowing, as though impressed with an extra blow from the die. Liberty's hair details and the stars above the eagle are equally well brought up. There is a bit of incomplete die polish along the top and bottom sides of the right wing. This is a common occurrence on branch mint proof dollars in the Morgan series, and while it is not entirely similar to a Philadelphia proof from this era, it is obviously a very special coin. Clearly, a great deal of care went into its production. The satiny luster over the devices plus the deeply mirrored fields produces a noticeable cameo contrast on each side. Even casual inspection reveals that this coin was produced differently from regular business strikes.

This coin has been submitted to both of the major grading services. According to Superior's January 1995 catalog description,

> "Superior submitted the coin to PCGS for grading. In a conversation with PCGS' principal shareholder, Mr. David Hall, Larry Goldberg was told by Mr. Hall that in his opinion the coin is definitely something special, completely unlike regular issue New Orleans double eagles of the period. Only because he (Hall) wanted to insure a conservative estimate was it graded Mint State 63 by PCGS. (The service eschews the terms "Proof" or "Specimen" designations on most branch mint issues except for the few documented Proofs of which the mint has a record."

As a result, even though direct examination of the coin proves it was produced under controlled circumstances and it cannot be other than a special striking, PCGS would only certify it as an "MS63." NGC, on the other hand, recognized the special nature of this piece and was willing to certify it as such. There are, after all, other unquestionable proof New Orleans gold coins from this era: the unique 1844-O half eagle and eagle that both trace their pedigree to the fabled Parmelee sale of 1890.

Recalling the initial appearance of this rarity in the numismatic marketplace, Marc Emory recalled: "New England Rare Coin Galleries was contacted by a family, then living in Vermont. They inquired if we would be interested in purchasing a proof 1856-O double eagle. New England staff explained that no proofs were known of this issue. The party on the other end of the line patiently explained that, well, they had one, nonetheless. The New England staffer asked, rhetorically, or so he thought, if the prospective seller was a descendent of Bienvenu, the superintendent of the New Orleans Mint in the year 1856. All sarcasm was quickly forgotten when the seller on the phone responded, 'Yes.' "

In order to identify this important rarity, we point out the following surface irregularities which essentially "fingerprint" the coin. There are two small planchet flakes seen in the exergual area, one below the 8 in the date, the other at the top of the 5. Several others are located around stars 4, 5, 8, 10, and 13, and in the hair just above the bun. We stress that these are not post-striking imperfections, but small planchet flaws frequently found on proof gold coins from this period. On the reverse, a fine die crack runs from the rim through the D in the denomination and ends at the curve of the scroll.

The answer to the questions about the exact circumstances surrounding the striking of this coin may still be found in the New Orleans mint records from 1856. Unfortunately, mint records from this era are very sketchy, difficult to locate, and, in many cases, simply do not exist any longer. This piece is undoubtedly the highlight of Platinum Night in this memorable June Long Beach Sale. This is only the third appearance of this coin at public auction since its striking in 1856. When sold as part of The Eagle Collection in January of 2002, this piece realized $310,500, which seems like a relative "bargain" today, especially when one considers the strength of the overall market and in particular the strong prices double eagles have brought recently at auction.

Purchased from the New Orleans Mint at the time of issue by Mint Superintendent Charles Bienvenu; from him the piece was passed to his heirs; purchased by Marc Emory of New England Rare Coins directly from Bienvenu's family in 1979; sold by James Halperin later that year to Larry Demerer for approximately $215,000; sold to Superior for a reported $312,500 in late 1980/early 1981; The Premier Auction Sale (Superior, 1/95), lot 1645, where it realized $203,500 as a PCGS MS63; subsequently certified NGC MS63 Specimen; The Eagle Collection (Heritage, 1/02), lot 4147, where it brought $270,000.(#9061)

IMPORTANT GEM PROOF 1867 LIBERTY DOUBLE EAGLE Ex: TROMPETER

6373 1867 PR65 Cameo NGC. This coin was previously offered as lot 7574 in our Philadelphia 2000 Signature Sale, where it was partially described as: "Only 50 proof Double Eagles were produced in 1867, half of which were delivered on March 5 and the other 25 pieces on July 2. The number of survivors is believed to number no more than a dozen coins. Akers suggests that many of the 50 pieces struck went unsold at year's end and were subsequently melted. As with all other Double Eagles of this period, 1867 proof Twenties are exceedingly rare, and the splendid preservation of this specimen along with its impeccable pedigree place it in a category all its own.

"The digits used in the date are taken from the Silver Dollar logotype. The date is placed high in the exergual field with the 1 close to the bust. An extra outline around the bust of Liberty is broken just above the 18 in the date, and extra outlines surround the inner points of all the peripheral obverse stars. The denticles are well apart except in the area of the date, where they are minutely closer than elsewhere. A tiny Mint-made dash (die scratch) is noted just to the right of star 8. On the reverse, a small area of incomplete die polish is seen to the left and right at the top of the first vertical stripe in the shield. The middle arrowshaft is weak and wavy from die polishing. The lowest arrowhead touches the scroll, and the tip of the left (facing) wing just touches the E in UNITED. The denticles on the reverse are well spaced on the bottom half of that side, with incomplete die polish noted between the denticles over NITED STATES OF.

"The visual impression left by this proof Double Eagle is simply astonishing. The fields sparkle with intense, deeply mirrored reflectivity, and close examination reveals the fine, orange-peel texture often seen on 19th century proof gold. The devices are thickly frosted and are set against the limitless mirrored fields, yielding a profound two-toned cameo effect. We seen no superficial flaws on either side of this remarkable piece. For pedigree identification, the only reliable markers we see are three tiny ones that originated at the Mint some 133 years ago: on the obverse, a tiny planchet flake is noted by star 3; set in the field equidistant between the B in LIBERTY and stars 7 and 8 is a minute lintmark; and a small, vertical streak of grease that was struck into the coin, located on the upper portion of Liberty's neck."

Ex: Major William Boerum Wetmore (S.H. & H. Chapman, 6/27-28/1906); Clapp; Eliasberg (Bowers and Ruddy, 10/82), lot 918, where it realized $44,000; Ed Trompeter Collection of Proof U.S. Gold.

From The Greenwich Collection, Part One.(#89082)

SPECTACULAR 1869 PROOF DOUBLE EAGLE ONE OF NO MORE THAN 12 COINS BELIEVED EXTANT

6374 1869 PR64 Cameo NGC. This is an exquisite proof Twenty whose eye appeal alone would do justice to an even higher grade. The cameo contrast is profound, so much so that one is left wondering why NGC did not provide a Deep Cameo designation. The devices are richly frosted in finish and set atop glistening, mirrored fields that appear to "go black" when the coin rotates away from the light. The overall color is an orange-gold shade, this feature, as well as all others, being fully appreciable in the absence of sizeable contact marks. In fact, we are unable to locate any singularly useful pedigree markers, although accuracy compels us to mention a couple of wispy slidemarks on the obverse over and before Liberty's cheek. Were it not for these light handling marks, this coin would easily warrant a full Gem grade.

Proof Double Eagle production at the Philadelphia Mint amounted to just 25 coins in 1869. Breen (1988) estimates that a mere 10-12 pieces are extant, a range that Doug Winter and Mike Fuljenz also credit in the 1999 book *Type Two Double Eagles 1866-1876: A Numismatic History and Analysis*. This is the first proof 1869 Double Eagle that we have offered at auction in recent memory, and its appearance marks an event that is surely not soon to be repeated.

From The Greenwich Collection, Part One.(#89084)

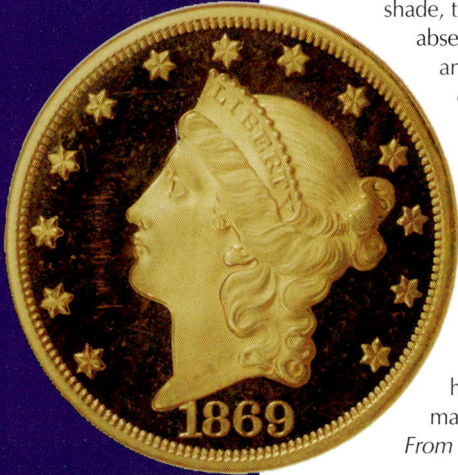

CHOICE CAMEO PROOF 1879 DOUBLE EAGLE, FROM THE GENAITIS COLLECTION

6375 1879 PR64 Cameo NGC. As with the other gold denominations struck in this year, only 30 proofs were produced of the 1879 Double Eagle. Of that number, Akers estimates that only 10 or 11 pieces are extant, while Breen states that only 8-10 pieces have survived. This is a spectacular cameo proof that has deeply reflective mirrors in the fields and heavy mint frost on the devices which produces the stark field-to-device contrast seen on each side. Rich orange-gold color covers both obverse and reverse. The only identifying mark we see for future pedigree purposes is a slight discoloration, i.e., a light alloy spot, on the obverse rim at 12 o'clock. Exceptional quality combined with exceptional rarity.

Ex: Atlanta ANA Sale (Heritage, 8/2001), lot 8200.

From The Greenwich Collection, Part One.(#89095)

CHOICE 1884 LIBERTY DOUBLE EAGLE
A RARE AND COVETED PROOF-ONLY ISSUE

6376 1884 PR64 PCGS. An issue that needs no introduction among gold specialists, the 1884 was produced solely in specimen, or proof format. The official mintage is 71 coins, which is fewer than those of the proof-only 1883 and 1887 deliveries. Perhaps not surprisingly, the 1884 is the rarest issue of this trio, but just *how* rare has been a matter of debate within numismatic circles. For years, Walter Breen's estimate of 16-20 pieces extant was widely accepted as fact. However, Mike Fuljenz and Doug Winter offer a range of just 15-17 coins in the 2000 book *Type Three Double Eagles 1877-1907: A Numismatic History and Analysis,* and we have also seen estimates of as few as 12 pieces receive credit. Regardless of which of these estimates is closest to the truth, there can be no doubt that our offering of the present specimen represents a numismatic event of undeniable significance.

We are aware of only five other auction appearances for the 1884 Double Eagle over the past nine years:

1. Ex: Harry W. Bass, Jr. Collection (Bowers and Merena, 10/1999), lot 1891, where it realized $46,000. This coin was certified PR63 by PCGS at the time of the sale.

2. Ex: Dallas Bank Collection (Stack's/Sotheby's, 10/2001), lot 94, where it realized $48,875. Cataloged as "Choice Brilliant Proof."

3. Ex: Eagle Collection of Double Eagles (Heritage, 1/2002), lot 4149, where it realized $54,625. Graded PR64 Cameo at NGC.

4. Ex: FUN Signature Sale Platinum Night—The North Shore Collection (Heritage, 1/2004), lot 3225, where it realized $149,500. An exquisite NGC PR66 Cameo specimen.

5. Ex: Long Beach Signature Sale (Heritage, 1/2004), lot 7590, where it realized $103,500. Certified PR63 PCGS.

We do not know the prior pedigree of the specimen that we are offering in the present sale, but we are fairly certain that it is not one of the pieces listed above. This coin is identifiable by a tiny planchet flaw (as produced) in the obverse field before Liberty's brow.

Needle sharp striking definition and dominant reddish-gold color are seen on both sides. The color becomes somewhat variegated in select areas in the obverse field and through the center of the reverse, but all features are uncommonly mark-free for a gold coin of this size. The uniformly reflective finish sparkles as the coin rotates under a light.
From The Greenwich Collection, Part One.(#9100)

IMPORTANT 1889 DOUBLE EAGLE, CAMEO PROOF 63 NGC

6377 1889 PR63 Cameo NGC. Ex: Bass Collection. Only 41 proof Double Eagles were struck in 1889, and estimates of survivors vary from perhaps 12 pieces (Akers, 1981) to as many as 12-15 (Breen, 1988). Both Breen and Bowers (in the Eliasberg catalog) make a point of mentioning that of the few known survivors, quite a few are nicked or somehow damaged, and 2-3 pieces are impounded in museums, further reducing the number of collectible specimens.

This is a truly spectacular coin whose warm rose tinted surfaces are deeply mirrored in the fields and contrast sharply against the thick mint frost on the devices. There are a few hairlines scattered about in the fields and these hairlines keep this amazing coin from grading even higher. The pedigree of this important proof can be easily confirmed by noting a small toning spot between the tops of the 1 and 8 in the date. This is one of the finest proofs known of this Type Three issue. Population: 1 in 63, 3 finer (4/04). *From The Greenwich Collection, Part One.*(#89105)

AMAZING GEM CAMEO PROOF 1891 LIBERTY TWENTY DOLLAR

6378 1891 PR66 Deep Cameo NGC. The 1891 Double Eagle was struck in a year when the vast majority of large gold coin production was earmarked for the San Francisco facility, certainly a practical policy since nearly all newly mined gold ore originated in the Pacific West. As a result, only 1,390 business strikes were produced along with 52 proofs. Both are predictably elusive today, with the tiny quantity of business strikes almost always seen with some degree of circulation and fewer than half of the proof mintage believed to be extant.

The surfaces on this spectacular proof Double Eagle display the slightest haziness over fields of uncanny depth of mirrored reflectivity, while the central features are heavily frosted, and the resultant contrast is extreme. Solid Condition Census quality on this difficult and sought-after proof Double Eagle issue. Population: 3 in 66, 1 finer (4/04).
From The Greenwich Collection, Part One.(#99107)

PITTMAN'S CHOICE PROOF 1902 DOUBLE EAGLE

6379 1902 PR64 PCGS. Ex: Pittman. This meticulously struck sunrise-gold near-Gem exhibits flashy mirrored fields and has impressive eye appeal. A few wisps of milky gray patina are noted on the reverse, above the I in PLURIBUS and the field near the arrowheads, but there is scant evidence of the wispy hairlines that often accompany proof gold coins. Only 114 proofs were struck, and far fewer than the quantity survive in unimpaired grades. Although the PCGS population for the PR64 grade is 22 pieces, it is very likely that most of that population reflects resubmissions from a dealer or two attempting to achieve the elusive PCGS PR65 grade, which only a solitary example has attained.
Ex: John Jay Pittman Collection, Part One (Akers, 10/97), lot 1178; earlier purchased by Pittman from Max L. Justus on 11/22/59 for $945.(#9118)

LIGHTLY CIRCULATED HIGH RELIEF DOUBLE EAGLE

6380 1907 High Relief, Wire Rim AU58 ANACS. Fully and intricately detailed on each side, the surfaces are bright and retain almost complete mint luster in the fields. A lightly handled example of this classic coin design.(#9135) (Registry values: N2998)

HIGHLY DESIRABLE NEAR-MINT MCMVII HIGH RELIEF SAINT-GAUDENS TWENTY

6381 1907 High Relief, Wire Rim AU58 PCGS. A Choice example for the near-Mint level, the surfaces are free of sizeable and/or individually distracting abrasions. The color is a pleasing yellow-gold shade, and the devices retain ample evidence of the powerful impression for which this first-year issue is known.(#9135) (Registry values: N2998)

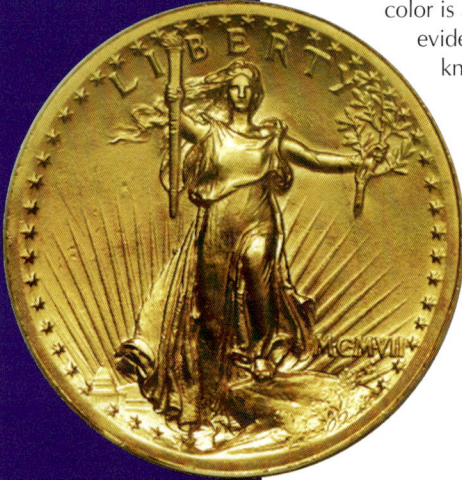

ATTRACTIVE 1907 HIGH RELIEF TWENTY MS62

6382 1907 High Relief, Wire Rim MS62 PCGS. Honey-gold in sheen, both sides display the boldness of definition that explains the unflagging popularity of this first-year issue. The fields of this attractive example are especially smooth and only a nominal amount of stacking friction about the reverse periphery appears to preclude a Select rating.
From The Barry Donnell Collection.(#9135) (Registry values: N4719)

RADIANT NEAR-GEM 1907 HIGH RELIEF TWENTY

6383 1907 High Relief, Wire Rim MS64 NGC. A high quality representative of this popular gold issue, the surfaces are bright with radiant yellow-gold features. Every device is sharply impressed, and the number of wispy abrasions is consistent with the near-Gem grade level.(#9135) (Registry values: N7079)

NEAR-GEM MCMVII HIGH RELIEF DOUBLE EAGLE

6384 1907 High Relief, Wire Rim MS64 NGC. No important rare coin auction would be complete without a high grade offering of the beautiful and always-popular High Relief Saint-Gaudens Double Eagle of 1907. This coin is an example of the more prevalent Wire Rim variety, a feature that was created when metal was forced between the dies and the collar during repeated impressions. The surfaces exhibit a khaki-gold sheen with isolated blushes of orange-gold color evident at a few angles. A few faint marks in the vulnerable obverse field are all that seem to bar this otherwise smooth looking example from a full Gem grade.(#9135) (Registry values: N7079)

HIGH GRADE (MS64) WIRE RIM HIGH RELIEF TWENTY

6385 1907 High Relief, Wire Rim MS64 PCGS. The exact mintage of the High Relief twenties has always been a subject of controversy, but whatever the exact mintage a high percentage of better grade (MS60 and better) coins were set aside at the time of issue and remain so today. This particular coin has an even wire rim around each side and the striking details are well defined throughout. Pale reddish patina is seen over both obverse and reverse with the usual strong presence of underlying satiny mint luster. An exceptionally pleasing, problem-free example of this popular gold type coin.(#9135) (Registry values: N7079)

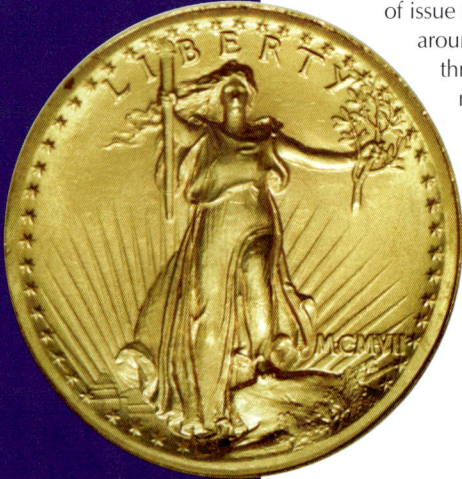

EXCEPTIONAL MS64 MCMVII TWENTY

6386 1907 High Relief, Wire Rim MS64 NGC. The term "upper-end" is used frequently in numismatics, some would say overused, but few would quarrel with calling this coin upper-end for the grade. The surfaces have rich golden-orange coloration and the swirling die polish marks in the fields impart a brightness to the satiny mint luster that is most attractive. The only blemishes of any note are a short, shallow, angling mark below the olive branch on the obverse, and on the upper reverse there is evidence of some sort of strike-through over STAT(ES OF AM)ERICA—a very unusual occurrence on a High Relief and the first such error we can recall having seen. Crisp striking definition is seen on all the devices as well.(#9135) (Registry values: N7079)

FLASHY 1907 HIGH RELIEF TWENTY AU58, FLAT RIM

6387 1907 High Relief, Flat Rim AU58 PCGS. Although technically not Mint State, this is a particularly flashy representative of the scarcer flat rim variant. Bright yellow-gold surfaces reveal just the slightest trace of friction on the highpoints when carefully examined.

From The Barry Donnell Collection.(#9136) (Registry values: N1)

NEAR-GEM 1907 HIGH RELIEF DOUBLE EAGLE

6388 1907 High Relief, Flat Rim MS64 NGC. In our experience, the Flat Rim is several times more difficult to locate than its Wire Rim counterpart, although collectors of this beautiful design rarely distinguish between the two sub-varieties. Both sides of this well preserved representative display a first rate strike and are just a few wispy blemishes from Gem status.(#9136) (Registry values: N7079)

ELUSIVE CHOICE UNCIRCULATED 1909/8 TWENTY DOLLAR

6389 1909/8 MS64 PCGS. The 1909/8 is the only Saint-Gaudens overdate and it is most often seen in XF or AU condition—often enough that it doesn't carry a significant premium. The situation changes quite drastically at the Uncirculated level, where true Mint State coins are few and far between. This example is absolutely Choice with full frosty mint luster and sharp definition. There is very little toning and the color is a nice bright yellow-gold. For accuracy we must mention a few very small contact marks on the eagle's wings and one under Liberty's right (facing) arm. This coin will please even the most particular collector of Saint-Gaudens twenties. Population: 55 in 64, 11 finer (3/04).(#9151) (Registry values: N4719)

SCARCE 1909-D TWENTY, MS64 PCGS

6390 1909-D MS64 PCGS. As might be expected, finding a Choice Uncirculated example of this low mintage issue is very difficult. This piece is quite pleasing with good luster and a hint of yellow-golden patina over each side. The surfaces have a few light, scattered marks but none are particularly obtrusive. Population: 93 in 64, 10 finer (3/04).(#9152) (Registry values: N4719)

REMARKABLE GEM 1911 TWENTY DOLLAR, MS66 NGC

6391 1911 MS66 NGC. With a mintage of 197,350 pieces one would think the 1911 would be more available in high grades than it is. The fact is, it is very elusive in Gem (MS65) condition, and as an MS66, only 11 pieces have thus far been graded by both services combined, with 1 finer (4/04). Fully struck throughout, the rich orange-gold surfaces show excellent luster characteristics and there are no mentionable abrasions on either side.(#9157) (Registry values: N7079)

ATTRACTIVE 1913 DOUBLE EAGLE MS64

6392 1913 MS64 PCGS. Quite lustrous with an attractive reddish tint over both sides. The obverse has a few scattered contact marks both in the fields and on Liberty's gown, while the reverse is generally quite smooth. The lower mintage 1913 Saint is nearly unobtainable (and quite expensive) any finer.(#9161) (Registry values: N2998)

LUSTROUS 1913 DOUBLE EAGLE, MS64 PCGS

6393 **1913 MS64 PCGS.** Lightly toned with thick mint luster, the devices are sharply struck. There are a few small and medium sized abrasions present on the reverse that serve to limit the grade. A scarce issue, particularly in this high grade, that is always in demand by collectors. Population: 110 in 64, 6 finer (3/04).(#9161) (Registry values: N2998)

CHOICE BU 1913 SAINT-GAUDENS TWENTY

6394 **1913 MS64 NGC.** A scarcer date in all three issues of this year, the '13-P is actually the most difficult of the three (with the release of a small hoard of 1913-S Saints) and is an important condition rarity above the MS 62-63 grade range. This is an impressive, matte-like specimen with some reddish-golden color in the recessed areas.(#9161) (Registry values: N2998)

FULLY LUSTROUS 1913-S TWENTY, MS64 PCGS

6395 1913-S MS64 PCGS. This issue boasts the third lowest mintage of the series, 34,000 pieces, and the normal grade encountered is a high grade AU (55-58). Only a small group of Uncirculated pieces that surfaced several years ago has enabled the collector to have a legitimate chance to acquire a strict Mint State example. The color of this specimen is a medium yellow-gold with very bright luster showing on both sides. The strike is uniformly sharp, including the crescent at the lower portion of the obverse that is sometimes blunt on '13-S Double Eagles. A collection of small marks and abrasions limits the grade to MS64.(#9163) (Registry values: N4719)

LOW MINTAGE 1913-S TWENTY MS64 PCGS

6396 1913-S MS64 PCGS. Always a popular issue among Saint-Gaudens collectors due, in part, to its low mintage. While usually available in lower grades, the '13-S is a scarce and worthwhile date in MS64 and better grades. This piece is well struck and shows rich golden luster overall. A few contact marks overall serve to limit the already high grade.(#9163) (Registry values: N4719)

LUSTROUS ORIGINAL 1913-S TWENTY DOLLAR

6397 **1913-S MS64 PCGS.** A crisp strike and rich orange-gold patina are the hallmarks of this lustrous near-Gem. The obverse side has a few mentionable luster grazes typical of the grade, while the reverse field is somewhat cleaner. With its mintage of just 34,000 pieces, the 1913-S has long been a popular target for hoarders and speculators.(#9163) (Registry values: N4719)

LIGHTLY CLEANED, LIGHTLY CIRCULATED 1921 DOUBLE EAGLE

6398 **1921—Cleaned—ANACS. AU Details, Net AU50.** It has long been obvious that most of the original half million coin mintage of the 1921 Double Eagle was melted at a later date. Experts in the field earlier estimated as low as 15 pieces extant (Breen) and 40-50 pieces (Akers). In reality, the number is probably somewhere around 100. The bottom line is still that there are not very many available to meet a constant demand for this popular issue. This coin is well struck with a few contact marks. Evidence of cleaning is observed upon close examination, but this does little to diminish the overall visual effect and appeal of this legitimate rarity. *From the Virgil Farstad Collection, Part Two.*(#9172) (Registry values: N7079)

HEAVILY MELTED 1924-D SAINT, MS63

6399 1924-D MS63 PCGS. A modestly abraded representative of this condition scarcity, with soft, frosted luster and pleasing coloration. Only a minority of '24-D Saints survive at the Select or better grade level.(#9178) (Registry values: N2998)

SCARCE 1924-D SAINT, MS63 PCGS

6400 1924-D MS63 PCGS. Once considered a prime Double Eagle rarity, the 1924-D has occupied a new position on the rarity scale due to the emergence of several small hoards. Nevertheless, this issue is anything but common in today's hobby, and survivors are equally as elusive as those of the 1925-D and 1926-S issues. This satiny finished example is awash in pleasing golden-rose and yellow color that highlights the appreciable cartwheel luster effects. Both sides are well struck with a typical number of small abrasions for the MS63 grade level.(#9178) (Registry values: N2998)

SCARCE 1925-D TWENTY DOLLAR, MS63 NGC

6401 **1925-D MS63 NGC.** Although valued less, the '25-D Double Eagle is similar in rarity to the 1926-D and 1929. Of the 200 or so pieces believed extant today, most fall into the lower Mint State categories. While the present piece shows a few scattered abrasions throughout, the surfaces are nicely struck (save for some of the highpoint detail on the obverse), and richly frosted. Vibrant yellow-gold color envelops both sides. In sum, this is an attractive representative of this scarce and desirable D-mint issue.(#9181) (Registry values: N4719)

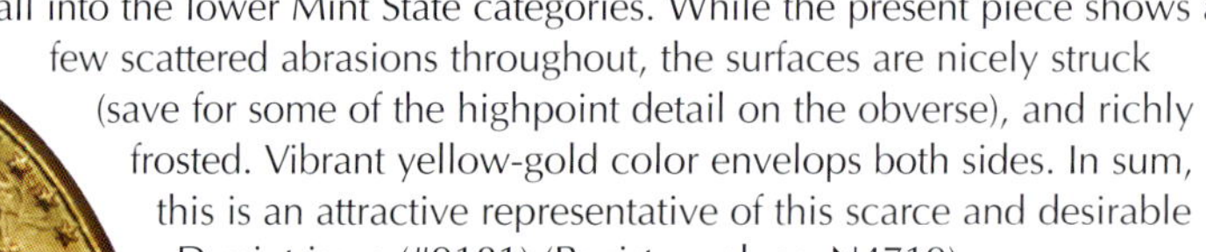

SUPERB, UNSURPASSABLE 1926 SAINT-GAUDENS TWENTY

6402 **1926 MS67 NGC.** The strike has a medal-like clarity of detail and the surfaces are accented by bright, satiny luster and medium yellow-gold color. There are also no individually mentionable abrasions visible on either side. In researching our archive file, we find this is the single finest 1926 Twenty Dollar coin we have had the pleasure to offer since we began keeping records. Simply, a must-see item for the specialist. Population: 2 in 67, none finer at either service (4/04).(#9183) (Registry values: N4719)

SUPERB GEM 1928 SAINT-GAUDENS DOUBLE EAGLE

6403 **1928 MS67 PCGS.** Truly exceptional quality. The mint luster is uncommonly bright, even for this well-produced issue, and colorfully toned in variegated shades of pink and orange. Very sharply struck, the reverse is nearly perfect and there are just a few shallow abrasions on the obverse. These do not have any significant effect on this Superb type coin's overall eye appeal. Population: 57 in 67, 0 finer (3/04).(#9189) (Registry values: N4719)

SCARCE GEM GRANT / STAR COMMEMORATIVE HALF DOLLAR

6404 **1922 Grant with Star MS66 NGC.** Medium silver-gray toning blankets each side of this unusually smooth example. A small area of reddish-golden color is detected at the lower portion of the reverse and the corresponding part of the obverse. One small vertical abrasion is detected on Grant's forehead. Population: 35 in 66, 4 finer (4/04).(#9307) (Registry values: N4719)

GEM MISSOURI 2X4 HALF DOLLAR

6405 **1921 Missouri 2x4 MS66 PCGS.** Highly lustrous beneath swirling, original shades of silver-gray accented with some limited mottled russet-brown hues. Better grade examples of this early key commemorative are often overlaid in somewhat oppressive toning, not so with this uncommonly frosty and vibrant piece. Population: 11 in 66, none finer at either service (3/04).(#9331) (Registry values: N4719)

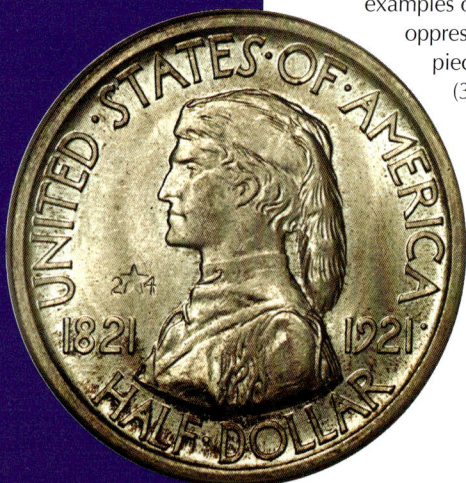

SUPERB GEM WISCONSIN HALF, MS68 ★ NGC

6406 **1936 Wisconsin MS68 ★ NGC.** Even close examination fails to produce a mentionable mark or abrasion on either side. The dove-gray centers are greatly enhanced with rich multicolored iridescence at the border areas. A fully original, Superb specimen worthy of the finest collection. Population: 15 in 68, none finer at either service (4/04).(#9447) (Registry values: N2998)

EXCEPTIONALLY ATTRACTIVE 1853 U.S. ASSAY OFFICE TWENTY DOLLAR

6407 1853 Assay Office Twenty Dollar, 900 Thous. MS63 NGC. K-18, R.2. Lustrous and bright, both sides exhibit rich, yellow-gold coloration. A few scattered contact marks serve to limit the grade, the most notable of which is a small dig in the obverse field under the A of STATES. The powerful strike is free of criticism. Although this issue is the most readily available Double Eagle that the U.S. Assay Office of Gold produced in 1853, it is not an easy coin to locate with this much pleasing eye appeal. This lot clearly represents an important bidding opportunity for advanced territorial gold collectors. Listed on page 292 of the current *Guide Book.*(#10013)

POPULAR 1860 CLARK, GRUBER & CO. "PIKES PEAK" TEN DOLLAR

6408 1860 Clark, Gruber & Co. Ten Dollar AU Details, Burnished, NCS. K-3, R.5. The start of the Colorado Gold Rush followed that of California by almost exactly ten years. Two settlements, Auraria and Denver City (the present day Denver), formed on opposite sides of the South Platte River, and by 1860 Auraria was absorbed by Denver City. During this time, the risk of loss in bullion trading was great due to increased robbery and little in the way of organized local security. The stage was set for a local mint, and there to fill the void was Clark, Gruber, & Co. Commerce in Colorado took a significant turn when they arrived.

C, G, & Co. bought three lots in Denver City on which to build their mint, and a two-story brick "Assay and Coinage Office" was erected on the corner of McGaa and G Streets (the present 16th and Market). Coinage began quickly and totaled approximately $120,000 between July and October of 1860. The entire area was known as the "Pike's Peak District," leading to the legend PIKES PEAK GOLD DENVER seen on the Clark, Gruber, & Co. 1860 ten and twenty dollar gold. In 1863, the federal government bought out the firm under the pretense of setting up a branch mint. Of course it was more than 40 years before that actually occurred. This minimally worn, but rather subdued example was harshly cleaned at one time, stripping the coin of its natural luster. Listed on page 302 of the 2004 *Guide Book.*(#10137)

HIGHLY ELUSIVE 1861 CLARK-GRUBER DOUBLE EAGLE

6409 1861 Clark, Gruber & Co. Twenty Dollar XF Details, Whizzed, NCS. K-8, High R.5. This is a seldom-seen Colorado private issue. We have been privileged to offer only a couple of 1861 Twenties at public auction over the past twenty years. This piece has unnaturally bright surfaces, having obviously been cleaned at one time. A bit softly struck, as always seen, there is also a small area of attempted repair below the eagle's tail. Still, a very important listing and worthy of a close examination. Listed on page 303 of the 2003 *Guide Book*.(#10142)

ELUSIVE 1851 HUMBERT $50 OCTAGONAL SLUG

6410 1851 Humbert Fifty Dollar, 880 Thous., VF Details, Improperly Cleaned, NCS. K-5, Low R.5. A lower grade Humbert Fifty that saw extensive use in the channels of commerce. The bright green-gold surfaces have a number of small rim bumps on the obverse in addition to the relatively inoffensive cleaning. If one is seeking an elusive Humbert slug without raiding the college fund, this piece has all the heft without the big price tag. Listed on page 289 of the 2004 *Guide Book*.(#10211)

UNCIRCULATED 1851 HUMBERT FIFTY DOLLAR 887 THOUS.

6411 1851 Humbert Fifty Dollar, 887 Thous. MS61 NGC. Reeded Edge. K-6, R.4. An important Mint State example of this large format territorial gold coin. The Assay Office in San Francisco actually did very little in 1851 to help alleviate California's need for a circulating medium. What they did under Humbert's leadership was to convert the raw gold dust, that had previously been used as currency, into these large $50 so-called "slugs." Smaller denominations would follow, but these are the initial emissions from the Assay Office, an official U.S. government office that acted as a *de facto* Mint until the actual Mint opened in 1854.

Many of these "slugs" have numerous rim bumps and nicks due to their massive size, as does this example. Minor rim irregularities that were on the planchet at the time of striking are noted at 1 o'clock on the obverse and at a similar position on the reverse. The target reverse has a vertical blemish above and just to the left of center and a few others of relatively minor consequence. An attractive reddish patina highlights the lustrous green-gold surfaces and the strike displays normal deficiency on the obverse devices. Listed on page 289 of the 2004 *Guide Book*.(#10214)

FINEST KNOWN 1849 MOFFAT HALF EAGLE

6412 1849 Moffat & Co. Five Dollar MS67 NGC. K-4, R.5. John Moffat was born in Goshen, New York on February 21, 1788. A veteran of the Southern Appalachian Gold Rush of the 1830s, he and Curtis, Perry, and Ward traveled to California and established Moffat & Co. on the San Francisco waterfront. After relocating to the southwest corner of Clay and Dupont Streets, the firm of Moffat & Co. began to advertise its new smelting and assaying business from June 21, 1849. Numismatists believe that the firm began to issue its famous rectangular gold ingots at this time. The cumbersome qualities of these ingots, however, made them almost worthless as a circulating medium of exchange and, after the Bavarian-born engraver George A. Ferdinand Kuner joined the firm from New York, Moffat & Co. enacted plans to produce actual gold coins. Kuner fashioned his coins after the federal Coronet gold issues of the era and, while they were not the first private issues of the California Gold Rush, their workmanship and composition was of such high quality as to ensure Moffat & Co.'s place as the leading private mint of their day.

Kuner's 1849 Half Eagles were issued from the fall of 1849 through early 1850. Kagin lists three distinct varieties. These are similar in overall appearance and differ only in the presence or absence of die cracks. The scarcest of the three varieties, as represented by the present piece, is the one which lacks both the die crack on the reverse rim below DOL. and the crack that bisects the eagle's breast. Despite characteristic softness of strike on the hair curls and eagle's talons, the crisply delineated features of this specimen speak volumes for the coinage skill of Kuner in particular and Moffat & Co. as a whole. The incredible, lustrous surfaces exhibit a pronounced granular texture as well as pastel avocado-golden patination. The balance of the coin is exceptionally smooth, having obviously been carefully preserved for over 150 years. Since many of Moffat & Co.'s gold issues were melted to provide bullion for the San Francisco Mint's first coinage of 1854, the rarity of this Superb Gem Half Eagle should be plainly evident to the territorial gold specialist. This is the single finest example thus far certified by either service (4/04).(#10240)

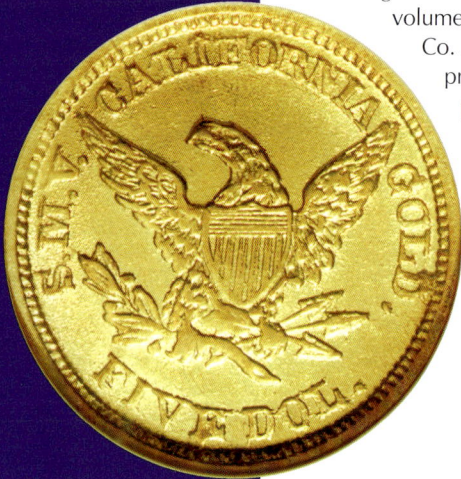

IMPORTANT GEM 1836 GOBRECHT GOLD DOLLAR, JUDD-67 PATTERN

6413 1836 Gold Dollar, Judd-67, Pollock-70, R.5, PR65 PCGS. The obverse features a Liberty cap surrounded by numerous glory rays, similar in design to certain contemporary Mexican issues. The reverse features the denomination "1 D." within a coiled palm frond, with the date below and UNITED STATES OF AMERICA above. Christian Gobrecht is credited with both designs. Struck in gold alloy with a plain edge. Judd-67 has considerable historical importance, as it is the first Federal gold pattern as well as the first Gold Dollar issue. Originals are likely quite rare, although a number were restruck in the 1860s, one of which was struck over an 1859 Gold Dollar. This bright yellow-gold Gem has a needle-sharp strike and highly reflective fields, while the reverse has bold mint-made striations.(#11260)

DESIRABLE 1836 GOLD DOLLAR PATTERN IN SILVER, JUDD-69

6414 1836 Gold Dollar, Judd-69, Pollock-72, High R.7, PR64 PCGS. The obverse features a Liberty Cap surrounded by a sunburst, very similar to that seen on certain Mexican coins of the time. The word LIBERTY is inscribed in the cap. A coiled palm frond encircles 1D. on the reverse with UNITED STATES OF AMERICA around. The design was attributed to Christian Gobrecht. Struck in silver with a plain edge. Considered a probable restrike by Judd. The fields glitter with deep reflectivity and there is a trace of blue and gold toning around the outer margins on each side.(#11264)

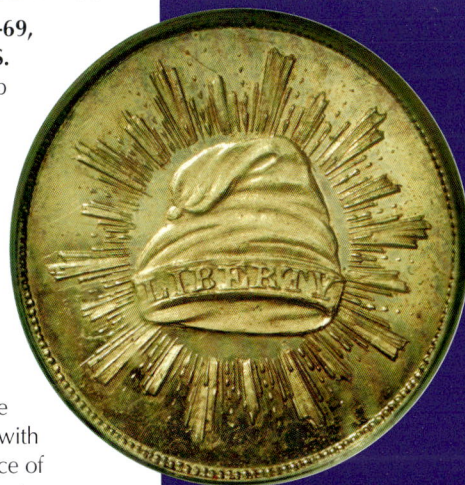

FLASHY 1838 KNEASS HALF DOLLAR PATTERN, JUDD-72

6415 1838 Half Dollar, Judd-72, Pollock-75, R.5, PR65 NGC. The William Kneass design for the Half Dollar that features a draped bust of Liberty facing left with stars on the left and right, date below. The reverse shows a stately drop-wing eagle without shield. Struck in silver with a reeded edge. Believed to be an earlier restrike (circa 1858), as there is little evidence of die rust and only slight softness in the centers. The reverse is medallically aligned to the obverse. Attractive peripheral toning in dappled shades of golden-violet and turquoise enlivens highly reflective surfaces.(#11282)

OUTSTANDING 1850 THREE CENT SILVER PATTERN, JUDD-125

6416 1850 Three Cent Silver, Judd-125 Original, Pollock-147, R.4, PR66 NGC. Similar in design to the famous Judd-67 Gold Dollar pattern from 1836, however, the date has been moved to the obverse below the cap, and the denomination within the palm frond is expressed with a large Roman numeral III. Struck in silver with a plain edge. This outstanding representative is by far the nicest we have ever handled. Bright, noticeably striated surfaces are essentially untoned through the centers while displaying occasional russet and charcoal peripheral accents.(#11536)

WELL PRESERVED 1855 FLYING EAGLE PATTERN, JUDD-168

6417 1855 Flying Eagle Cent, Judd-168 Original, Pollock-193, R.4, PR63 Red and Brown PCGS. The design shows a large eagle surrounded by 13 stars on the obverse, while on the reverse ONE CENT is surrounded by a thick laurel wreath which is, in turn, surrounded by UNITED STATES OF AMERICA. Struck in copper or bronze with a plain edge. Very scarce with any of the original red color remaining, this piece shows a significant amount around the outer margins with emerald-green surfaces otherwise and nice reflectivity in the fields. Identifiable by a large planchet flaw in the field above the N in ONE.(#11721)

ELUSIVE 1863 THREE CENT SILVER IN ALUMINUM, JUDD-322

6418 1863 Three Cent Silver, Judd-322, Pollock-387, High R.7, PR66 Deep Cameo PCGS. Although described in the literature as "regular dies trial pieces," these are actually restrikes made in the early 1870s and sold as part of complete off-metal sets with the silver coinage of this year containing quarter, half dollar, and dollar which had the reverses of 1866 with the motto IN GOD WE TRUST above the eagle. These three cent dies were made from a hub which had the D in UNITED broken and may be a backdated novodel. Struck in aluminum with a plain edge. The obverse is this high quality specimen is heavily striated and, while similarly reflective, the reverse lacks this feature. A bit of striking softness is noted along the left side of both obverse and reverse.(#60479)

EXTREMELY SCARCE 1866 THREE DOLLARS IN NICKEL JUDD-543

6419 1866 Three Dollar, Judd-543, Pollock-608, High R.7, PR64 PCGS. An elusive regular dies trial striking after James B. Longacre's adopted design. Struck in nickel, interestingly with a reeded edge. The silver-gray planchet, while almost totally free from post-minting disturbances, exhibits heavy pitting from die rust on the headdress and more subtle graininess near the base of the wreath and in intermittent areas over the balance of the coin.(#60741)

1869 DIE TRIAL HALF DOLLAR IN ALUMINUM PR67, JUDD-761

6420 1869 Half Dollar, Judd-761, Pollock-845, Low R.7, PR67 NGC. Regular die trials issue for the Seated Half Dollar. Struck in aluminum with a reeded edge. These pieces were deliberately struck by the Mint for sale to collectors as part of off-metal sets. Fewer than a half dozen are known today and this piece is certainly among the finest extant. The fields are deeply mirrored and show no traces of oxidation. The devices are heavily frosted and present a strong cameo contrast against the deeply reflective fields. A pair of tiny U-shaped lintmarks to the left of the portrait can be used for attribution on this Superb aluminum pattern.(#60992)

1870 STANDARD SILVER HALF PR66, JUDD-952

6421 1870 Standard Silver Half Dollar, Judd-952, Pollock-1095, Low R.7, PR66 NGC. The obverse shows a Bust of Liberty facing right, encircled by the peripheral legend UNITED STATES OF AMERICA, with the motto IN GOD WE TRUST on a scroll below. Miss Liberty is wearing a diadem inscribed LIBERTY, and her hair is tied in a bun. The reverse displays the denomination 50 CENTS and the date 1870 within a wreath of cotton and corn, with the inscription STANDARD above. Struck in silver with a plain edge. This sparkling, fully brilliant specimen is potentially the finest known example of this elusive Standard Silver pattern.(#61198)

IMPORTANT 1870 TWENTY DOLLAR IN ALUMINUM JUDD-1039

6422 1870 Twenty Dollar, Judd-1039, Pollock-1174, High R.7, PR64 Cameo PCGS. A possibly unique die trial striking from regular issue 1870 Double Eagle dies, but struck in aluminum with a reeded edge. Examples of aluminum strikings are also known for the other gold denominations of this year, which were likely produced as presentation pieces. Specimens are also known in copper and in nickel. The primary source of these important patterns is the 1954 auction of the King Farouk holdings, also the origin of this aluminum representative. A small flip that accompanies attributes the piece to the Palace Collection, although it is not signed like the 1885 $5 aluminum pattern later in the sale.

This specimen appears to have escaped the harsh treatment received by many of the Farouk coins, its bright, watery mirrors being totally void of hairlines. A squiggly hairline planchet crack that angles down from Liberty's upper lip is nearly expected of early aluminum strikings and a few paper thin grease stains are noticed on the portrait. The only post minting blemish we can find is a shallow frost break on Liberty's neck. Of course, these rather trivial distractions are made even more inconsequential by the uniqueness of this important offering.

Ex: Palace Collection (Sotheby's, 1954), lot 1833.(#61288)

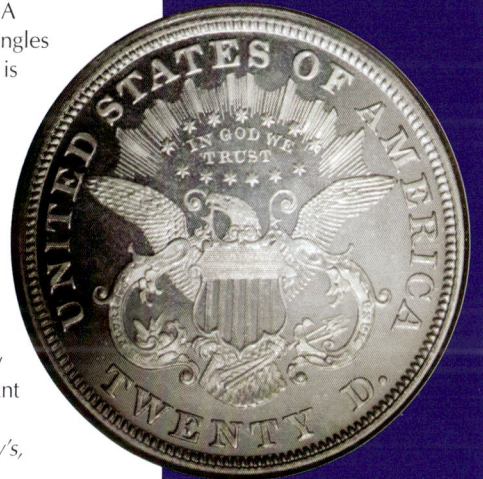

This Coin Is From the
PALACE COLLECTION
of Former
KING FAROUK
of Egypt
Sold to..........
Attested..........

RARE 1872 AMAZONIAN SILVER HALF DOLLAR PATTERN JUDD-1200, PROOF 66 NGC

6423 1872 Half Dollar, Judd-1200, Pollock-1340, Low R.7, PR66 NGC. A representation of Liberty is seated left on the obverse with her right hand outstretched and resting on the head of an eagle. Her left hand holds a sword, and that arm is propped up on a shield. Thirteen stars encircle the border and the date 1872 is below. The reverse depicts an eagle with spread wings and three arrows in its right talon. The left talon supports a shield, in front of which is an olive branch and over which is draped a ribbon inscribed with the motto IN GOD WE TRUST. The legend UNITED STATES OF AMERICA is at the upper border and the denomination HALF DOL is at the lower border. Struck in silver with a reeded edge.

The Amazonian patterns of 1872 are attributed to William Barber. Long considered one of the most beautiful designs in U.S. coinage history, the term "Amazonian" appears to have originated with the Lorin G. Parmelee Collection Sale of June 1890. The catalogers for that sale, H. P. Smith and David Proskey, apparently likened Liberty to the mythical female Amazonian warriors because of her warlike pose with sword and shield. No more than 12 examples of the present variety are believed extant, some of which have been owned by such numismatic luminaries as William H. Woodin, Harry W. Bass, Jr., King Farouk of Egypt, and Byron Reed.

This important Gem is the single finest certified 1872 Judd-1200 Amazonian Half Dollar at NGC and PCGS (10/02). Hazy apricot-gray toning drifts over both sides with blushes of lavender color at the left borders. We have no complaints about the sharp strike, and both sides are distraction-free save for an obverse spot in the field above the eagle's left (facing) wing that should be useful for pedigree purposes.

Ex: Robert E. Branigan Estate Sale (Bowers and Ruddy, 8/1978), lot 1859; William R. Sieck Collection (Bowers and Ruddy, 7-8/1981), lot 224.

From the Harold Hoogasian Collection. (#61471)

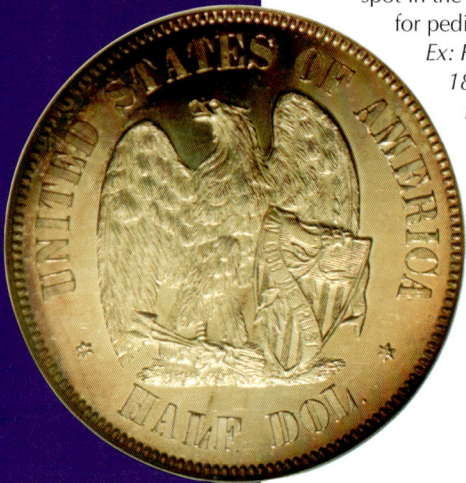

1873 TRADE DOLLAR PATTERN IN SILVER, JUDD-1310

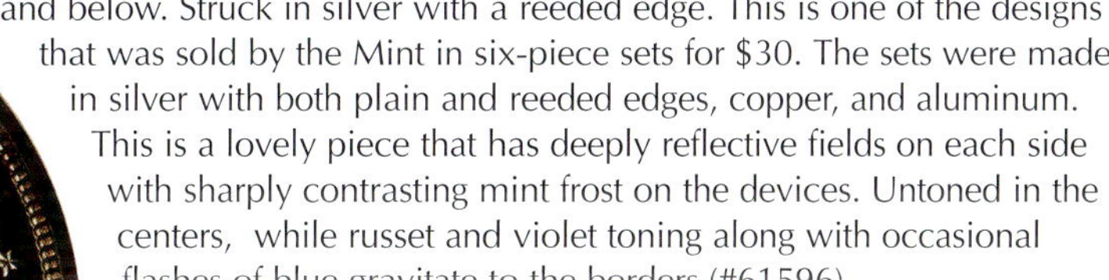

6424 1873 Trade Dollar, Judd-1310, Pollock-1453, R.4, PR64 NGC. A Trade dollar design struck in the year of its regular issue debut that shows Liberty seated on the obverse wearing an Indian headdress, Liberty pole and cap in her right hand, left hand resting on a globe, and conjoined flags behind. The reverse has a small eagle in the upper half with the weight and fineness below and the statutory legends on scrolls both above and below. Struck in silver with a reeded edge. This is one of the designs that was sold by the Mint in six-piece sets for $30. The sets were made in silver with both plain and reeded edges, copper, and aluminum. This is a lovely piece that has deeply reflective fields on each side with sharply contrasting mint frost on the devices. Untoned in the centers, while russet and violet toning along with occasional flashes of blue gravitate to the borders.(#61596)

BEAUTIFUL GEM 1875 TWENTY CENTS IN COPPER, JUDD-1408

6425 1875 Twenty Cents, Judd-1408, Pollock-1551, Low R.7, PR65 Brown PCGS. The obverse is very similar to the adopted design, but the date is smaller and LIBERTY is incuse on the ribbon. On the reverse, the denomination 1/5 OF A DOLLAR is surrounded by a laurel wreath. UNITED STATES OF AMERICA is above, and another expression of the denomination, TWENTY CENTS, is below. Struck in copper with a plain edge. This lovely Gem specimen has needle sharp detail and the glittering surfaces are accented in lovely aquamarine iridescence.(#61715)

BEAUTIFUL GEM 1878 PATTERN HALF EAGLE IN COPPER JUDD-1574

6426 1878 Five Dollar, Judd-1574, Pollock-1766, R.6, PR66 Red and Brown PCGS. William Barber's design that shows the head of Liberty wearing a band inscribed LIBERTY incused with E PLURIBUS UNUM around the margin. This portrait is similar in design to the famous $4 Flowing Hair Stella pattern. The reverse has an erect eagle with raised wings. Struck in copper with a reeded edge. The beautifully preserved surfaces are seemingly carbon-free, and display deep reflectivity, with bright orange-red patina in the more protected areas of each side. A highly desirable example of this beautiful pattern Half Eagle. Population: 1 in 66, 0 finer (3/04).(#71937)

POPULAR GEM PROOF 1882 PATTERN SHIELD NICKEL, JUDD-1690

6427 **1882 Liberty Head Five Cents, Judd-1690, Pollock-1892, R.5, PR65 NGC.** The obverse appears the same as the regular die of 1883, however, it is actually struck from an obverse die with a slightly different arrangement of the stars. The reverse is as the first variety of 1883, the "nickel without cents." Judd comments, "Often seen circulated." Very deeply mirrored, especially so for a nickel product, each side is covered with dusky gray patina with pale underlying rose and lilac accents.(#62095)

RARE 1885 ALUMINUM HALF EAGLE DIE TRIAL, JUDD-1754

6428 1885 Five Dollar, Judd-1754, Pollock-1967, R.8, PR64 Cameo PCGS. From regular issue 1885 Half Eagle dies, but struck in aluminum with a reeded edge. Examples of aluminum strikings are also known for the other gold denominations of this year, which were perhaps made for presentation purposes. Pollock was able to trace only two examples of this rare die trial:

1. Ex: King of Siam Sale (Bowers & Merena, 10/87), lot 2259; Auction '88 (Superior, 10/88), lot 293.

2. Ex: Palace Collection (Sotheby's, 1954), lot 2014, the present specimen.

A small flip that accompanies, signed by Sol Kaplan, attests to the King Farouk origin. The only noticeable distraction on this Choice specimen is a lamination from the eagle's left (facing) wing to the T in UNITED.(#62197)

This Coin Is From the
PALACE COLLECTION
of Former
KING FAROUK
of Egypt
Sold to
Attested Sol Kaplan

INTRIGUING 1928 STANDING LIBERTY QUARTER ON CENT PLANCHET ERROR

6429 1928 25C—Quarter Struck on a Cent Planchet—MS63 Brown SEGS Sovereign Series (MS60 Brown). 3.04 grams. Standing Liberty quarters are very rare with any type of error and even the slightest off-center coin brings a huge premium when one is offered for sale at public auction. This is easily the most dramatic and unusual error we have ever encountered on a Standing Liberty quarter.

The silver specks are a most interesting aspect of this piece and are easily seen, most especially on the upper reverse above the CA in AMERICA. Dies pick up silver "dust" from repeated strikings that is then transferred to the next coin. This is not noticeable on same-metal strikings, but on off-metal strikings they can be seen as fingerprints of the dies that struck the coin.

The dies themselves that struck this particular coin do indeed look authentic. Even with the three prominent die cracks, the details are still quite sharp. It is very unusual to find Standing quarters with die cracks. In fact, we cannot remember the last time we encountered one. This particular piece has two pronounced ones on the obverse and one on the reverse. It is also unusual to locate cents that are lightweight. The ones we have weighed in the past show very little variation in weight. After considering the above factors, the conclusion we have come to after studying this piece is that it was struck in the Mint, probably on a mostly complete fragment of a cent planchet by a pair of discarded quarter dies.

The coin itself is off-center with most of the date showing, but nothing visible above the top of the shield. The surfaces have taken on the appearance of aged copper with a deep brown and blue patina over much of each side and traces of pinkish-red around the devices. Sharply defined with a trace of rub over the highpoints. The planchet is somewhat irregular in shape, as would be expected since it was essentially struck without a collar. The devices at the margins are slightly distended, again as one would expect, as seen on other wrong planchet errors.

The pedigree of this piece is also quite interesting. This particular coin has an entire page devoted to it in Jay Cline's third edition of his book on the series. It was purchased by a Midwest collector at the 1958 ANA convention in Los Angeles for "a few hundred dollars." The collector took the coin over to a well-known Philadelphia dealer and after he did not receive an offer to his satisfaction, he took the coin home and tossed it in his safe deposit box. It wasn't until 1983 that the collector found the coin once again and showed it to Cline, who wrote an article for Coin World in September of that year and reprinted it in his book.

The insert of the holder is hand-signed by SEGS finalizer Larry Briggs. This is a most intriguing study piece for the general error specialist as well as those who collect Standing Liberty quarter errors.

PCGS CERTIFIED 1867 PROOF SET, COMPLETE THROUGH SILVER DOLLAR

6430 A Ten-Piece 1867 Proof Set PR62 to PR64 PCGS. The set includes:

Cent PR64 Red and Brown. Well struck and exquisite with intermingled orange and lilac patina.

Two Cent Piece PR64 Red and Brown. A needle-sharp near-Gem with essentially undisturbed surfaces. Bright honey color competes for territory with lavender hues.

Three Cent Nickel PR63. This silver-gray specimen features a curly mint-made lintmark on Liberty's jaw. Crisply struck aside from the centers of the first two pillars of the denomination.

Three Cent Silver PR63. Golden-brown, ruby-red, and ocean-blue colors appear when this boldly struck and nicely preserved example is rotated under a light. Business strikes and proofs combined for only 4,625 pieces.

No Rays Nickel PR62. Fletcher's IIa Reverse. A meticulously struck dove-gray piece with a few wispy hairlines on the reverse.

Half Dime PR62. Mauve and electric-blue colors embrace this nicely struck and lightly hairlined specimen. A low mintage date, since just 8,625 proofs and commercial strikes were coined.

Dime PR63. Navy-blue and golden-brown patina cedes to a lightly toned reverse center. The 18 in the date is lightly repunched. Silver coins did not circulate during this era except in the far west, and between proofs and business strikes only 6,625 pieces were issued.

Quarter PR63. Orange, mauve, and sky-blue colors bathe this lightly hairlined piece. Just 625 proofs were struck, along with a mere 20,000 business strikes.

Half Dollar PR63. An exquisitely struck example that has deep honey, aqua, and navy-blue patina. A few hairlines and handling marks are evident upon thorough examination. Elusive due to a stingy proof mintage of 625 pieces.

Silver Dollar PR63. This boldly struck Seated Dollar has carefully preserved surfaces and deep apple-green, mauve, tan, and pearl-gray patina. A desirable type in proof format. *From The Paulsboro Collection.* (Total: 10 Coins)

HIGH QUALITY 1893 PROOF SET, CENT THROUGH DOLLAR

6431 1893 Proof Set PCGS Certified. A dazzling set of primarily cameo proofs that includes:

Cent 1C PR64 Red and Brown. Mostly pinkish-tan with a touch of haziness over both sides. Small carbon spot connects the bases of AM in AMERICA.

Nickel PR65 Cameo. Strong reflectivity for a nickel striking and just a few wispy contact marks above the denomination.

Dime PR66 Cameo. Fully brilliant with glassy fields and heavily frosted features that result in dramatic contrast.

Quarter PR65 Cameo. A nice match for the Dime, with crystal clear fields and equally chalky central devices.

Half Dollar PR65 Cameo. Just a hint of golden toning is seen at the margins of this otherwise brilliant specimen.

Dollar PR64 Cameo. Well detailed for this often substandard issue and boasting eye catching contrast over untoned surfaces. Most often downgraded by wispy hairlines, this lovely proof Morgan derives its less-than-Gem rating from a well concealed milling mark in the curls over Liberty's ear. (Total: 6 Coins)

ONE-OF-A-KIND 1898 GOLD PROOF SET QUARTER EAGLE THROUGH DOUBLE EAGLE

6432 An awe-inspiring set of 1898 proof gold coinage, Quarter Eagle through Double Eagle, as follows:

Quarter Eagle PR67 Deep Cameo PCGS. Unbelievable depth of mirrored reflectivity in the fields boldly contrast with chalky yellow-gold features. From an original mintage of 165 pieces, of which half or less are estimated to have survived, only a dozen or so pieces could possibly compare with the technical supremacy of this specimen. Population: 7 in 67 Deep Cameo, 8 finer (4/04).

Half Eagle PR68 Deep Cameo NGC. The glittering, glassy fields form an impressive backdrop for starkly contrasting devices. The surfaces are a tinted a delicate reddish-orange and the only noticeable imperfection is a tiny, U-shaped lintmark between stars 2 and 3. Just 75 proofs were originally produced and just one other specimen has matched this piece in terms of numerical rating, that being a PR68 Cameo. Population: 1 in 68 Deep Cameo, 0 finer (4/04).

Eagle PR67 Deep Cameo NGC. Another drop-dead gorgeous cameo proof, this sparkling example boasting a bright yellow-gold appearance that is essentially as struck. A mere 69 Eagles were produced for collectors in a year that American Imperialism reached a fever pitch and survivors represent about 75 percent of the original mintage. Population: 3 in 67 Deep Cameo, 1 finer (4/04).

Double Eagle PR67 Deep Cameo NGC. Of course Twenty Dollar denomination is always the centerpiece of any four-piece set of gold coinage, and the dazzling specimen offered here certainly does not disappoint. The contrast is every bit as struck and the peerless surfaces are on equal footing with the other three. The proof mintage here, like the Half Eagle, was limited to 75 pieces, and specimens at this nearly flawless grade level are more of a dream than a reality. Population: 2 in 67 Deep Cameo, 0 finer (4/04). (Total: 4 Coins)

MEMORABLE 1899 FOUR-COIN GOLD PROOF SET SUPERB CAMEOS

6433 An incredibly preserved set of 1899 proof gold coinage, Quarter Eagle through Double Eagle, as follows:

Quarter Eagle PR68 Deep Cameo NGC. A seemingly flawless proof specimen with just a slightest blush of reddish patina at the margins. The contrast on this piece, like all four coins offered here, is simply outstanding. Proof mintage of 150 pieces. Population: 5 in 68 Deep Cameo, 0 finer (4/04).

Half Eagle PR68 Deep Cameo NGC. Intensely reflective, yellow-gold surfaces possess the exceedingly rare combination high quality production with almost perfect preservation. From an original mintage of 99 proofs, only a handful could possibly compare in quality or in eye appeal. Population: 2 in 68 Deep Cameo, 0 finer (4/04).

Eagle PR67 Cameo NGC. Rich golden color is amplified by the coin's dazzling contrast and wondrous technical merits. Just 86 proofs were minted and this piece is surely among the finest survivors. Population: 3 in 67 Cameo, 0 finer (4/04).

Double Eagle PR67 Deep Cameo NGC. A solid Gem specimen with instantly appealing contrast and tinges of reddish-orange peripheral color. Wispy die polishing on the portrait is not to be confused with hairlines. Fantastic quality from a proof production of a mere 84 coins. Population: 2 in 67 Deep Cameo, 0 finer (4/04). (Total: 4 Coins)

PCGS GRADED 1903 PROOF SET CENT THROUGH SILVER DOLLAR

6434 **1903 Proof Set PR64 to PR66 PCGS.** The set includes:

Cent PR64 Red. Lemon and peach hues enliven this meticulously struck near-Gem. A few tiny carbon flecks do not remove the eye appeal. Although proof Indian Cents had higher mintages than their silver and gold denomination counterparts, full Red examples are elusive.

Nickel PR66 Cameo. Lovely rose, gold, and powder-blue patina graces the impressively preserved surfaces of this well struck premium Gem. Originally toned Cameos are scarce, since many proofs have been dipped to make their white on black nature more apparent.

Dime PR64. Waves of sea-green and apricot color embrace this beautifully preserved near-Gem. A mere 755 pieces were produced, the same low mintage as the other proof silver denominations for the year.

Quarter PR66 Cameo. Peripheral qua-marine, peach, and electric-blue colors frame the lightly toned centers. An essentially pristine premium Gem. Due to a lapped die, a mirrored surface (as made) is noted within and below Liberty's ear.

Half Dollar PR64. Rich golden-brown, steel-gray, and mauve patina embraces this sharply struck and carefully preserved Choice Barber Half. A prize for the collector who covets originally toned silver proofs.

Morgan Dollar PR64. Lovely tan, rose, and apple-green colors dominate this nicely struck and nearly undisturbed near-Gem. A thin planchet streak (as made) below the eagle's below is strictly of mint origin and does not affect the technical grade. (Total: 6 Coins)

EXEMPLARY FIVE-PIECE 1911 PROOF SET, PR66 TO PR67 PCGS

6435 A Five-Piece 1911 Proof Set PR66 to PR67 PCGS. The set includes:

Cent PR66 Red and Brown. Golden-brown color dominates the reverse, while lilac hues endow the majority of the reverse. An exquisitely struck and seemingly immaculate premium Gem. Population: 13 in 66 Red and Brown, none finer (3/04).

Nickel PR66 Cameo. A well struck specimen that exhibits lovely powder-blue and peach colors. The obverse is essentially flawless, and the reverse has only a couple of minute flecks of green debris. Population: 10 in 66 Cameo, 5 finer (3/04).

Dime PR66. A magnificently struck premium Gem with flashy mirrors and deep olive, rose, and aquamarine patina. A beautiful example of this low mintage issue. Population: 27 in 66, 17 finer (3/04).

Quarter PR67. Iridescent apricot, sea-green, orange, and rose-pink colors enrich each side. A razor-sharp strike and undisturbed surfaces further the eye appeal of this imposing specimen. The Barber Dime, Quarter, and Half Dollar for this year each have a scant production of only 543 pieces. Population: 22 in 67, 7 finer (3/04).

Half Dollar PR66 Cameo. The snow-white devices have pleasing contrast with the mirrored fields, and the untoned surfaces are essentially pristine. This sharply struck premium Gem would be a highlight of any proof Barber collection. Population: 7 in 66 Cameo, 1 finer (3/04). (Total: 5 coins)